BLACK HISTORY AND
BLACK IDENTITY

BLACK HISTORY AND BLACK IDENTITY

A Call for a New Historiography

W. D. Wright

PRAEGER

Westport, Connecticut
London

Library of Congress Cataloging-in-Publication Data

Wright, W. D. (William D.), 1936–
    Black history and black identity : a call for a new historiography / William D. Wright.
        p.   cm.
    Originally published: 2001
    Includes bibliographical references and index.
    ISBN 0–275–97442–1 (alk. paper)
    1. African Americans—Historiography.   2. African Americans—Ethnic identity.   3.
    African Americans—Race identity.   I. Title.
    E184.65.W75   2002
    973′.0496073′0072—dc21   2001036709

British Library Cataloguing in Publication Data is available.

Library of Congress Catalog Card Number: 2001036709
ISBN: 0–275–97442–1

First published in 2002

Praeger Publishers, 88 Post Road West, Westport, CT 06881
An imprint of Greenwood Publishing Group, Inc.
www.praeger.com

Printed in the United States of America

The paper used in this book complies with the
Permanent Paper Standard issued by the National
Information Standards Organization (Z39.48–1984).

10 9 8 7 6 5 4 3 2 1

To Georg Iggers,
Mentor and Friend

When you're Black and analyze American history, you start with racism, slavery, racist segregation, denial of human rights, denial of political and civil rights, public humiliation, and individual, mob, and government violence. You do not get democracy out of that. What you get is a *Blackcentric Perspective* on Black history, White history, and American history.

Contents

Acknowledgments

I wish to thank Professor Richard Garner of the Classical Languages Department of Yale University and his graduate student, John Dyan, as well as Margaretha and Johann Bischoff, for their assistance in translating passages in ancient Greek and Latin. I also wish to thank colleague Samuel Andoh for his assistance in identifying the word "black" in several African languages, which were the languages of the black people taken from the island continent to the Western hemisphere as slaves over a period of three and a half centuries.

I also wish to thank Regine Bence for her critical observations, patience, and support.

Chapter 1

Introduction

The subject of Black history in America became an accepted academic discipline in the 1960s, and became one of the most popular fields of study in the 1970s. This popularity continued in the 1980s and on into the 1990s. And this historical scholarship has and continues to throw much light on the history of Blacks in America. But what the historiography over the last few decades has not done has been to clarify who Black people have been and who they presently are in America. Are they Africans, Afro-Americans, African Americans, Blacks, blacks, Black Americans, or black Americans? This question and these many possible identities for Black people in America, all of which are in use, indicate, emphatically, that historical research and writing have not cleared up this matter.

Indeed, Black historiography has added to the disrupted and confused thinking, because all of these identities appear in it, with some individual writings evidencing almost all of these identities. The question is then raised: How should Black history be described? Another question is, What is the identity of Black people in America? This book endeavors to answer these two questions; namely, by arguing, based on historical evidence and sociological analysis, that Black people are to be described as Black, Blacks, and Black Americans, and that Black history is to be described as Black history and Black American history when viewed in its broadest scope.

Resolution of the questions of the description of a historiography and the identity of a group of people have become two of the most important cultural tasks facing Black Americans. The importance is not only from the standpoint of legitimate scholarship, or knowledge, or truth. The two questions and the answers they receive also relate directly and profoundly to the social, cultural, economic, political, and historical development of Black people in America. They also relate directly and profoundly to how Blacks in America relate to other black people in the world, particularly in the Western Hemisphere and Africa, and also to the world itself. The cultural tasks have been made more pressing because of the efforts of some Blacks to persuade Black people in America that they are and should refer to themselves as Africans or, more often, as African Americans.

This effort is being led by some Black middle-class people: scholars, politicians, print and electronic journalists, public school teachers, clergypersons, social workers, and professional community organizers. For the past few years such individuals, some in a concerted and cooperative way, but most others by emulating others, have been engaged in an effort to persuade Blacks in America that they are African Americans, and are seeking to oblige Whites and other Americans to accept this identity.

There are Black historians who are part of this political–cultural effort as individuals among the cooperating ones, or as emulators of others, particularly other Black historians, who write about Black history in America as if it were African history or African history in America. Such historians are very concerned to investigate and disclose the extent of the retention of African culture, or "Africanism," in Black life in America (or in American life in general), to help provide legitimacy for the political–cultural project and to validate their own contention that Black people are and should be referred to as African Americans and that Black history should be designated African American history or African American historiography. Historian Joseph Holloway recently asserted in his edited book on African cultural and social retentions in Black America and in America in general that Blacks should refer to themselves as African Americans, and that as far as he was concerned, debate on this subject was closed:

This debate had come full circle, from African through brown, colored, Afro-American, Negro, and *black* to African, the term originally used by blacks in America to define themselves. The changes in terminology reflect many changes in attitude, from strong African identification to nationalism, integration, and attempts at assimilation back to cultural identification. This struggle to reshape and define blackness in both the concrete and abstract also reflects the renewed pride of black people in shaping a future based on the concept of one African people living in the African diaspora.[1]

Holloway was correct to refer to a debate going on among Blacks in America as to who Black people think they are and the name they should go by. But he was wrong in saying that the debate had closed, or that it had come full circle back to the original African identity of Black people. This book represents a continuation of the debate, and some of the points it will make is that Black people, as a people in the United States, *never* had for themselves, originally or throughout their history in America, the name African. Further, as overwhelming historical evidence indicates, Black people as a people in America have never had a *strong* African identity. A series of polls in the 1990s showed that Blacks overwhelmingly rejected an African identity for themselves, and showed a preference to be referred to as *black* or *Black*.[2] One of those polls showed that 66 percent of Whites in America rejected an African identity for Blacks and believed that they should be called Blacks.[3] Historically, white people rarely referred to Black people in America as Africans. Thus, a White rejection of this name and identity is not surprising. But, of course, it is not up to white people to determine the identity of Black people, which was something they did in the past. The identity of Black people has to be determined by Black people, and others in America have to accept that determination.

But the question is, What collective or group identity will Black people decide upon? As the polls indicated, Blacks have already made that determination: that they are Blacks and Black Americans and not Africans or African Americans. In the 1960s and 1970s, and even in the 1980s, Black people proudly and publicly proclaimed that they were Black, and even talked about black (race and color) and Black (meaning ethnicity) being "beautiful." But it was in the 1980s, especially, that some Black historians and other Black scholars, and other educated and professional Black people, began to stress that Black people were Afro-Americans. The emphasis then shifted to Blacks being African Americans, where an emphasis presently lies with such people.

There are Black historians whom I call Second-Wave Black historians, who not only accept the African American identity of Black people, but who seek to uncover historical or cultural evidence to prove it; namely, the "Africanisms" evidenced in Black cultural and social life. These historians contrast sharply with older generations of Black historians, whom I call precursor Black historians and

First-Wave Black historians, who commonly referred to Blacks as Negroes or Colored People, or as Negro Americans or Colored Americans, and indicated at the same time that such people were not Africans, but people of *black African descent* in America. Chapters 2 and 3 are about the three successive groupings of Black historians in America and their approach to writing Black history, including the names they used to describe Black people in their historical writings.

Closely associated with the various names of Black people in America, and reflected in the writings of Black historians over generations of historians and schools of historiography, is the spelling of these names and identities. The spelling of words in language study is called orthography. Black historical writing, from the nineteenth century to the present day, reflect how the names and identities of Black people are mired in orthographic problems. But Black writing of almost any kind, historically or presently—fiction writing, poetry writing, literary criticism, or journalistic writing—reflects the orthographic problems and encumbrances to clarifying who Black people have been and are in America. It has not only been "what name" or "What is in a Name" in Black history and Black life in America, as Black literary critic Henry Louis Gates, Jr. has recently indicated.[4] It has also been a matter of how a name and identity, or names and identities, were spelled.

The spelling of words not only reflects grammatical rules and protocol, it also refers to social values or certain forms of social behavior. Malcolm X understood this matter rather well. A complaint he used to have of white critics (adversaries) when he was a member of Elijah Mohammad's Muslim group was the way they referred to the group as the "Black Muslims" and not the "black Muslims." The first description, as Malcolm X saw it, was not just a nominative description, but was used by critics and enemies of his religious group to suggest that they were not really authentic Muslims, but rather some peculiar kind of Muslim religious group, isolated from and not part of the worldwide, authentic Muslim or Islamic religion. That association and authenticity, Malcolm X felt, would have been expressed by the description of "black Muslims," because this would have been a reference to Muslims who happened to be black racially, as opposed to other Muslims in America, or in the world, who were white, brown, or yellow racially. Nominative and adjectival spellings of words or names, as Malcolm X saw, could have social and political implications or uses. Unfortunately, Malcolm X did not develop his criticism of orthographic practices in America, and there was no one who sought to take up the matter as a historical or linguistic problem that has affected the history and lives of Blacks in America, as well as the writing of Black history.

A large truth that Malcolm X had focused on with his very small discussion was that language and even the spelling of words (i.e., orthography, which was not a formal term that he used) could be used as instruments of domination, control, and exploitation, and that, indeed, white people had used such devices as weapons to promote such objectives in their historical relationship with Black people in America. The various spellings and uses of the word *black* (as well as the spellings and uses of other names and identities of Black people in America, such as Negro and Colored) have sown and continue to sow confusion among a number of Blacks, especially educated and professional Blacks, about an authentic (i.e., Black) identity in America, and has them seeking to promote the false Afro-American and African American identities among Black people. Thus, the orthographic problems surrounding efforts to establish a *Black* identity in America have to be discussed and will be in Chapter 4.

Of course, resolving orthographic problems cannot resolve the question of Black people's identity in America. This matter also cannot be decided by a simple choice; that is, Black people deciding to call themselves Black, as opposed to some other name. In short, the decision cannot be based simply on ideology or rhetoric. All identities are historically formed, and thus it is fundamental to history that people turn to see who they have been and who they presently are. The argument of this book is that history had indicated that Black people are Black people, and not Africans, Afro-Americans, or African Americans, and that this is the identity that Black people have to settle upon, that is to say, choose (as opposed to some other identity for themselves, which would also be based on history, because the latter invalidates or jettisons other identities). The Black people of the Joint Center for Political and Economic Studies Poll (1990), the ABC News–*Washington Post* poll (1991) and mid-1990s polls reported in *Jet* magazine were reflecting their historical sense and feeling of being *black* and *Black*, and were expressing adherence to and acceptance of these historical identities.

Second-Wave Black historians, those historians who emerged in the 1960s and thereafter, strongly contribute to the orthographic problems surrounding a Black identity, and, in a strong manner, to the general disrupted and confused thinking about the identity of Black people in America. This is actually ironic, because it is primarily Second-Wave Black historians who insist that Black people are Afro-Americans or African Americans, and have pressured other Black historians to accept these identities. But Second-Wave Black historians, just as often or even more often in their historical writings, refer to Black people as Black people, using various kinds of descriptions to do so, such as "black," "Black," "blacks," and "Blacks." Orthographic problems are clearly present in Second-Wave historical writings. These problems, and not being clear as to whether Black people are Africans, Afro-Americans, or African Americans, makes Second-Wave Black historian guidance out of the difficulties regarding a Black identity in America rather dubious.

A number of Second-Wave Black historians are Black nationalists by their own disclosure, or are dubbed so by others. But oddly enough, such historians rarely refer to themselves as "Afro-American nationalists," or "African American nationalists." They also rarely talk about Afro-American or African American nationalism in Black history in America. References to or discussions of nationalism are usually about Black nationalism. But if Black people, as Second-Wave Black historians assert, are Afro-Americans or African Americans, should not their historical discussions be about Afro-American nationalism or African American nationalism? And, indeed, since these identities are not the same, should there not be some clarification as to which of these nationalisms has been a part of Black history? Thus, does Black history in America reflect two different kinds of nationalism? Or three: Afro-American nationalism, African American nationalism, and Black nationalism?

Confusion marks not just Second-Wave Black Historiography regarding the forms of nationalism in Black history; it is true of First-Wave Black historians as well. They also employ the concept of nationalism itself in a confused manner in their writings. Nationalism is a reference to a nation-state or country, with nationalism itself as the ideology that rationalizes or seeks to legitimate the existence or guide the construction of a nation-state or country. First- and Second-Wave Black historiography sometimes reflects this kind of understanding of nationalism, and the role this kind of nationalism has played in Black history. But as a rule, First- and Second-Wave Black historians misemploy the concept of nationalism, as they usually equate it with such historical and social realities as ethnicity or community, thus equating Black ethnicity; the Black community, its existence, and functioning; or any kind of Black separate cultural or social reality or activity (existing or occurring apart from white people or other Americans) with nationalism or nationalistic happenings, when they are nothing more than ethnic or community realities or happenings.

Discussions of Afro-American nationalism, African American nationalism, Afrikan nationalism, or Black nationalism in First- and Second-Wave Black historical writings are invariably distortions of Black history and Black life in America. Another critical observation to be made is that a number of Black historians, especially Black nationalist Second-Wave Black historians, substitute Black nationalist ideology or rhetoric—or Afro-American or African American nationalist ideology or rhetoric, as it might be referred to—for historical evidence and historical fact, which either suppresses Black historical and social realities or distorts them. The nationalist issue and its problematic relationship to Black history, Black identity, and Black historical writing in America will be taken up in a full manner in Chapter 7, which will critique the works of two Black nationalist Second-Wave Black historians, Sterling Stuckey and V. P. Franklin, and their works, *Slave Culture* and *Black Self-Determination*, respectively.[5] Both authors show the deleterious effect that ideology or rhetoric can have on historical scholarship.

But in making these remarks, I do not want to leave the residual impression that I think ideology or rhetoric are necessarily detrimental to historical scholarship, or that political thinking or political motivation, which are essentially the same thing, are necessarily detrimental to it. Purists among historians (or historical Platonists) have always argued so. But purist historians have rarely understood their own romanticism and strong subjectivism, even while spouting views from what they regard as an objective canonical posture. Historical writing in America itself since the nineteenth century has shown how political thinking and political motivation have identified areas for historical research and writing, have opened up or expanded areas for research and writing, or have helped to augment historical interpretation, knowledge, and truth.

The political thinking and political motivation of a number of Black and white historians in the 1960s and 1970s led to new and vigorous research into Black history, and to a greater and more truthful telling of that story. One could make the same observation about the way political thinking and political motivation—ideology and rhetoric—have expanded research, knowledge, and truth about the history of women in America. The legitimate question has always been not whether political thinking or politics relate to historical research and writing, but how they relate. Do they augment historical research, knowledge, truth, and understanding, or do they obstruct achieving these objectives? History has recorded both realities.

As said at the outset of this chapter, an evaluation of how Black people and their history should be described in America would be determined not only by historical evidence, but also by sociological analysis. A critical historical writing or evaluation requires a critical sociology. History, after all, as subject matter or reality, as opposed to the academic discipline designed to investigate and explain this subject matter or reality, is human behavior in time and over time. This automatically brings sociology directly to historical research, writing, and explanation. Some historians have understood this matter, and the sociology of Karl Marx, Max Weber, Antonio Gramsci, C. Wright Mills, and Talcott Parsons has appeared in historical works. But none of these sociologies would be adequate to help explain American history or American society, because none has the necessary critical capacity to do so. Namely, none exhibit a racist analysis or a racial analysis, or the employment of these forms of analyses along with a class and gender analysis. And what they also lack as a prerequisite for a critical analysis of American history and society is the hierarchical racist-inundated White over Black social structure and social system, the centerpiece of American history and society and the broad analytical framework in which all other forms of analysis of American history and life take place. Determinism and indeterminism existed in this structure and system, and both were also capable of change and development.

W.E.B. Du Bois devised the White over Black hierarchical structure and system and broad critical analytical framework without ever providing it with a label, which I have done for him. Du Bois was the progenitor of scientific sociology in the United States, developing it between the 1890s and World War I, putting him in the company of Émile Durkheim in France and Max Weber, who were also putting science into sociology in Europe. Du Bois made a racist analysis and the racist-inundated hierarchical social structure and social system the centerpieces of his historical and sociological analyses.

He inaugurated his interest in the study of social life, and thus his early interest in investigating sociology, when he was a teenage journalist in Great Barrington, Massachusetts. He wrote articles about Black life in his village for New York Black newspapers.[6] These articles reveal his perception of a basic White over Black social relationship in Great Barrington that helped to determine the culture and social life of the village, which both Whites and Blacks participated in in an unequal manner. As a student at Fisk University, and thus living in the South, Du Bois saw the great division between Whites and Blacks, and Black life and White life, not only in Nashville, Tennessee, and surrounding areas, but, on the basis of his reading and studying, all over the South.

In that region, Du Bois saw the stark reality of the White over Black hierarchical social relationship that stood at the center of Southern life, that was characterized by racism and race, and that directly and profoundly affected that life in all of its major cultural and social dimensions. He also saw how Blacks were excluded from much of the culture and social life of the South, and how they were subordinated or suppressed when they participated in them. He further saw the distinctive White and Black social worlds of the South, with the White social world dominating the Black social world. Du Bois described the racist–racial social realities of the South in an unpublished article written in 1887, entitled, "An Open Letter to the Southern People":

For twenty-five years you have more than intimated that there is little in common between White and Black in the South. . . . The Negro has at last come to consider that whatever is for the benefit of the White man is for his detriment. Nor is it strange he should jump at such a conclusion; a blind prejudice has too often heaped injustice of the grossest kind upon him: the rights dearest to a freeman, trial by peers, a free ballot, a free entrance into the various callings of life, have been ruthlessly wrestled from him in multitude of cases. Arguing him into an inferior being you have forced him into the gallery, the hovel, and the "Jim Crow" car; arguing his ignorance have rendered nearly seven millions of people practically voiceless in politics; in the face of this you have refused his children equal educational advantage with yours.[7]

In his published doctoral dissertation of 1895, *The Suppression of the African Slave Trade to the United States,* Du Bois only adumbrated the view that white people initially established a White over Black hierarchical social structure and social system in early American history as foundational or ontological structures of the history through which American history and social life were produced and reproduced.[8] In *The Philadelphia Negro* and a plethora of other sociological, historical, and political writings between the 1890s and the time of his death in 1963, Du Bois, without conceptualization, described and discussed what he regarded as the general social structure and social system in American history and American society, using them as the basic framework to analyze that history and society, and particularly relations between white people and Black people in those contexts.[9]

Du Bois's historical and sociological argument was that white people, owing to their racist beliefs and attitudes and other motivations—connected to those beliefs and attitudes, and even often stimulated by them—initially divided America, broadly and hierarchically, between two races, the white race and the black race, with the white race at the top of the hierarchy and the black race at the bottom. This established the basic or fundamental social relationship in America, initially during British colonial history in North America and then throughout the length of American history. The hierarchical interaction between the white and black races occurred within American culture and social institutions, from the colonial period throughout American history, creating the general racist-inundated hierarchical social structure and social system that the white race continuously participated in in a superordinate and dominating and controlling manner (that is to say, from the top down), and that the black race continuously participated in in a dominated, subordinated, and suppressed manner (that is to say, from the bottom up).

In interacting with the black race in the American hierarchical racist-saturated social structure and social system, the white race adhered to two sets of racist beliefs: *white supremacy* and *ebonicism*. The first body of beliefs referred to the alleged innate superiority of white people, and the other to the alleged innate inferiority of the black race. These beliefs went beyond race and established "race," something that did not exist and was a fanciful abstract construction, but that the white racist believed did exist and had embodiment. White supremacist racist beliefs established a white "race" that amounted to a "race" of "godly" or "godlike" "entities," believed to be real, with concrete embodiment, and a black "race" of "nonhumans" or "subhumans," believed to be such material or biological entities. The two forms of racism were always expressed simultaneously (i.e., *white supremacy/ebonicism*), even if one of the forms was not explicitly stated or readily detectable. To engage in ebonicistic racism already implied white supremacist racist thinking, beliefs, and motivations. Ebonicism was applied to black people (race) and Black people (ethnic group), declaring both to be nonhuman or subhuman. Ebonicism is not to be mistaken for "ebonics," which is a description of the dialect spoken by many Blacks in this country. There are, in fact, numerous forms of racism, such as maleism (that alleges the innate superiority of men) and *sexism* (that alleges the natural inferiority of women), which function in a combined manner as maleism/sexism. There is also *anti-Jewism* (which is more accurate than anti-Semitism), *redicism* (alleging the innate inferiority of American and Western Hemispheric Indians), and *xanthicism* (alleging the natural inferiority of yellow or Asian people). All these forms of racism have and continue to function in

America, but the primary racist expression has and continues to be white supremacy/ebonicism, which will be the focus in this study. I refer readers to my book, *Racism Matters,* for a discussion of the different forms of racism in American history and life.[10]

Figure 1.1 is a diagram of Du Bois's unlabeled but sociologically conceived and discussed White over Black hierarchical social structure and social system, which functioned nationally, regionally, and locally, wherever Whites and Blacks lived and interacted with each other.

As Du Bois asserted in his sociological and historical (and even his political) writings, and as seen in Figure 1.1, the White over Black hierarchical social structure and social system involved

Figure 1.1
Du Bois's Hierarchical Social System

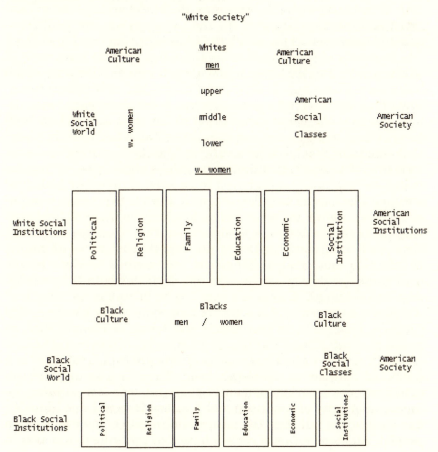

people, culture, and social institutions. White people were at the top of the structure and system as a race and large group of people, subdivided into genders, social classes, and individuals, who participated in a culture and social institutions. At the bottom of the hierarchical social structure and social system were Black people as a race and smaller group of people, subdivided into genders, social classes (not fully developed or crystallized), and individuals. Du Bois asserted that Blacks were made the bottom of the racist-filled hierarchical social structure and social system legally, as legally established slaves, but also by racist thinking and racist political and social practices. He also argued that American history, American society, and American civilization were constantly mobilized against Black people to maintain them as a subordinate people in the country and as the structural bottom of American history and society.

Du Bois contended that the White social classes in the racist-stained hierarchical social structure and social system were actually *American* social classes, that White social institutions were actually *American* social institutions, and that White culture was actually *American* culture. But white people, acting as racists, enslavers, and segregationists, usurped *American* culture, social classes, and social institutions and made them "White" culture, "White" social classes, and "White" social institutions. They also made *American* society "White society," and *American* civilization "White civilization." It was usurpation, as Du Bois saw it, because he argued that Black people had helped, in an important manner, to construct American culture, American social classes, American social institutions, American society, and American civilization, but white people had absorbed and appropriated their contributions and then had excluded them from the constructions and the rewards that they had provided, or at least had primarily excluded them from the constructions and rewards that they had helped to produce and to which they had been fully entitled, based on their contributions.

The White over Black hierarchical social structure functioned as a social system; that is, evidenced motion, moving parts, and dynamism when Whites and Blacks interacted with each other. The interaction, as said before, occurred from top to bottom and from bottom to top. Whites interacted with Blacks from an ascendant and dominant position, and thus from top to bottom in the social structure and social system. Generally speaking, this was the White social world interacting with the Black social world, which was the macro social interaction that made the White over Black hierarchical social structure function as a social system. But it also functioned as a social system when Whites functioned in their specific manifestations as a large racial group, and in their genders, social classes, and as individuals, and interacted with Blacks on these bases. This interaction occurred through culture and social institutions, and whenever Whites interacted with Blacks, as a race, in genders, in social classes, or as individuals, it was primarily and strongly done in a racist manner. This was so because the top part of the White over Black social structure and social system were inundated with White racist beliefs, values, and attitudes, which were strongly imparted to Whites and which the top part of the structure and system, as well as the general social structure and social system, reinforced in them throughout their lives. As Du Bois saw it, the racist socialization of white people, carried out by the White over Black social structure and social system as a partial entity or as a whole entity, was a lifelong activity.

The White over Black hierarchical social structure functioned as a social system when Blacks interacted with Whites and the top of the hierarchical structure from the bottom up. They did this on the basis of their broad social world, but also as a race, in their genders, their social classes, and as individuals. The social structure functioned as a social system in its most dynamic manner, from bottom to top, when Blacks, functioning through some of their social institutions and (more or less) as a people, related to Whites in a direct, physical manner or in American culture and in American social institutions, which Whites claimed for themselves and for their exclusive use. When Blacks interacted with Whites and the top part of the racist-inundated hierarchical social structure and social system from the bottom up, it was for the purpose of mitigating the racist character and the oppression of the structure and system; or, as another motivation, to free themselves from White domination, control, and exploitation, and to be able to integrate, as individuals, genders, and a group of people, and as equal individuals, genders, and a group of people, in what they regarded as *American* culture, *American* social classes, *American* social institutions, *American* society, and *American* civilization.

Thus, Blacks and Whites sought to make the White over Black hierarchical social structure and social system function in different ways. Whites sought to maintain the structure and system to make them function to reproduce White racism and White racist power and the White domination and control of America, as well as the domination, control, and exploitation of Black people. Blacks, on the other hand, functioning from a dominated, suppressed, and exploited position and from the bottom of American society, sought to mitigate the oppressive functioning of the hierarchical social structure and social system to be able to progress and develop as a people. Or they sought to get rid of the structure and system so that they could be fully included in America, and fully free in it.

The previous lengthy discussion now needs a modification. The White over Black structure and system originally began as a racist-inundated racial hierarchical structure and system, with the white race over the black race. Du Bois never deviated from this view. I find it necessary to modify it, as an extension of Du Bois's position. In time, black people, the original black Africans, became an ethnic group in America, Black people. This made them one among many ethnic groups to be found among the black race that existed from Africa to the Western Hemisphere. The white race in America at the time exhibited many ethnic groups: Anglo Saxon, German, French, and, later in the nineteenth century, Irish, Greek, and numerous others. These were "white ethnics," meaning ethnic groups of the white race. But the white ethnic groups also formed a large White ethnic group, as denoted by such phrases as "White culture," "White America," or "White society." Any ethnic group has a racial dimension as well as cultural and social features. The Black ethnic group is a manifestation of the black race, and the White ethnic group is a manifestation of the white race.

In using the term White over Black structure and system, as done over the previous pages and as will be done throughout the book, the focus will be on the White and Black ethnic groups. But since white people function as a race and ethnic group in this country, and relate to Black people as both, it is possible to refer to white people in racial and ethnic terms, as "white" and as "White." White people, in fact, relate to Black people more as members of the white race than as members of the White ethnic group, and thus, the word "white" or the phrase "white people," or similar lower-case usages, will be frequently employed in this book. This explains why white is most often spelled in the lower case in this book, because white people mainly relate to black or Black people out of their racial orientation.

White historians invariably, or primarily, write American history as if only white people have made that history and as if Black people have not done so, or not in any substantial manner, and as if Black people have not affected the way white people have made history in the country. In short, white historians, as a rule, write American history focusing on the top part of the White over Black hierarchical social structure and social system and ignoring or excluding, or only meagerly including, the bottom part of the structure and system. But even Black historians, generally, are not significantly aware of the White over Black hierarchical social structure and social system of American history and American society, although they would have no difficulty knowing that Black and white people have made history in America, and that Black people have made a large contribution to the historical, cultural, and social development of the country. Some of these historians even indicate how Black people have impacted and contributed to the way Whites have made history in the country. Black historians who insist that Black people have always thought of themselves as Africans and have historically had a strong African identity in America and presently retain it—regarding themselves as African Americans—show an acute lack of knowledge of the White over Black hierarchical social structure and social system. That structure and system has historically ridiculed and even denigrated the name and identity of African as well as Africa itself, which usually resulted in the Blacks who were aware of the name African or of the African continent ignoring both or deprecating both and avoiding close association with both.

The White over Black hierarchical social structure and social system has functioned strongly in American history and society to compel Whites not to accord Blacks an identity that would convey dignity and status on them or equality with Whites. It compelled Whites to think of Blacks as being "nonhuman" or "subhuman," or as an identity based on their race and, namely, the color of their skin, both of which were publicly deprecated. Blacks have historically been pressured in America by the White over Black hierarchical social structure and social system to accept a public, group, and personal identity of "nonhuman" or "subhuman," or the view that their identity was not a matter of history or culture, but simply of biology; that is, race and color, and particularly the latter.

These kinds of pressures alone have historically stood as roadblocks to Blacks thinking of themselves as Africans and having an African identity, or even wanting one. Then there were the other names and identities for Black people that the White over Black hierarchical social structure and social system strongly insisted upon historically—Negro, Colored, nigger, and black—that made an African identity for Black people unreal, unthinkable, unreachable, unwanted, and nothing more than just a romantic or fanciful identity if chosen. The White over Black hierarchical social structure and social system functioned in America to distort and confuse the thinking of Black people, including Black historians and other Black scholars or intellectuals, about who Black people have been and are in America.

For exposition convenience, the White over Black hierarchical social structure and social system will hereafter be referred to as the White over Black structure and system, or simply as the structure and system. That structure and system continues on in American history and American life. It would have to be conceived more broadly now to include more racial peoples in America and the ethnic realities of the country, which Du Bois knew about but did not make significant elements of his macro method of analyzing American society and history. But even though there is a broader reality of a racist-embedded social structure and social system in America, the White over Black portion of it is still the central portion of it and the primary determinant portion of it; that is, the part of the racist-imbued structure and system that primarily functions to reproduce American history, culture, and social life.

Since a purpose of this book is to show that Black people in America are Black people and not Africans or any variation of that identity, it will be necessary to focus attention on the origin of the name and identity of African and the role this name and identity have played in history. Precursor Black historians made the assumption that the name Africa was given to a large land mass by the millennial black people who lived there, and it was further assumed by them that these people called themselves Africans. First- and Second-Wave Black historians—virtually to a historian—accept the same assumptions and write their historical works upon them. But the historical truth is, as will be detailed in Chapter 5, neither the words nor names of Africa or African have their origins with the millennial black people who have lived on what history, for more than two thousand years, has called Africa.

The word "Africa" is an ancient Greek word, and it was the ancient Greeks, as well as the Carthaginians and the Romans, who gave the name Africa to a land mass, that resulted in the people of the land being called Africans. Europeans after the Romans, and for centuries, used the words Africa and African, which were not even known or used by most people who were supposed to be the Africans and were known by other people in the world as Africans, living in Africa. If the people of the continent known in history as Africa did not call the vast area in which they lived Africa and did not, historically, for over two millennia, call themselves Africans, then why do people on that continent presently call themselves Africans and their homeland Africa?

If the black people who came to the Americas and the West Indies as slaves did not know themselves to be Africans and did not call themselves Africans, why are there Black historians in America, particularly Second-Wave Black historians, trying to prove that Black people in this country are Africans, Afro-Americans, or African Americans? And how legitimate is it for such historians to talk about a "Pan-African" consciousness or orientation among the black people who came to the Americas and the West Indies as slaves? Chapter 6 will focus on the African identity as it relates to Black people and their history in America. Chapters 5 and 6 will both raise questions about what I call a "retrospective African identity," with Chapter 5 providing a discussion of this identity as it relates to Africans and Africa, and Chapter 6 providing a discussion of how this identity relates to Black people and their identity and history in America.

Another question that will be raised by this work is the legitimacy or proper usage of such phrases or concepts as "Afrocentric" or "Africancentric." There are First- and Second-Wave Black historians seeking to use the Afrocentric phrase or concept especially, and are endeavoring to vest it with historical meaning and historical, cultural, and social analytical capability. They are making, therefore, an effort to devise an Afrocentric Perspective on Black history, and even on African history. A phrase or concept associated closely with this effort to develop an Afrocentric Perspective on Black history or African history is the "African diaspora." I object to this latter phrase on historical grounds. Diaspora, as a word, means dispersal. First- and Second-Wave Black historians use this word, and usually in its larger construction of African diaspora. They argue that an African diaspora was created in the Americas and West Indies, or what is called the Western Hemisphere, by the African slave trade that dispersed Africans to this part of the world. There were black Africans dispersed to the Middle East and Asia by a slave trade that preceded the black African slave trade to the Western Hemisphere by centuries, but those who employ the African diaspora concept usually do not draw these areas and these peoples into their understanding of this concept. This ignores as well as suppresses the history of black Africans and their descendants.

Thus, the African diaspora concept does not give a sense of the vast global presence of black Africans and their descendants. Nor does it convey the millennial reality and history of this reality. And that history and reality go back to the first human beings, who were black people. About 180,000 to 90,000 years ago, black people left Africa and began migrating to other parts of the world and, in turn, became the human basis for the evolution of all humanity. At one time the only human presence in the world, that is, *homo sapiens sapiens*, was the black race that had emerged in Africa and that spread about. As the first human beings, black Africans initiated human history, human language, human culture, and human social organization and spread them to other parts of the world. The African diaspora concept does not put any Black or black person in touch with this tremendous understanding, not only of black people, but of human beings and human history. There were even black Africans in the Western Hemisphere long before a slave trade dispersed them there. Ivan van Sertima showed in *They Came Before Columbus* that black Africans were part of the Olmec civilization of Mexico that went back thousands of years before the slave-trade dispersal.[11] Indeed, a human skull was recently found in south central Brazil that has been declared to be 11,500 years old and is a skull, nicknamed Luzia, of a black woman, not an Asian or Indian woman: "A reconstruction of her cranium undertaken in Britain this year indicates that her features appear to be Negroid rather than Mongoloid, suggesting that the Western Hemisphere may have initially been settled not only earlier than thought, but by a people distinct from the ancestors of today's North and South American Indians."[12]

The African diaspora concept, as it is usually used, puts black Africans into Western hemispheric history and reality much too late. As it is usually used, it is a term employed to try to show the similarities between Jewish and black African history, even using the notion of the Jewish diaspora as the example and basis for talking about an African diaspora. The African diaspora, if that term were used properly, would be an automatic reference to the vast millennial black African global presence preceding the Jewish dispersal into the world by scores of millennia.

But Black historians and other Black intellectuals do not use the African diaspora concept properly. They primarily use it in a very restricted ideological sense, for a number of ideological and not historical reasons: to equate black African history, that part associated with dispersal, to Jewish dispersal history, to argue that all black people in the Western Hemisphere are Africans, to try to bolster the concept of Pan-Africanism, to talk about some "universal black African culture" from Africa to the Western Hemisphere, and to be able to use the term "African American" to refer to all black people in this Hemisphere, as if there were no historical, cultural, or identity distinctions among them. All this amounts to a romantic, ahistorical point of view.

To replace the concept of African diaspora, I have devised the concept of *African Extensia*. It might be considered a needless proliferation of concepts, but a new investigative and exploratory approach, as offered in this book, requires some new concept construction. A concept like African diaspora, which is so rigidly ideological, romantic, and ahistorical; which distorts, neglects, and suppresses so much of the history and reality of black Africans and their descendants in the world; and which seems to be irrevocably tied to these crippling dispositions, is a concept that should be replaced. The African Extensia concept is predicated on the paleontological and historical understanding that black people (or it could be said, black Africans) were the original human beings, and that they were the basis for the evolution of all humanity, as well as the progenitors of human history, language, culture, and social organization and institutions. The concept is an instant recognition and acceptance of the vast millennial reality and global presence of black people or black Africans as the first contributors to world history, culture, and social life. I have broken the general concept into four subdivisions: the *Southern African Extensia*, the birthplace and original homeland of black people and human beings; the *Eastern African Extensia*, referring to the migration of the original black Africans into the Middle East and Asia, and their descendants; the *Northern African Extensia*, the movement of original black Africans into Europe, and their descendants; and the *Western African Extensia*, referring to the movement of original black Africans into the Western Hemisphere and their descendants. The general term and its subdivisions are predicated on the historical reality that there is a distinction between black Africans and those who would now be referred to as black people of black African descent, who are no longer Africans, historically, culturally, socially, or in terms of identity, but who exhibit traces of black Africanness, in terms of race and culture in their present lives.

An argument of this book is that an Afrocentric concept or an Afrocentric Perspective on Black history or black African history are inadequate to deal with these realities. There are no "Afros" in this world and have never been; also meaning that the concepts of "Afro-American" or "Afro-Americans" are bogus, because such people have never existed in this country or in any part of the Western Hemisphere. What originally existed were black Africans and then their descendants, including those, like Black people in America, who can only claim a black African descent status, not a black African or African identity. And while Black Americans can be referred to as creoles, as some Black historians and other Black intellectuals do, this identity in no way helps Black people know who they are. Creole is a concept and identity that could easily and legitimately be applied to a white or yellow person, as well as a black one. A person born of English, Dutch, French, Spanish, Chinese, or Lebanese parentage in the Western Hemisphere would technically be a creole. An abuse of the term creole is to associate it exclusively with mixed-racial parentage, as has been commonly done. Since a creole identity does not denote Black or refer directly to a Black identity, and indeed obscures or suppresses it, it is an identity or designation that is better left alone.

I prefer the terms Africancentric and an Africancentric Perspective, which I feel can be properly applied to describing and analyzing black African history and peoples from the earliest time to the present. These terms could also legitimately be employed to discuss and analyze the migration of the early black people from Africa to other parts of the world, and thus the global black African presence. But these concepts would not be able to deal with the descendants of the black Africans where they have become a different people, making history differently, possessing a substantially different culture, and adhering to a different identify, such as describing themselves as Asians, or Europeans, or South Americans; or, more limited, as Yemenites, or Germans, or French, or English, or American, or Jamaican, or Barbadian. The latter are national identities, and many black people in the world think of themselves primarily or substantially in terms of their national identity, and do not think of themselves as Africans at all; at best only as black people of black African descent, and sometimes, as in the case of black people in the Fiji Islands or Hawaii, not even of black African descent. Black people in the United States are no longer Africans, but are of black African descent.

That is the argument of this book, and I have devised the concepts of *Blackcentric* and the *Blackcentric Perspective* to emphasize that; to show that Black people in this country are distinct and different from all other black people on this planet, and are not to be mistaken for any other black people. The Africancentric Perspective and explanation applies to them up to the point they began to emerge as a distinct and different ethnic group of the black race, which exhibits a myriad of such groups worldwide. The Africancentric Perspective argues, as per its chief theorist and developer, Molefi Asante (who uses the term Afrocentric), that "centeredness" or "place" is its core concept, meaning "the groundness or observation and behavior in one's own historical experiences."[13] This core conception of Africancentricity excludes Black people in America—not totally, but in an overwhelming way—because they have not been centered in an African historical, cultural, and social experience. Their centeredness has been in Black chattel slavery, Black ethnicity, English colonial and American national life, and Western civilization. Asante considers all black people on the planet to be Africans, rejecting the concept of black African descent, and regards efforts to separate black African people from each other as being "short-sighted, analytically vapid, and philosophically unsound."[14] He sees this as an attempt to "disconnect" Black people in America and other black people around the world from "thousands of years of history and tradition." This disconnection occurred when black African people took different historical, cultural, and social paths in this world, living away from the African continent; that is, separating space and time from place and reinvesting them elsewhere, in another place. It is not a matter logically or historically about disconnection, therefore, but in what way, and on what legitimate historical, cultural, and philosophical basis, a "reconnection" can be made, if it can be at all. Black centeredness is away from Africa and has been for centuries, making black Africa peripheral, although yet meaningful to Blacks in America.

Black people have been evolving within a Blackcentric context with respect to their history, identity, culture, and social life and for analytical purposes since the seventeenth century, when they became slaves in the country. The Blackcentric Perspective is in need of extensive development, and will receive it, not only at the hands of Black historians, but also from Black social scientists, literary critics, novelists, poets, playwrights, theologians, philosophers, and other kinds of Black intellectuals. It will also receive help from rank-and-file Black people who, after all, initially, as slaves, launched the construction of the Blackcentric Perspective.

But Black historians have to play a leadership role in further augmenting the development of a Blackcentric Perspective, as they have further to develop the knowledge, truth, and understanding about Black history in America. It seems to me that to accomplish both of these efforts more fruitfully it is necessary to go beyond First- and Second-Wave Black historiography, which have significant restraints on their efforts, to be discussed in the text. I propose a new approach to researching and writing Black history, a Third-Wave Black historiography that will incorporate aspects of First- and Second-Wave historiography. This will be discussed in Chapters 7 and 8. The centerpiece of this historiography will be the critical sociology of Du Bois, which includes his critical macro analytical framework, which I have called the White over Black hierarchical social structure and social system. This entire book is written from the stance of Third-Wave Black historiography, which includes not only critical Du Boisian sociology, but also the Blackcentric and Africancentric Perspectives in their legitimate usage.

In a word, Third-Wave Black historiography is critical sociological history or critical historical sociology. It declares several purposes. It seeks to be a critical approach to studying and writing Black history. It seeks to clarify the identity of Black people in America and how Black history itself should be designated. It seeks to clarify and emphasize the distinctiveness and uniqueness of Black history, which involves not only writing on Black history in America, but also entails showing how the realities of America, Europe, the Western African Extensia, and African history have helped to shape Black history and its distinctiveness or uniqueness, and how such historical factors continue to perform these determinant and shaping roles. Third-Wave Black historiography also has space within its philosophical, conceptual, and methodological orientations to proffer and employ Black history as a critical, heuristic device to evaluate the way white people have made history in America, the way American history itself has been made, and even the impact of Black people in America on the history and culture of America and Western Europe. Finally, Third-Wave Black historiography seeks to be an asset to the efforts of Blacks to achieve full inclusion and freedom in America.

Chapter 2

First- and Second-Wave
Black Historians I

Black historical writing emerged in America later than White historical writing, but followed the same path of development, originating as lay or nonprofessional historical writing and then, at a later time, advancing to professional historical writing. Lay or precursor Black historians, as well as the later Black professional historians, were always up against White racist thinking, which included the racist thinking of white historians, that declared that Black people were "nonhumans" or "subhumans," and thus a people not only without history but lacking the innate capacity to make it. The early Black historians sought to rend this racist thinking and argument, and in their efforts laid the foundation of determination, rebellion, and contrary historical writing that Black professional historians would inherit and build upon. They had their own stages of development, as First- and Second-Wave Black historians, as I depict them in this and the succeeding chapter, and made Black history a fully professional project, fully serviceable to Black people.

Lay Black historians emerged in America in the early nineteenth century, immediately catapulted into existence, in part in reaction to white lay historians who were endeavoring to write national histories that glorified white men and America and that simultaneously, in conjunction with other forms of writing, including newspapers, denigrated Black people. Precursor historians also emerged, motivated by their interest in providing public historical knowledge about Blacks, and also some positive public images of them. As a rule, Black lay historians were not as skillful as white ones in research, the use of documents, or narrative ability. But Black lay historians were revolutionary in their approach to writing Black history. Individuals like William Cooper Nell, William Wells Brown, and George Washington Williams sought to tell a different story about Black people. Their interest was not to revise the story told by white lay historians, but to provide historical knowledge and a historical understanding of Black people in America not to be found in white lay historical writing. George Bancroft, for instance, wrote of Black people that they were "gross and stupid, having memory and physical strength but . . . undisciplined in the exercise of reason and imagination."[1]

Early Black historians were not revisionist historians, that is, historians who accepted certain historically interpreted premises but sought to revise or modify them. These historians were not interested in accepting and revising racist premises or racist interpretations of the history of Blacks in America. They rejected such thinking and premises. They established, based on the kind of research they did, using the Bible (which white lay historians also used), newspapers, letters, speeches, or various official documents, their own factual and interpretive premises from which they wrote Black history, such as that the black race was not inferior to the white race; that the black race had made contributions to ancient history and Greek and Roman history (which white lay historians denied); that it was not the inferiority of the black race that led to its enslavement, as white lay historians said, but the power, cruelty, and greed of white people that was responsible for it; and that Blacks had made numerous important contributions to American history, culture, and social life (which white lay historians denied).

But some of the lay Black historians were revolutionary in another way in their historical writings: They used Black history as a basis to critique the way Whites made history in America, and the larger American history itself. In his book, *The Colored Patriots of the American Revolution*, William Cooper Nell not only discussed how despised Black men, as soldiers, helped the former English colonies defeat England—and how white people, ironically, were dependent upon such despised and supposedly inferior people for their survival and the survival of the new nation-state—but how Black soldiers and other Black people upheld the ideals of America better than most white people.[2] William Wells Brown made similar observations in his *The Negro in the American Rebellion: His Hero-ism and His Fidelity.*[3]

George Washington Williams talked of Black contributions to America's war with England and the war between the United States and the Southern Confederacy, and the ironic character of this Black participation in these wars, in his two-volume history of Black people, *History of the Negro Race in America,* which saw Black sol-diers acting more patriotically than white soldiers in both wars.[4] But Williams carried the theme of irony beyond American history and further back in time. In the first volume of his history of Black people he discussed the ironical situation of White/European civili-zation having its intellectual and cultural roots in ancient black civilizations such as Egypt and Meroe (Ethiopia). Dickson Bruce, Jr. referred laudably to the irony to be found in Black precursor historiography, arguing that it enabled these historians to develop a distinctive Black perspective on the American past, "a perspec-tive that differed significantly from the point of view with which white scholars of the same period approached the nation's history. For these early black scholars, the course of American history and of key historical events appeared almost overwhelmingly ironic."[5] Bruce further wrote that white historians did not develop an ironic perspective until the early twentieth century, and this change oc-curred initially among some professional historians. But even then it was not until the 1950s that professional white historians in larger numbers began to pay serious attention to the ironies in American history, which were themselves contradictions and paradoxes in that history.

This greater interest in ironic history was stimulated by a theo-logian and philosopher Reinhold Niebuhr, rather than by a histo-rian.[6] Thus, while early Black historians lagged behind early white historians in research and narrative skills, Black historians had a keener insight into American history than many lay and professional white historians, and even many professional white historians of to-day. Moreover, even when professional white historians deal with iro-nies or contradictions and paradoxes in American history, it does not usually change their basic views on American history. White histori-ans noting the irony of slave laws and slavery promoting the lib-erty and rights of white slaveholders (vis-à-vis other Whites, and against Black slaves and nonslave Blacks), do not conclude that slaveholders had a peculiar idea of liberty and rights that violated universal and idealistic views of liberty and rights, and which were devoid of ethics, humaneness, and a sense of justice.

In short, they had a view of liberty and rights that was synony-mous with a view and practice of license. Many white historians, noting the contradictory situation of White racism, slavery, segregation, and a hierarchical class stratification of Whites in America involving differentials in power, status, wealth, and social and cultural opportunities for the different social classes—the great inequality of American life even for white people, let alone between white people and Black people—still argue that the Age of Jackson, which reflected these disparities, was still a democratic period in American history. Some white revisionist historians, such as Edward Pessen and Harry Watson, have argued that America was not as democratic during the Jackson Era as past historians had said, but that it was still democratic.

Harry Watson was utterly confusing in presenting his historiographical view. In *Liberty and Power* he wrote, "The democratic developments of the 1830s and 1840s did not change as many things as some supporters and others feared." He also said the following things: "Direct popular democracy, moreover, was never a reality in Jacksonian America"; "There was no burst of complete social or political equality then or later"; "at its best . . . Jacksonian politics expressed a contradictory version of democracy"; "At its worst, moreover, 'Jacksonian democracy' was not democratic at all"; and "Jacksonian equality did not apply to women, either."[7] Watson was saying that democracy did not exist during the Age of Jackson in America, but he was unable to stay with that view and wrote, contradictorily, that it was democratic. The revision of the democratic premise was so thorough that there should have been a rejection of it. But Watson, not for evidentiary reasons, could not reject it; that is, he could not be revolutionary in his interpretation of the Jackson Era in America.

Like many white historians past and present (but unlike many Black historians, who have never bothered to question the democratic premise), Watson did not make a distinction between representative government and democratic government. Representative government grew in America between the 1820s and 1840s, but not democratic government. And a society of strong racism, with slavery, racist segregation, hierarchical class stratification, gender domination, and unequal power, status, wealth, and opportunity, was certainly not democratic during these decades. Still less could it be argued, as it has been by some white historians, that the South between the late nineteenth and early twentieth centuries, evidenced a "new democracy"—not with the widespread political disenfranchisement, and the vast political, economic, and social suppression of Blacks and Whites during those years.

Another important way of looking at this matter is to note that the recognition of irony in American history by white historians does not usually lead to a focus on the tragic character of American history, and thus does not take such historians to that deep analytical level of betrayal, subversion, and deformities or congenital defects in American history, culture, and social life. To recognize and write about ironies or contradictions and paradoxes in American history and not to mention or explore these areas of reality is to engage in quasi-critical (i.e., superficial), and even self-deceptive historical writing.

The racist-inundated White over Black structure and system plays a primary role here. Historically, that structure and system, invested in and reflected in the personalities, thoughts, and social behavior of white people, has conditioned them always to think of themselves as guiltless, innocent, and nonresponsible, and to think of other people, namely Black people, as guilty and culpable people. Did not white slaveholders blame the slave existence of Black people on their inferior nature and believe themselves to be guiltless, innocent, and nonculpable in maintaining the institution? Was this not part of the Pro-Slavery Argument? And did not Abraham Lincoln and other white people blame Black people for the war between the United States and the Southern Confederacy, taking white people off the hook? Talking to a group of Black men in the White House in August 1862, Lincoln said:

See our present condition—the country engaging in war!—our white men cutting one another's throats, not knowing how far it will extend; and then consider what we know to be true. But for your race among us there could not be war, although many men engage in war on either side do not care for you one way or another. Nevertheless, I repeat, without the institution of slavery and the colored race as a basis, the war could not have an existence.[8]

Early or precursor Black historians, especially those writing in the late nineteenth century, or even some in the early twentieth century, such as William Crogman and Benjamin Brawley, were strongly motivated to write their histories to justify what they described as the emancipation of Blacks from slavery and Black participation in the political and social life of America from the Reconstruction years onward.

But it has to be said that even early Black historians, while displaying an ironic perspective on American history, did not focus in a strong or clear way on the betrayals, subversions, deformities, or tragedies of American history. They mainly pointed to those realities of America without discussing them deeply or extensively in their writing. The White over Black structure and system played a primary role here as well. That structure and system said to Black people—and functioned to get to them to accept the conclusion by holding them in slavery, by verbal racist assaults, by public humiliation and denigration, and by racist practices that presupposed Blacks to be nonhumans or subhumans, nothings and nobodies—that they had nothing to say that white people needed to hear or needed to respect. That structure and system also said to white people that if Blacks were publicly critical of Whites or of a White-dominated America, or sought to project knowledge and images of themselves that contradicted White (i.e., racist) understandings and images of Blacks, Whites were to ignore or even suppress—through admonition, censorship, or violence—such Black efforts.

Thus, precursor Black historians realized that white people were not going to pay much attention to their historical writings on Blacks or America, and that these writings would not have much impact on the relationship between Whites and Blacks in the country. But they felt compelled to write their histories anyway and to present different kinds of public knowledge about Blacks, and also to present some different understandings about Whites and America. But these early Black historians softened their observations about Whites and America, thinking this might be a way to get material published, or to get some Whites to read works, or to prevent the full suppression of Black historical writing.

In his discussion of early Black historians, Earl Thorpe advanced the criticism that these historians did not write about the tragic dimensions of Black history or about tragedies in Black history and social life. Even when they discussed slavery, it was not at the level of the tragic or of tragedies. Precursor Black historians, as Thorpe said, were very optimistic in their historical writings, preferring to talk about the progressive moral, cultural, and social development of Blacks and their continuous, progressive efforts to attain inclusion and freedom in America.[9] Thorpe's argument was not without merit, but it was overdrawn. Early lay white historians, such as Jared Sparks, Walter Prescott, or George Bancroft, wrote optimistically about white people in America and focused on the continuous "progressive" development of white people, American history, and American society. Such historians were not slowed one iota by racism, segregation, slavery, or the suppression and extermination of Indians in writing their histories.

In short, such white historians essentially stayed away from writing on the tragic dimension of White history in America or the tragic dimensions of the larger American history. If early white historians would not write about these flaws and failings of White history and the larger American history, why should early Black historians write about such realities in Black history and Black life in America?

Moreover, there was another motivating factor for precursor Black historians. They were fully aware of how white people publicly denigrated and ridiculed Black people, which was done daily throughout the nineteenth century and on into the twentieth century.

For precursor Black historians to have focused on the tragic or negative features of Black history or Black people, or even to have said substantial things about them in their historical writings, would have fed the White racist thinking about Black people and the vile public images of them in America that white people insisted upon projecting for Whites and Blacks to see. In fine, early Black historians would have shown themselves and their scholarship to be in the full grip of the White over Black structure and system, which in many ways encouraged Blacks to denigrate or suppress themselves. Precursor Black historical writing was an attack against White domination of America and the White over Black structure and system that made the former possible, even if that attack in both instances was rather muted.

Where early Black historians did show themselves still to be in the strong grip of the White over Black structure and system was the varied and confused way they described Black people in their historical writings. In an individual work, Blacks would usually be described by three different names: Negroes, Colored people, and blacks, spelled with a small b. Sometimes Blacks would be spelled with a capital B, and would appear as Blacks, while the names and identities of Negroes and Colored might be spelled uncapitalized, as negroes and colored. The word black might be employed as an adjective or a noun in precursor historical writing. The same might be true of the word Negro even when capitalized, as when early Black historians spoke of the Negro race, employing the word Negro synonymously with the word black and meaning the black race. Sometimes the phrase or description "African race" would be used by precursor historians when they meant the black race.

But on the other hand, early Black historians did not regard all Africans in what they understood to be Africa as being Negroes. For instance, in the first volume of his *History of the Negro Race*, George Washington Williams wrote, "But in our examination of African tribes we shall not confine ourselves to that class of people known as Negroes, but call attention to other tribes as well.[10] In talking about the black people who came to America as slaves, Benjamin Brawley, a college teacher of English literature but also a lay Black historian of the early twentieth century, in his *A Social History of the American Negro*, remarked, "Those who came were by no means all of exactly the same race stock and language. . . . A number of those who came here were of entirely different race stock from the Negroes; some were Moors, and a very few were Malays from Madagascar."[11]

What Brawley and Williams were evidencing with their comments, which was also true with other lay Black historians, was confusion about race (biology), ethnicity, and nationality, mainly because this confusion existed widely among intellectuals in America and Europe. Race, ethnicity, and nationality were often projected in scholarship and other kinds of writings as being synonymous; even the word "nation" would appear in scholarly or other kinds of writings and would be employed to mean race or ethnicity. Precursor Black historians, like other intellectuals in the nineteenth and early twentieth centuries in America and Europe, did not appreciate the biological or physical variation that might appear in a given race, and this was particularly true when the focus was on the black race.

In America, as in Europe, when white or black people thought, wrote, or spoke of black people, meaning the black race, they meant the people who were understood to be Negroes; that is, people with "Negroid" features, such as black skin, kinky hair, broad noses, thick lips, and rounded behinds. Racism was involved here, to which even precursor Black historians acceded. Owing to their racism, white people in America and Europe felt that all black people looked alike; that is, they all had "Negroid" features, which, of course, were denigrated in a racist manner, to demean and belittle them and to reinforce the notion of their singularity within the black race. People of the black race—which white people (as well as Black people), called the "Negro race" or the "Colored race," employing all terms interchangeably—who did not have all "Negroid" features or such easily identifiable features, and especially if they exhibited a different language and culture, would not be called Negroes or black people, meaning "Negroid" people, and would be called by an ethnic or national name instead.

In America, determining who was or was not Negro or black could sometimes be a complicated matter. There were Black people, people who were regarded and designated as Black and black, but who were very light, yellowish in color, or even white in color. It could not always be determined, on the basis of eyesight, whether such people were Negroes or black. But Whites, in strong racist fashion, usually took the position that if any "Negroidness" or "blackness" could be discerned in light-skinned black people, they were to be considered Negroes, Colored people, or black people. Some were sometimes referred to as mulattoes or quadroons (although not a widely used phrase in North America), when they looked more white than anything, having only a "quarter" reality of blackness in them.

The black race in America, therefore, and Black people as an ethnic group (a realty to be discussed more fully in Chapter 4), had people among them who were not really black in color, but who were considered by white people to be black, Negroes, or Colored, although they were sometimes treated better than Black people who were darker and obviously Negro, Colored, or Black. Black people also accepted designated mulattos or quadroons as black and Black people, owing to kinship and blood ties, and because of the White imposed reality.

Precursor Black historians accepted, as did other Blacks, the White racist manner of describing and defining black people and the black race as Negroes and the "Negroid" race. They also accepted, like other Blacks in America did, the designation of people as black people, Negroes, or Colored people who were not black in color and who might be rather, or purely, white in color. When writing about the history of Blacks in America, precursor historians did not put an emphasis on the racial variation or the racial complexity of Black people. They wrote about Black people, for the most part, as if they were all of the same racial group, no matter what their complexion.

Precursor Black historians also accepted the existence of what was understood by some in America to be Africa, although it was not always understood by them that Africa was a continent and not a country. These historians, therefore, also accepted what was publicly understood by some in America to be African, namely black people with "Negroid" features who came from Africa. Other people in Africa who they might think were not Negroes were usually not their serious historiographical interest. Drawing what they understood to be Africans into their historical efforts, precursor Black historians focused on those Africans they regarded as having "Negroid" features, or who were to them Negroes.

Thus, in this historical scholarship, Negroes and Africans were synonymous. But precursor historians did not regard Black people in the United States to be Africans, but rather black people of black African descent or, as it was also asserted, Negroes of negro African descent. When they were writing about Black people in America and not about Africa or Africans, early Black historians rarely used the word African, which was generally rarely used in the United States. When they used the word African to refer to some black person in America, it was someone they thought to be an African, having just arrived in North America, or who still had a strong African orientation, who had not become an American Black person; that is, a Negro or a Colored person. On occasion, a precursor Black historian would refer to Black people in America as Africans, but this was not done with much conviction, and was likely a literary usage of the name or an emotional comment by the author. William Cooper Nell demonstrated this behavior. In *The Colored Patriots of the American Revolution*, he wrote,

It is not surprising, that in the time of the Revolutionary War, when so much was said of freedom, equality, and the rights of man, the poor African should think that he had some rights, and should seek that freedom which others valued so highly.[12]

Nell usually referred to Black people as Negroes, Colored people, or blacks in his book. Other precursor historians did the same. Accepting, as they did, that Blacks in America were people of African descent, precursor historians accepted the historical, cultural, social, and even psychological transformation of the black people who had come to America as slaves. They had more clarity about this than the name of Black people, a single one of which they could not or, at least, did not settle upon. This represented continued confused thinking about the Black identity in America, and as to how Black history itself should be designated, as precursor Black historians saw it as Negro history and Colored history, and sometimes as black history, spelled in the lower case. They passed this confusion on to their successors, those whom I call First-Wave Black historians.

The precursors also passed some rather positive things on to their successors. They generally rejected White racist historical writing about Black people, and provided different historical knowledge and understandings and different images of Black people. This was the legacy of revolutionary historical writing that precursors passed on to their successors. These early historians left the knowledge and understanding that neither Black people nor Black history had their origins in America or in slavery, but rather in what they understood to be Africa. They left the revolutionary viewpoint that the black race (the race of "Negroid" physical features, or the Negro race, as they often said), was not inferior to the white race and to white people, and that it had been a race that had built advanced cultures and civilizations and had benefited white people and the cultures and civilizations they constructed. The early historians also left a legacy of using Black history as a heuristic means to critique the history of white people in America and the larger American history, although this critical view was not fully developed and employed.

The successors to the early Black historians initially appeared in the 1890s, actually in the form of one person: William Edward Burghardt Du Bois—W.E.B. Du Bois—who was educated and trained as a historian at Harvard University and who also studied at the

University of Berlin, receiving his Ph.D. from Harvard in 1895. This was the same year that the *American Historical Review* was founded, and eleven years after the establishment of the American Historical Association, which later established the *Review* as part of its general effort to institutionalize historical research and writing and the teaching of history in American colleges and universities, and to help produce professional historians. In the 1880s and 1890s a trend evolved to replace the lay or amateur historians and the way they did research and wrote history, with their emphasis on narration, their strong romantic orientation, and their sweeping historical syntheses or generalizations.

The new movement toward professionalization in writing history sought to produce as a model a historian who had been college or university educated, who had been trained as a historian (with that training including a method of historical research that had a scientific orientation that emphasized specialization in historical research and knowledge), who had attained a Ph.D., and who wrote monographs on specialized and limited historical subjects.[13] Professionalization also became the interest of philosophers, economists, psychologists, political scientists, and eventually sociologists, all of which, like history, equated professionalization with a college or university education, specialized training, a Ph.D., and a scientific method of research.

Du Bois was the first Black person to undergo education and training as a professional historian. Other Blacks underwent the process in the early twentieth century, and also receiving Ph.D. degrees. What I call First-Wave Black historians and First-Wave Black historiography were launched. In an article in the mid-1980s, John Hope Franklin provided a discussion and assessment of the kinds of Black historians who had been produced in America since the 1880s, which coincided with the development of professional history in the United States, and which differs from my perspective on the history and functioning of Black historians in this country.[14] Franklin argued that there had been four generations of Black historians. The first generation had begun in the 1880s with George Washington Williams when he published his two-volume history of Blacks in America in 1882. This generation, as Franklin said, included W.E.B. Du Bois and Booker T. Washington, owing to the latter's two-volume history of Blacks in America, *Story of the Negro*, which was published in 1909. The latter date marked the end of the first generation of Black historians.

The second generation of Black historians, as Franklin contended, was inaugurated by Du Bois, who was also of the first generation. The second generation were professionally trained Black historians. Du Bois inaugurated this group with the publication of his doctoral dissertation in 1895. The second Black Ph.D. in history was Carter Woodson, who got his degree from Harvard in 1912. Woodson has usually been regarded as the "father" of Black history, a status that Franklin accepted, given his prodigious effort to create professional Black historians and to promote Black history in America. In 1915 Woodson founded the Association for the Study of Negro Life and History, and in 1916 founded the *Journal of Negro History* and also Associated Publishers, to publish his own books as well as those of other Black historians.

In 1926 Woodson established Negro History Week so that there could be an annual public observation of the contributions that Black people had made to American history, society, and civilization. With the success of Negro History Week, Woodson then, as Franklin remarked, "launched the *Negro History Bulletin*, a magazine for students, teachers, and the general public." Franklin also noted, "Fifty years after the beginning of the *Negro History Bulletin*, the American Historical Association was still wrestling with the idea of a popular history magazine for students and the general Public."[15]

Part of Woodson's own promotional activities, over a period of decades, were his own publications. There were a number of them, such as *Education of the Negro to 1861*, *The Negro in Our History*, *The Mind of the Negro as Reflected in Letters Written during the Crisis, 1800–1860*, *The African Background Outlined*, and *African Heroes and Heroines*.[16] Describing Woodson's efforts to advance Black historical writing and Black history and to create professional Black historians, John Hope Franklin wrote,

Woodson was the dominant figure of the period. He was not only the leading historian but also the principal founder of the association, editor of the *Journal*, and executive director of the Associated Publishers. He gathered around him a circle of highly trained younger historians whose research he directed and whose writings he published in the *Journal of Negro History* and under the imprint of the *Associated Publishers*. Monographs on labor, education, Reconstruction, art, music, and other aspects of Afro-American life appeared in a steady succession.[17]

Over several decades, Woodson made interest in Black history a movement of sorts among Black people, but he also drew a number of white people into it, including professional white historians, to have them take an interest in Black history and write articles for the *Journal of Negro History*. In the 1930s and 1940s a number of Blacks gained Ph.D.s in history, such as Rayford W. Logan, Luther Porter Jackson, Lorenzo Johnston Greene, Lula M. Johnson, Helen G. Edmonds, William Sherman Savage, Alrutheus Ambush Taylor, Benjamin Quarles, John Hope Franklin, Elsie Lewis, Lawrence D. Reddick, Charles Wesley, and Merze Tate. These individuals, along with Du Bois and Woodson, as well as other Black historians, made up what I call the First- Wave Black historians.

Under Franklin's classification of second-generation Black historians, these historians were strong and predominant until about the 1950s. The third generation of Black historians then emerged fully on the scene, which Franklin said had its origins in the 1930s. This generation was initiated by Du Bois with his publication of *Black Reconstruction*, and lasted until the close of the 1960s.[18] Many of the historians of the third generation were historians of the second generation. Franklin saw the difference between the second and third generation to be their historiographical interests. The second generation, as had the first generation, produced a "contributionist" historiography, writing about individual Black and Black group contributions to American history and life. The third generation of Black historians focused their historiographical attention on

the interaction of blacks and whites, and more to the frequent antagonisms than to rare moments of genuine cooperation. They tended to see Afro-American history in a larger context, insisting that any event that affected the status of Afro-Americans was a part of Afro-American history even if no Afro-Americans were directly involved."[19]

Many of what I call First-Wave Black historians and that John Hope Franklin called second- and third-generation Black historians got their Ph.D.s or master's degrees in history at a time, in the 1930s and 1940s, when Blacks were making a strong effort to integrate themselves more fully into American culture, social institutions, and social life (what I call the top part of the White over Black structure and system), to reduce its racist orientation, and to mitigate its racist oppressiveness to create more and better inclusion. The Black thrust for greater integration and for more freedom in America was also stimulated by World War II and the perceived changes that would come to the world and America, and to Black people and other oppressed people of dark hue in the world, changes that would give Black people and dark people more power, rights, and opportunities in the countries in which they lived. Black historians, caught up like other Black people in perceived or actual progressive, liberating trends in the world and in America between the 1930s and 1960s, focused their historical writing on the way Black people had been involved with Whites in American history and the cultural, social, economic, and political consequences this had produced.

In the 1970s, according to John Hope Franklin, the fourth generation of Black historians appeared in America. He regarded these historians as the largest group of Black historians ever, and perhaps the best educated and trained to be professional historians. Franklin called these historians, as well as all previous generations of Black historians, Afro-American historians, as he called Black history of America, Afro-American history, showing how he had been influenced by those Black historians, other Black scholars, and other kinds of Black intellectuals who had been arguing that Blacks were Afro-Americans or African Americans.

Franklin described the fourth generation of Black historians and their capabilities in the following manner:

The Afro-Americans . . . were trained, as were the white historians, in graduate centers in every part of the country, in contrast to those of the third generation, who had been trained at three or four universities in the East or Midwest. No area of inquiry escaped their attention. They worked on the colonial period, the era of Reconstruction, and the twentieth century. They examined slavery, the Afro-American family, and antebellum free blacks. Their range was wide, and they brought educational, cultural, and military subjects, among many others, under their scrutiny.[20]

John Hope Franklin was a little critical of what he called fourth-generation Black historians for not showing enough "grace . . . charity and . . . gratitude" toward previous generations of Black historians. But he also felt this criticism was relatively unimportant, because the work that these new historians produced was usually of high quality. Franklin was actually coming to the defense of fourth-generation Black historians. There had been criticism of some of them for not observing the canon of historical research and writing as it had been sanctioned by the history profession, or for being too ideological or too romantic in their historical writing. Franklin was not only aware of these criticisms, but had them for some of the new Black historians himself. But it was clearly his view that fourth-generation Black historians were generally competent historians, equal to the generality of professional historians, and that they wrote important and enlightening historical works that, in fact, had received this kind of public acknowledgment.

Much of the praise that both white and Black historians placed on what John Hope Franklin called second- and third-generation Black historians was because of the belief that such historians accepted the canon of scientific historical research and writing as it evolved in the late nineteenth and early twentieth centuries, with the new professionalization of historical research and writing, which centered on the dream and value of objectivity. Precursor Black historians were not professional historians, but rather amateur historians, although some, such as George Washington Williams, or William Brawley in the twentieth century, made an effort to be as canonical as they could in their writings.

What I call First-Wave Black historians adhered to the canon of professional historical writing with zeal so that white historians would not say they had ignored, deprecated, or abandoned the standard, and with the understanding or, at least, the hope that historical knowledge about Black people gained from the same scientific methodology used by white historians would have more credence with professional white historians as well as with the White and Black publics in America. In drawing his classification of historians in terms of generations, Franklin, in his conception of first-generation Black historians, ignored a number of earlier historians and put Du Bois in with the earlier lay historians who wrote history between the 1880s and 1909, such as William Crogman and Archibald Grimke. It seems necessary to divide Black historians between the earlier lay historians, who I call precursor Black historians, and who Earl Thorpe referred to as the "Beginning School" in *Negro Historians in the United States*, and Black professional historians.[21]

It is important to note that some of these lay historians went beyond 1909, such as William Brawley, but also Alain Locke and J. A. Rogers. Brawley, a university-educated and trained specialist in English literature and an author of books on the subject, took a strong interest in historical writing. He was actually, as a lay historian (but trying to adhere to canonical historical research and writing), the specific precursor of Black intellectual and cultural history with his book *The Negro in Literature and Art*, published in 1910, which was expanded in subject matter and reissued in 1937 as *The Negro Genius*.[22] Alain Locke, a Ph.D. in philosophy, was also a lay Black historian writing in the area of Black intellectual and cultural history, as reflected in his books, *The Negro and His Music*, published in 1936, and *The Negro in Art*, published in 1940.[23]

J. A. Rogers was a lay black historian, a West Indian (a Jamaican) living in the United States, who not only took an interest in Black history in the United States but also in the history of the black race and how that race, emanating from Africa, made history around the world, or what I call the African Extensia. The African Extensia, which it could be said had its origins millions of years ago when prehistoric creatures initially left Africa and migrated to the eastern, northern, and western parts of the world, forming the prehuman populations of those worlds and creating whatever existed as prehuman culture and social life. About 180,000 to 90,000 years ago a migration ensued from Africa, this time of *homo sapiens sapiens* or human beings, with consequences for human history and human beings to which I have already alluded.[24]

J. A. Rogers's historical works, which were actually a mixture of history and physical and cultural anthropology, reflected knowledge of the two great migrations from Africa, even if he did not have any conceptualization of them and did not separate the two migrations clearly in his thinking or historical writings. Rogers was concerned to show the presence and impact of what he regarded as black African people and people of black African descent on the world. He wrote a number of books to reveal this presence and impact, such as his three-volume *Sex and Race* and his three-volume *World's Great Men of Color*, the latter of which were written on a biographical basis, similar to the way a number of Black precursor histories were written, and for the same reasons: to identify individual black people and their accomplishments and to preserve them for posterity, which was not something that white historians would be interested in doing and which would be a glorious legacy for black people in America, Africa, and elsewhere.[25]

J. A. Rogers sought as much historical documentation for his works, as a rule, as he could uncover. He also relied upon photographs and artwork, paintings, and sculptures to verify his assertions about black people in the world and their historical, cultural, and social efforts. Sometimes Rogers could do no more than just infer the black African or black African descent presence, and would just leave the matter there. But talking about a black African presence in world history, culture, and social life when such a thing was ignored or denied, not only by white professional historians but even by some Black historians who were walking too closely in the shadows of white historians, thinking like them that Africa was the "dark," meaning blighted continent, and that black Africans were primitive, was revolutionary historical writing. J. A. Rogers should be classified, as I classify him, as a primary precursor black historian of what I call, and will discuss more fully in the next chapter, Second-Wave Black historiography, and also of what I call Third-Wave Black historiography, which will be discussed fully in the last chapters of this book.

W.E.B. Du Bois once said of J. A. Rogers, "No man living has revealed so many important facts about the Negro."[26] Before Rogers, and also before Carter Woodson, it had been Du Bois of whom it could have been said what Du Bois later said of Rogers. As the first Black professional historian in America, Du Bois took much of his historical writing cues from precursor Black historians in America. This could even be said of the entire group of what I call First-

Wave Black historians. Du Bois and other First-Wave Black historians were like precursor historians in that they were also historians of the Western African Extensia. Du Bois as well as other First-Wave Black historians, and this was particularly true of Carter Woodson and those historians he trained or influenced, wrote about Black contributions to American history, culture, and social life. Those same historians in the 1930s and 1940s and thereafter concentrated their historical writing, as John Hope Franklin said, on historical Black and White social interaction and involvement in America.

Precursor Black historians used "contributionism" to talk about Black and White interaction and involvement in America, and pointed to the ironies that this involvement produced in American history. First-Wave Black historians also dealt with ironies and paradoxes, although they said much more than precursor Black historians about how Black involvement with Whites impacted American history, culture, and social life. Finally, like precursor Black historians, First-Wave Black historians usually referred to Black people as Negroes or Colored people, and usually as people of Negro African descent; sometimes, the description "blacks" would be used, spelled with a small b. Black history itself was usually described by this first wave of professional historians as Negro history or Colored history; sometimes, black history, spelled with a small b.

In the 1960s and 1970s and thereafter, some new and younger Black historians joined the ranks of what I call First-Wave Black historians, such as Nathan Huggins, Nell Irvin Painter, Darlene Clark Hine, and Bettye J. Gardner. These historians and others like them use the name Afro-American or African American to describe Black people. But such people also describe Black people as Black, Blacks, black, and blacks in their writings. Older generations of First-Wave Black historians who are still writing history, such as John Hope Franklin, have been influenced by the new, younger members of their ranks, as well as by Second-Wave Black historians in referring to Black people as Afro-Americans or African Americans, but like these same younger historians, they refer to Blacks as being Blacks as well, spelling it various ways. All these historians, ascribing so many identities to Black people, are showing confusion in their thinking and scholarship.

It also shows a refusal to look sharply at historical evidence that points to the identity of Black people in America and does not designate them as Africans, African Americans, or Afro-Americans. It should also be said that there are First- and Second-Wave Black historians who seem not to be disturbed in the slightest that they play around with the name of Black people, and are abusive with it and thus with Black history and Black people. This means that they do not see how, in this particular matter, they are strongly in the grip of the racist-inundated White over Black structure and system, doing the work of racism and the structure and system by abusing Black people and their history themselves, something that the racist-inundated structure and system always sought to encourage Black people to do.

Third-Wave Black historiography would stop playing around with the name of Black people and abusing Black people and their history and doing the work of the White over Black structure and system in any way. It would reinforce in a very consistent way what has been a tradition of Black historical scholarship even when that tradition was not implemented totally or consistently: that it was a weapon to be used against White racism and the White over Black structure and system, and an instrument to help Black people achieve full inclusion and full freedom in America.

Chapter 3

First- and Second-Wave
Black Historians II

It was John Hope Franklin's view that Du Bois's long life of ninety-five years enabled him to "span three generations" of his classification of four generations of Black historians in America. He died just as the Second-Wave of Black historians were emerging. He would have an influence on some of them, and also some of the later members of this new wave, particularly with his writings on black Africa and the relationship between black Africans and black people in the Western African Extensia. There would be Second-Wave Black historians over the years who would be impressed and impacted by Du Bois's vast and varied writing output, including his vast and varied writing about Black people. In writing about Du Bois, John Hope Franklin stated that he did not have a singular interest in history, but also had an interest in "sociology, anthropology, political science, education, and literature." One could have also said philosophy, philosophy of social science, socialist theory, and other intellectual pursuits. In Franklin's view, "Du Bois became one of the few people ever who could be considered truly qualified in the broad field of Afro-American studies."[1] It could be said that Du Bois pioneered Black Studies in America with his published doctoral dissertation, *The Philadelphia Negro, The Souls of Black Folk*, the Atlanta University studies in ethnographic sociology (eighteen volumes in all), *The Negro, The Gift of Black Folk, Black Reconstruction, Black Folk Then and Now*, and other writings between the 1890s and his death in 1963.[2]

John Hope Franklin said, mistakenly, that Du Bois, trained as a professional historian, "deserted the field shortly after he entered it." Du Bois remained a historian all of his life, as he remained a sociologist, philosopher, literati, political analyst and theorist, and even journalist all of his life. Du Bois did not abandon history; he never fully accepted the canonical version of a professional historian, or of professional historical research and writing, when it was evolving in the 1880s and 1890s or when they became full-blown realities over the subsequent decades. Du Bois's doctoral dissertation, though usually not indicated as such by scholars, was not strictly history, but rather historical sociology. Du Bois wrote some strictly historical pieces, but they were articles, not books. His monographic historical writings were writings in historical sociology. *John Brown*, published in 1909, and a book that Du Bois regarded as one of his favorites, was historical biographical sociology.[3]

The history profession ultimately turned against Du Bois; that is, white historians, for the most part, ultimately turned against him because of his association with American Communists from the late 1940s and for joining the American Communist Party in 1962. There was no mention of Du Bois's name, or any memorial to him in the *American Historical Review* or any other American professional historical journal, when he died in Accra, Ghana, in 1963. But the history profession had more or less turned against Du Bois as a historian long before the 1940s. There was a negative reaction to his *John Brown*, which was criticized because it did not employ much primary documentation, relied too heavily on secondary sources, and only a few of them at that, and because it used overlong quotations. *The Negro*, written six years later, was criticized for its philosophical viewpoints and its incorporation of so much anthropological information. Du Bois's *Black Reconstruction* was criticized strongly by a number of historians for being a Marxist work—that is, an ideological writing, and of one of the worse kinds—for relying too heavily on secondary sources, and for using very long quotations. The update of *The Negro*, published in 1939 as *Black Folks Then and Now*, was criticized for being a Marxist writing and for being too sociological.

A point of clarification to be made was that Du Bois was never a Marxist, something that even Herbert Aptheker indicated, which was why he was critical of Du Bois as a political thinker.[4] Manning Marable interviewed Aptheker extensively to write his biography of Du Bois, *W.E.B. Du Bois: Black Radical Democrat*, and thus it was strange to see him regard Du Bois as a Marxist in his work.[5] And he was still less correct to suggest that Du Bois was an evolving Marxist–Leninist. My own unpublished dissertation, "The Socialist Analysis of W.E.B. Du Bois," made it quite clear that Du Bois was neither a Marxist nor a Marxist–Leninist at any time in his life.[6] He was always a Du Boisian socialist, as he was a Du Boisian historian and a Du Boisian sociologist.

Du Bois, in the area of scholarship, whether it was done in the academy or not, was always primarily a sociologist. He used many forms of human (also academic) knowledge to help him understand things sociologically, and to engage in sociological analysis. He used history to help him engage in sociological analysis and, in turn, used sociological analysis to understand history. Du Bois was educated and trained as a scientific historian, but he was also, at the same time, developing scientific sociology in America. As said earlier, he was the progenitor of scientific sociology in the country.

But Du Bois rejected a strong (i.e., strict natural science) orientation for scientific historical writing, and for a scientific sociology. In regard to the latter, he was like Max Weber in Germany, his contemporary, who was also endeavoring to develop a scientific sociology and who, like Du Bois, rejected the positivistic viewpoint, gaining ground in Europe and America, that a scientific sociology had to follow strictly along the lines of natural science. Du Bois and Weber, in independent efforts, concluded that history and the social sciences had to focus on more than what was thought to be objective reality. They both had to focus on subjective reality as well, which also had to be studied scientifically and had to be part of any *scientific* investigation of historical and social phenomena. In 1904 Du Bois wrote that a scientific sociology had to focus on subjective and objective factors in human behavior, and how they interacted with each other:

Now whatever one's whims and predilections no one can wholly ignore either of these criticisms: if this is a world of absolute unchanging physical laws, then the laws of physics and chemistry are the laws of all action. . . . On the other hand . . . men after experiencing the facts of life have almost universally assumed that in among physical forces stalk self-directing Wills, which modify, restrain and re-direct the ordinary laws of nature. The assumption is tremendous in its import. It means that from the point of view of science this is a world of Chance as well as law.[7]

Du Bois did not believe that human behavior was strictly determined by history, culture, and social life that patterned behavior and made it regular on a daily basis and over a period of time. Human beings, on the basis of their intellect, wills, desires, and interests, could interdict and alter patterns of behavior, and thus the course of history, culture, and social life. Human beings, as Du Bois saw it, always held onto their "inner life" (subjectivity) that interacted with their "outer life" (objectivity), producing observable behavior. Du Bois believed that statistics were needed to help research and understand human behavior in a scientific manner.[8] But he also felt that statistics could be abused, especially when they replaced focusing on actual human behavior, including the "inner life," or actual social facts, and when human behavior was just understood mathematically: "It may take a statistical turn and the student becomes so immersed in mere figures as to forget, or to be entirely unacquainted with, the concrete facts standing back of the counting."[9]

Du Bois felt that scientific sociology had to be motivated by intent, involvement, and commitment, but also had to be conducted with a certain amount of disinterest, detachment, and neutrality. These were not contradictory approaches to scientific sociological investigation, but different approaches that were both required. These different approaches not only represented aspects of methodology; they were values as well. Du Bois believed that values were necessary or integral to scientific sociological research and study. He rejected the positivistic view that was taking over historical research and writing in America in the late nineteenth and early twentieth centuries and that would engulf sociology in the early twentieth century, and that said that values should be divorced from scientific inquiry; that this inquiry should be "value-neutral."

Du Bois rejected this positivistic view because it would function to squeeze imagination and creativity out of historical and scientific sociological research and explanation, and social science research and explanation generally. He also argued that values could either aid scientific research or hinder or suppress it, like racist values did. A strict positivistic or strict natural science approach to sociological or social science study, or even to historical study, would not be a scientific approach. It would suppress an effort to be scientific, which for historical and social phenomena had to take in human motivation (subjectivity) and not just external behavior (objectivity). Positivism, or the natural science approach, had to be mixed with the interpretive approach. This was the more complex view of science that Du Bois held to for sociology and for historical research and writing. Du Bois criticized sociologists who attempted to make sociology a natural science discipline, which would call for an overstress on statistics or mathematics: "Sociology carried it to its logical limits and has become a mere statistical guide to calculate facts lifelessly like mathematics. It is perhaps unnecessary to illustrate the effect of this deadening technique upon real scholars."[10] Du Bois also criticized historians who took the natural science (the exclusive objectivity) approach to research and writing:

It has long been a point of honor with historians trained in modern seminar methods to allow themselves no expression of moral indignation. They seek the aloofness and imperturbability of the biologist who dissects bugs or the geologist who hammers stone. The difficulty is that history does not deal simply with bugs and stones, but with human beings; and if it is written honestly and truthfully, it is impossible to be entirely and continuously unperturbed, or to avoid sometimes getting plain mad. Of course, if the indignation precedes a knowledge of facts, or supplants honest and endless effort to know the truth, history becomes a dangerous pastime. . . . If, after studying the history of Africa in the last sixty years, and studying it carefully and exhaustively, a writer can put down these facts with cold detachment; without bias or moral indignation, he is not a human being. The object of many historians seems to be just that: to avoid being human.[11]

While Du Bois did not have the conceptualization, he did have the discussions to indicate that he regarded the efforts of historians and social scientists to be natural scientists in their research and writing efforts; to be what some present-day critics of such an approach say it is: "scientism," or pseudoscience. He looked upon the history profession's interest in producing "objective history" as scientism. Other than having a different conception of science when he wrote history, Du Bois also had intellectual attributes that were exhibited by lay historians of the nineteenth and twentieth centuries, Black and white, and especially the latter, such as a strain of romanticism, a strong interest in narrative, and a wish to synthesize history. *Black Reconstruction* evidenced all of these attributes, as well as Du Bois's conception of science. It also evidenced Du Bois's belief that ideas played a role in history, which was exhibited by his extended use of quotations. Du Bois's *Black Reconstruction* also reflected his socialist thinking and his own method of socialist analysis, which combined four different forms of analysis: racist, racial, class, and gender analysis, all in interaction with each other.

Du Bois, therefore, was unlike most First-Wave Black historians writing history from the 1890s into the early twentieth century, who fully accepted the canon of professional historical research and writing (i.e., the understood and sanctified approach), and who would advance their criticisms against Du Bois's historical writings, although they would also praise him or sympathize with him because of the important insights or the important knowledge or understanding he proffered, even if not following the strict canon of historical writing. Du Bois's *Black Reconstruction*, as negatively criticized by professional historians as it was, changed forever the way American historians would write about the Reconstruction period in American history. Du Bois's *Black Folk Then and Now* still remains an important work of historical sociology on the Western African Extensia. His published doctoral dissertation on the suppression of the African slave trade to the United States, another work of historical sociology, remains the foremost study on this subject more than a century after its publication. Du Bois predicated this work on extensive primary documentation, which would never be his research approach again in writing a historical monograph. In his other works, he would rely primarily on secondary sources and just simply endure the criticism. But it has to be said, as a point of interest as well as a statement of attitude, that Richard Hofstadter relied strongly on secondary research materials, and even Ph.D. dissertations, to write his historical works. He received Pulitzer prizes for his efforts, as well as great praise from the history profession.

Du Bois, of course, was fully aware of the racism and hypocrisy of the American historical profession. He was aware of how it reflected the society's racist practice of demanding that Black people observe professional or social standards that Whites often felt free to break. Du Bois was aware of how white historians would insist that Black historians observe all the features of the canon of professional historical research and writing, but for decades violated such standards when writing about Black people in American history or Black history itself. White historians also showed a concern and even fear of the critique that Black historians would make of the historical behavior of Whites in America and American history itself.

This is some of what precursor Black historians had done. They wrote histories of Black people that white historians could peruse, and in their histories they said things about white people and America that were different than what white historians said. Lay white historians of the nineteenth and early twentieth centuries, as well as professional white historians when they emerged in America, primarily ignored precursor Black historical writing. Most professional white historians ignored First-Wave Black historians who carried on in the historiographical tradition of their Black predecessors. These historians developed further what could be described as Black history and Black historiography, which was not given credence by most professional white historians or generally by the history profession; that is, Black history was not recognized to be a legitimate area of historical study within the history profession and as a recognized mini-area of American history.

In short, it was not history that white historians had to read, respect, or take into account, in the same way that white Americans felt that Black people had no rights or anything about their lives that they had to respect, such as their culture or their contributions to America. White people were part of the White over Black structure and system, the people component of it as opposed to the cultural and social elements of the structure and system, and they revealed their participation in it and the structure and system's influence over them. These remarks could also be extended to white historians who generally considered Black history and Black historiography outside legitimate historical research and interests.

But this was not true of all white historians, as some did think that Black history and Black historiography were legitimate history and historical writing in America. Moreover, such historians paid attention to the historical development of Blacks in America, and also to Black interaction and involvement with Whites in American history—the strong historiographical focus of First-Wave Black historiography from the 1930s on—that was a motivation and inspiration for such historians. Carter Woodson tried to encourage white historians to take an interest in Black history and Black people's interaction with and relationship to white people and America in the country's history (including an interest in Black contributions to American history and life). Woodson invited white historians to be members of and participate in the annual sessions of the Association for the Study of the Life and History of the Negro, to present papers and to engage in discussions, and he also encouraged them to write articles for the *Journal of Negro History*, which he published.

While Carter Woodson wanted white historians to write Black history and to know that history because the more historians disclosing the reality, knowledge, and truth the better, he did not for one second imagine Blacks abandoning writing Black history or relying upon white historians to do it. Black history was too important to Black people and their development and life in America to leave it in the hands of white historians. And Black historians had to be prepared to tell that story, as they saw it and as the evidence and their interpretation of the evidence would have it, and not be overly worried about White reaction to it, even the reaction of white historians.

What was important for Black historians to do, as Woodson saw it, was to present their knowledge and understanding of Black history to Black people and to make sure they got a view that was more accurate, more enlightening, and more helpful to them and that would be knowledge and truth about their own history that would enable them to resist and reject white lies and distortions about their history, the *miseducation* that Black people had continuously to endure in America. Woodson was interested in Black messengers for Black people, and so he tried diligently, before his death in 1950, to produce a plethora of Black historians.

By the 1950s, however, and as a consequence of their knowledge of Black history and the relationship of Black people to white people and American history, a number of First-Wave Black historians were thinking that Black history was necessary, indeed, central to understanding American history. John Hope Franklin made that observation in 1957 in "The New Negro History," and held that view thereafter, reiterating it in his article on Black historiography in the mid-1980s.[12] Benjamin Quarles expressed a similar view earlier, in 1974.[13] Younger Black historians who became more recent First-Wave Black historians, such as Thomas Holt, thought of Black history as the central history of America; namely, as providing a standpoint from which greater knowledge and understanding could be adduced by that history. In the mid-1980s, Holt wrote,

Thus Afro-American history becomes a window onto the nation's history, a vantage point from which to reexamine and rewrite that larger history. This is true not simply because Blacks should be included for a more accurate portrait, but more because their inclusion changes many of the basic questions posed, the methods and sources for answering those questions, and the conclusions reached.[14]

In the 1960s there were young Black historians who were not interested in First-Wave Black historiography, historiography that focused on Black history but also demonstrated an interest in showing how Blacks interacted with Whites and the larger American history and the impact that Blacks had on both, or the strong interest, at least philosophically, of viewing and employing Black history as a critical device to draw out more knowledge and truth about American history. These historians were primarily interested in focusing on Black history and telling the truth about it, which they did not feel that white historians wanted to tell or were capable of telling. Some of these historians were Black nationalist historians. But even when they were not Black nationalists or even Black nationalist–influenced historians, this newer group of young historians were interested in Black history and not White history or American history, or not much of either. They felt they could write Black history as it ought to be written and tell that story as it ought to be told, without being, in the case of some of these historians, particularly concerned about the White response to their writing.

One of these newer Black historians was Vincent Harding. Actually, Harding started out as a newer and younger member of the First Wave of Black historians. In 1971 he published an article, "Beyond Chaos," which was a bellicose but brilliantly argued assertion that Black history should be used as an analytical device to get at the "deeper" truths of American history.[15] But by 1973 this matter seemed less important to Harding than Black history itself and its development, its distinctiveness, and its truth. Sterling Stuckey, a confessed Black nationalist historian, had the same strong views. Both historians felt that an inadequate or false assessment of Black history was, at bottom, an assault against Black people themselves and their humanity. As John Blassingame said of the two historians in 1973, both demanded "an end to the distortion, deletion, and denial of Black humanity." Blassingame quoted some of Stuckey's remarks:

Whether writing about Afro-Americans during and since slavery . . . the historian must challenge the old assumptions about those on the lower depths—establishment homilies . . . —by revealing the internal values and life styles of the supposedly inarticulate. . . . As history has been used in the West to degrade people of color, black history must seek dignity for mankind.[16]

Blassingame wrote that Black historians like Harding, Stuckey, and others, including himself, were interested in seriously reducing the role of white people in Black history and concentrating on Black people as primary historical actors and the primary determinants of Black history. "Such an approach . . . has the virtue of automatically narrowing the focus of black history. . . . Then, too, an overwhelming majority of the lightly research[ed] and tangentially related works on blacks are eliminated from consideration. The number of works in this category alone is enough of a recommendation for taking this approach."[17] What Blassingame was expressing his concern about, which was the concern that other newer Black historians like himself had, was the way that people inside and outside the history profession felt that Black history amounted to nothing more than "race relations," especially when the role of white people in Black history was stressed or overstressed.

Black history in the view of Blassingame, Stuckey, Harding, and other similar newer and younger historians, such as Mary Berry, V. P. Franklin, Leslie Owens, John Roberts, Albert Raboteau, and Robert Harris, had to become a distinctive history discipline, a historical field of its own and accepted as that. These newer and younger historians, who initially emerged in the 1960s and have increased their numbers since, I call Second-Wave Black historians. These historians not only represented a challenge to white historians, both those who write in Black history and those who do not, but also to First-Wave Black historians in appreciable ways.

The horrendous political history in America and outside America in the 1960s and 1970s helped to produce Second-Wave Black historians, as it helped to add new and younger Black historians to the ranks of First-Wave Black historians. Blacks were engaged in a liberation struggle in America, which was also occurring in Africa, the Middle East, and Asia, which stimulated the Black struggle in America. Black intellectuals and Black leaders developed Black Power rhetoric and theories to help rationalize, justify, and guide the Black struggle. These individuals and masses of Black people publicly praised blackness (i.e., race, color, physiology). They all publicly chanted phrases such as "black is beautiful," "Black is beautiful," "Black and Proud," and "Black and Somebody," publicly defying and going against the racist and oppressive history of America and the White over Black social structure and social system that produced these historical realities.

During these years there were Blacks who described Blacks as Afro-Americans, and sometimes African Americans, but these names and identities were usually publicly projected by Black intellectuals or other individuals of the Black middle class in America. That included Black historians, and especially them. The newer and younger Black historians who joined the First-Wave Black historians and those who established the Second Wave of Black historians were rather widely disposed, in each instance, to use the name Afro-American in their writings, and in the 1980s and thereafter, although less frequently, to use the name African American. Both groups of historians, even more often, used Black, in various spellings, in their writings.

Second-Wave Black historians, since their inception in the 1960s, have come under the strong influence of Africa. African liberation movements and newly independent African countries have had an impact on them. Pan-Africanism, African Unity, the philosophy of Negritude, Kwame Nkrumah's concept of the "African Personality," and other specific political and intellectual happenings or trends have had an impact on them and their historiography. Some of these historians have also turned to individual historians as sources of inspiration and historiographical guides, such as the lay historians J. A. Rogers and John Jackson and the professional historians Josef ben-Jochanan, John Henrik Clarke, and Basil Davidson.

In recent years, Second-Wave Black historians have taken inspiration from Ivan Van Sertima and his *Journal of African Civilizations*. Van Sertima is a black historian and anthropologist from

Guiana, South America, living and teaching in America. He has gathered around his *Journal* professional and lay black and Black historians and other kinds of black and Black lay and professional scholars (as well as a number of white scholars). The *Journal's* general interest is in the African Extensia. It is specifically concerned with Egyptian civilization, and has also shown an important interest in the Western African Extensia. Second-Wave Black historians have been inspired and motivated to seek out the links between Africa and Black people in America—biological, historical, cultural, and others—which has also become an interest of more recent First-Wave Black historians. Both of these elements have had their interest in Africa and in their search for links stimulated by the National Black Studies Council and the Black Studies, Afro-American Studies, African American Studies, or Africana Studies, or the departments by these names at America's colleges and universities.

The National Black Studies Council, and various Black or Afro-American or African American Studies programs at colleges and universities, represent a massive and considerably coordinated effort to promote historical and other professional scholarship on Blacks in America, as well as on Africa, and to establish linkages, which has further been broadened to include historical, cultural, and social linkages between Black people and other black people in what is usually described as the African diaspora. Generally, then, there is a strong effort, with Second-Wave Black historians especially helping to lead the way with rhetoric and scholarship, to link Africa with what is called the African diaspora, but what I prefer to call the Western African Extensia.

Some Second-Wave Black historians have an interest in the general African Extensia, which increases in importance to them. Moreover, the interest of such historians is not just scholarship, but also politics, as is the case with other Black scholars and other kinds of Black intellectuals; namely, the unity of Africans and peoples of black African descent, particularly the unity of black Africans with people of black African descent in the Western Hemisphere. Sheila Walker remarked in the newsletter of the Center for African and Afro-American Studies at the University of Texas at Austin,

For the 21st century . . . we must go beyond such narrow, domestic considerations, because the politico-economic and socio-cultural definitions of reality will be international rather than local. Hence, it behooves African Americans in the United States to acknowledge the transnational reality of our history and present by understanding our historical ties and contemporary cultural links with people of Africa and of the rest of the African Diaspora in the Americas and elsewhere.[18]

This is rhetoric that Second-Wave and other Black historians could accept with great enthusiasm.

But rhetoric is not the same as scholarship, or even truth, and should not be permitted to be confused with either one or falsely linked with either. Such behavior could result in false political or other linkages. Second-Wave Black historians evidence (many of them) that they want to play a role in helping to forge the unity between Africa and black people of black African descent at the level of scholarship and in practical ways. But the fact is that Second-Wave Black historians, to the extent that they accept Robert Harris's conception of Black history (which many do), accept a rhetoric and rationale for a separate and distinct Black historiography that is seriously flawed, and from which they want to pursue scholarly and broad political objectives.

Robert Harris stepped forward in 1982 to provide a rationale for what he regarded as a separate and distinctive "Afro-American historiography" that had been developing since the 1960s and that by the early 1980s had reached fruition. In an article entitled "Coming of Age: The Transformation of Afro-American Historiography," Harris said,

Afro-American historiography, with its own conceptualization and methodological concerns, is now poised to illuminate the Afro-American past in a manner that will broaden or deepen our knowledge of Black people in this country. The writing of Afro-American History is no longer undertaken principally to revise the work of wrong-headed white historians, to discern divine providence, to show black participation in the nation's growth and development, to prove the inevitability of black equality, or to demonstrate the inexorable progress made by Afro-Americans. It is conducted as a distinct area of inquiry, within the discipline of history, with black people as its primary focus to reveal their thought and activities over time and place.[19]

It is to be noted that Robert Harris was critical of the historiographical thrusts of precursor and First-Wave Black historiography and the writing of what he called "wrong-headed" white historians writing on Black history. In another section of his article, Harris spelled out more of the historical, cultural, and geographical (i.e., spatial) scope of Black history: "Afro-American history has taken place within the context of American history, but it should not be overwhelmed by that fact. It is much broader than the activities of the American nation. Events on the African continent and in the African diaspora [Western Hemisphere] have profoundly affected Afro-American thought and action."[20] This latter thought will undergo examination later in this chapter. At this point it is necessary to focus critical attention on the rationale of the new

Afro-American historiography (i.e., Second-Wave Black historiography) expressed in the extended quotation of Harris, which, as said earlier, was seriously flawed.

Harris, for instance, argued that a separate and distinctive Black historiography rejected a "revisionist" approach to Black history—that is, as he understood revisionism (which was the same in the history profession), revising accepted interpretive historical premises—and wanted Black historians to cease seeking to revise "wrong-headed" white historians. As said in the previous chapter, Black historical writing was not and had never been revisionist historical writing. Black historians, from precursors to First-Wave Black historians, were not seeking to revise the racist historical writing of white historians, but to reject that writing and to write Black history from different premises.

Black historians have written revolutionary history, both precursors and First-Wave historians. These historians sought consciously to give white historians, lay and professional, different knowledge, truth, and understanding about Black people and their history and life in America. Carter Woodson brought white professional historians in on this revolutionary historical writing, who helped to expand it. Thus, what Black historians had to be concerned about was the revision of revolutionary Black historiography by white and Black historians that diluted, distorted, or suppressed this revolutionary approach to writing Black history or the political objectives of that writing. Racist white historians—or "wrong-headed" white historians—wrote Black history in a way to justify and help promote perpetual White ascendancy in America and perpetual Black subordination. Black history was written by precursor and First-Wave Black historians to help promote Black liberation and full Black freedom in America. Harris, by saying that Black historiography would no longer seek to "show black participation in the nation's growth and development, to prove the inevitability of black equality, or to demonstrate the inexorable progress made by Afro-Americans," was saying or, at least, was giving the strong impression, that he wanted Black historiography to give up its traditional and still important political objectives. Even an interest in the political objective of unity between black Africans and black people of the "African diaspora" should not be permitted to supercede or set aside these objectives. Black people, including Black historians, could have both sets of objectives, as two different kinds of objectives that could be viewed as related to each other. These would be the two separate but also interacting objectives of Black people that Third-Wave Black historians would accept.

Harris said, in the quoted comments but more clearly in his article, that a separate and distinctive Black historiography would be against a "contributionist" approach to Black history. It is hard to see how this could be justified when the contributions of Black women to Black history, American history, or even to European history, for that matter, had yet to be significantly disclosed. Harris argued in his article that the interactionist–involvement approach to Black history by First-Wave Black historians would not be a strong focus of a separate and distinctive "Afro-American historiography." This would mean, then, that Black women's interaction and involvement with white men and white women, and their impact on these two groups and the kind of history they have made in America, would not be a strong focus of this scholarship. It would gain strong attention from Third-Wave Black Historiography.

Harris also said that the separate and distinctive Black historiography would reveal the "thought and activities" of Black people "over time and place." Black people have had thoughts about America and their participation in it "over time and place." Are these thoughts no longer to be regarded as Black thoughts or as a part of Black history? Is Black thought to be only that thought of Black people that pertains directly and only to Black people? If so, what is the thought of Frederick Douglass, W.E.B. Du Bois, Anna Cooper, Francis Grimke, Ida Wells-Barnett, Alain Locke, Martin Luther King, Jr., or Toni Morrison to be called when it does not focus on Black people, but on white people or America? Or when Black people are drawn into these discussions to amplify or clarify matters? And, of course, Black people have engaged in activities with Whites, against Whites, inside American institutions, against such institutions, guided by American ideals, or against anti-American ideals, "over time and place," in American history. Black people are continuing to do this more so than ever. Should this kind of history not be called Black history, since Black people are making it?

What Harris's philosophical rationale for Black history and Black historiography show is that he does not want to accept the impact of white people and their history on Black people, and how white people and their history have helped to shape what can be described as Black history and even Black historiography. Black history has never occurred in a vacuum in America. It has always interacted with white people, White history, and the larger American history. The White over Black structure and system in American history and society, "over time and place," has always assured that. What the racist-imbued structure and system have always assured throughout American history is that White history would always impact and help determine Black history, and that Black history would always impact and help determine White history and the larger American history. This kind of interactive history would continue to occur in America if the White over Black structure and system were eliminated from the country, with the interaction between white and Black people, and each's impact on the other's history and life, being of different kinds.

Black history, therefore, has two dimensions: a Black dimension and an American dimension. Black history should properly be called *Black American history*, and the historiography should properly and fully be called *Black American historiography*. Harris and other Black historians of his orientation often refer to Black history as Afro-American history, or sometimes African American history. Thus, they recognize the double dimension of Black history in America, but only want to focus on one dimension of it, or primarily on the one dimension, what they call the Afro or African dimension, that they even more often or just as often in their writings refer to as either the black dimension or the Black dimension, showing that they themselves are not sure who Black people are or how to describe them, or how to describe Black history and Black historiography.

The full conception of Black history as Black American history points to another double and interactive dimension of Black history: its *separate* and *integrated* manifestations and their interaction. Black history has always moved on these two tracks, and interactive tracks at that, with each affecting the functioning, development, and reality of the other. This dynamic situation still characterizes Black history. It would be illogical to divorce these two dimensions of Black history from each other, because they impact each other and always have "over time and place" in America; they are two separate but interactive categories where Black "thought" and Black "activities" have occurred "over time and place" in America. The separate dimension of Black history (i.e., Black humanity, Black culture and social life, Black psychology, and Black spirituality) has always integrated into and interacted with the larger American history, which involved Black people with white people and American culture, social institutions, society, and civilization, helping to shape all of these realities. In turn, all these realities have helped to shape Black historical, cultural, social, psychological, and spiritual realities. All of this kind of double interaction, involvement, and impacting, derived from the separate and integrated dimensions of Black history, have been occurrences within that history (i.e., the broader Black American context) "over time and place" in America. Understanding this complex separate, integrated, interactive, and impactful character of Black history in America led Du Bois, in *The Souls of Black Folk* and other writings, to talk about the "double-consciousness" of Black people in America.

Black history, because of its great complexity, is not to be perceived, understood, researched, or written on the basis of *either–or* cognition, a form of cognition that cannot accept two different realities at the same time, seeing one reality as necessarily alien or contradictory and as something that has to be excluded or eructed from an intellectual (i.e., thinking) or social context. Either–or cognition that gives rise to either–or thinking would separate the various dimension of Black history from the integrated dimension for research and analytical and interpretive purposes. Another form, *domination–subordination cognition*, which gives rise to hierarchical thinking, would not separate one dimension of Black history from others and would not exclude one dimension from contexts, but would subordinate one dimension to the other, diminishing the reality that was subordinated. These two forms of cognition are generally invested in American history, culture, and social life, which means that both are invested strongly in white people as their methods of cognition and thinking. Black people are aware of these forms of cognition and thinking and have assimilated and internalized them to some extent. But Black people have not had a history in America where they could be dominant or have the power to exclude people, which would pack these forms of cognition and thinking into their minds and personalities.

Historically, Black people have sought to have their humanity and life recognized as realities in America, and this life and humanity recognized as equal to White humanity and life in the country. Thinking of things as being different but equal, as having individual integrity but also equal integrity, as being an independent reality but also an equal reality, inculcated what could be called a *diunital* form of cognition in Black people as their main form of cognition and *equi-thinking*, as their main form of thinking. The concept of diunital is taken, with modification, from a group of black/Black scholars who presented and discussed it in *Beyond Black and White*.[21] To define diunital cognition further, it perceives reality as comprised of independent existences, each with its own intrinsic character or authenticity (even if not morally acceptable), and seeks to have individual realities interact with each other horizontally (as opposed to hierarchically)—that is, on the basis of equality with each other (i.e., as each is constituted) that would result in the greater clarification or the change, augmentation, or dissolution of the realities. While not given the name diunital until the 1960s, this is the primary form of Black cognition that has occurred "over time and place" in America.

Mary White Ovington, for instance, one of the founders of the NAACP and a white person who knew Black people, as a people, rather well, wrote in 1911, "Few, if any Negroes hold logically to one ideal wholly to the exclusion of the other. They cannot be logical and live."[22] Mary White Ovington was not able to understand that the Black method of thinking expressed its logical form. The diunital cognition and logic of Black people was recognized more clearly by Lerone Bennett, Jr. when he said of it in the mid-1960s, without using the name diunital, "The creators of this great tradition respected the cutting edge of life; they understood that good and evil, creative and destructive, wise and foolish, up and down, were inseparable polarities of existence." Bennett also pointed out how white people, functioning from either–or cognition, could not clearly or fully understand Blacks or their culture and social life: "What is lacking in most white interpretations of Negro reality is a full-bodied evocation of the entire spectrum. By seizing on one element to the exclusion of the other white interpreters and other . . . white imitators of the Negro deform themselves and the total ensemble of the Negro tradition which stands or falls as a bloc."[23] Black psychologist Joseph White, Jr. said of Black cognition a few years later, "We should also recognize that black people have a great tolerance for ambiguity and uncertainty, for living with seemingly contradictory alternatives. As practitioners, then, we must eliminate the tendency to think in either–or terms with respect to the Black experience."[24] But it was W.E.B. Du Bois who showed the clearest perception of Black cognition, although he had no conceptual name for it. His perception was reflected in his conception of the "double consciousness" of Black people, and in the following remarks made in *The Souls of Black Folk*:

The history of the American Negro is the history of this strife,—this longing to attain self-conscious manhood, to merge his double self into a better and truer self. In this merging he wishes neither of the older selves to be lost. He would not Africanize America for America has too much to teach the world and Africa. He would not bleach his Negro soul in a flood of white Americanism, for he knows that Negro blood has a message for the world. He simply wishes to make it possible for a man to be both a Negro and an American, without being cursed and spit upon by his fellows, without having the doors of Opportunity closed roughly in his face.[25]

Harris (and this would also be true of other Black historians), while not wanting Black history to be seen in its strong relationship to white people and America or the European heritage of America, which was also the heritage of Black people, was evidencing that he did not know about the Black method of cognition and thinking, and that he had a preference for one of the usual White methods of cognition and thinking: the either–or method. Black history would be conceived in its separate existence to the exclusion, or the essential exclusion, of its integrated dimension, which would associate it closely with white people, America, and Europe and their impact on Black history and Black people.

Harris also adhered to the other usual method of White cognition and thinking when he made the following remarks in his article, reflecting his strong interest in the limited separate dimension of Black history (although he did seek, as Second-Wave Black historians especially have done, to widen that dimension and the dimension of a separate and distinctive Afro-American history):

Events on the African continent and in the African diaspora have profoundly affected Afro-American thought and action. The Haitian Revolution and the British abolition of slavery in the Caribbean touched Afro-Americans more substantially than Jacksonian Democracy. While Andrew Jackson broadened political participation for white Americans, the Haitian Revolt gave courage to Afro-Americans.[26]

As said earlier, the Jacksonian Era in American history was not a democratic era. At best, Jackson helped to broaden the political participation of white men in American elective politics.

But Harris's confident remarks have to be seen from another critical angle, which his methods of cognition, as well as his strong separate Black history orientation, calls forth. Blacks were suppressed politically during the Jacksonian Era, and also economically and socially. But this very suppression at the hands of white people, this kind of intense interaction and involvement with white people, had an ironic positive impact on Blacks. They were spurred into political organization and action during the Jacksonian Era. The first Black newspaper, *Freedom's Journal*, appeared at this time, in 1827. David Walker wrote his incendiary *David Walker's Appeal* two years later. In the early 1830s Blacks formed antislavery societies or joined white ones to integrate them. They also established the Black Convention Movement.

Northern Black churches became more vocal as agencies of protest against racism, slavery, and the Colonization movement's effort to deport Blacks from America. Other newly formed Black organizations and forums made the same protests. It was during the Jacksonian Era that precursor Black historians first appeared, such as Robert Benjamin Lewis and James W. C. Pennington, who sought, through their writings, to counter the public racist views of Black people. The Jacksonian Era was the time when a *Black Pub-*

lic and a *Black Public Voice* appeared in America, and these would remain institutionalized parts of Black and American existence. These were all Black and Black American historical occurrences of the Jacksonian Era, reflecting the impact of Whites and the Jacksonian Era on Black people and their historical "thought" and "activities" that Harris's narrow conception of "Afro-American historiography" could not glimpse or even have an interest in discerning. It also would not have an interest in Black history being employed as a critical device to analyze the history of white people or larger American history, and even, specifically, the Jacksonian Era itself, which would come out looking very different from how present White historical scholarship sees it in its most revisionist writings.

Nathan Huggins, in "Integrating Afro-American History into American History," provided a trenchant criticism of Harris's and other Second-Wave Black historians' views of Black history:

The danger, however, is that we see this work as the end and purpose of Afro-American history—creating a narrow specialty over which we establish a proprietary interest, squeezing our concerns to the point of historical insignificance. It is a danger because the American academic professions encourage such mindless territoriality, and because many are fearful to venture beyond their carefully cultivated certitudes.[27]

Another criticism of Second-Wave Black historiography is that much of it is too ideological and thus suppressive and distortive of Black history in many ways. This particular criticism has come from various historians, Black and White, especially the latter, who sometimes take their criticism to the point where they deny that history itself has been written because of its ideological inundation. Ideology can desecrate historical investigation, interpretation, and writing, and this can especially be seen in some of the Second-Wave Black historiography. But criticism of the strong ideological orientation of some of the Second-Wave Black historiography and its ravages by some white historians is rather hypocritical. It is a suppression and distortion of White history when Black history and its impact on that history is ignored or only meagerly included. This is White racism at work—racism as an ideology—and has been employed in White historical writing since the nineteenth century and continues to be exhibited today in much professional historical writing, albeit more subtly. White historians should never be so ready to cast the first stone.

Where Second-Wave Black historians have been most successful as historians, and have been most helpful to Black people, and this along with some of the newer First-Wave Black historians, has been to help disclose the history of Black slavery in America. A number of white historians have also played a large role here, perhaps even a larger role. Precursor Black historians wrote about slavery but did not focus on Blacks as slaves or the life of Black people as slaves. This was also essentially true of First-Wave Black historians up to the 1970s. In 1937, in "A New Interpretation of Negro History," First-Wave Black historian L. D. Reddick felt that a great deal had already been said about slavery. Indeed, he insisted that the topic had essentially been exhausted, and that it was "a further waste of time to continue to examine the few plantation records, the papers of masters, or the usually superficial impressions of travelers." But he felt that there were two areas where knowledge and light could still be thrown on Black slavery in America: on the attempts of Black slaves "to break the system . . . through suicide, flight, individual resistance and group insurrection," and the purely revolutionary historiographical effort, although this was not Reddick's phrasing, to see Black slavery "through the eyes of the bondsman himself."[28]

Herbert Aptheker ultimately took up Reddick's suggestion on the first point with his study, *American Negro Slave Revolts*, but the other project gained no historiography.[29] In 1947, ten years after Reddick, Richard Hofstadter argued that a full understanding of plantation slavery required seeing it from the standpoint of Black slaves. Kenneth Stamp made a partial effort to do this with *The Peculiar Institution*.[30] Stanley Elkins ignored the topic altogether in *Slavery*.[31] It was in John Blassingame's *The Slave Community* in 1972, George P. Rawick's *From Sundown to Sunup* in 1972, and Eugene Genovese's *Roll, Jordan Roll* in 1974 that the Black side of American slavery started coming to light.[32] Other historical studies in the 1970s cast greater light and revealed greater knowledge of the subject: Leslie Owen's *This Species of Property*, Albert Raboteau's *Slave Religion*, Thomas Webber's study of the informal social education of Black slaves on slave plantations, *Deep Like the Rivers*, Herbert Gutman's *Black Family in Slavery and Freedom*, Nathan Huggins's *Black Odyssey*, and Lawrence Levine's *Black Culture and Black Consciousness*.[33] There were collections of Black slave testimony published in the 1970s, such as George P. Rawick's *The American Slave: A Composite Autobiography*, and Norman Yetman's *Life Under the "Peculiar Institution."*[34]

So the historiographical basis for a deep and comprehensive study and understanding of Black slave life in America was laid in the 1970s and would be augmented in the next decade. First- and Second-Wave Black historians played roles in expanding this study and understanding. But this same scholarship of the 1970s and 1980s by Black and white historians received serious criticism. Laurence Shore was one who made this criticism; namely, that the scholarship on Black slavery in America in the 1970s and 1980s had essentially ignored the tragic dimension of Black slavery and Black slave life:

For all their attention to Southern slave society, most historians have not created a tragic representation of the slave experience; they have sought to engender in their readers a catharsis of the tragic emotions—pity and fear. Struggle, defeat, isolation are not in the foreground of these historians' writing.[35]

Shore argued in his writing that Black historians, and white historians sympathetic to them, always talked about Black slave culture and social life in positive ways, refusing to see much or anything negative about them or refusing to recognize and accept the social and psychological afflictions of Black slave life that slavery produced and that the Black slave culture and social life could not prevent, the tragic character of Black slave life that Black slave culture and social life could not offset. The answer to Shore is the same one directed to Earl Thorpe's comments in Chapter 2, where he was critical of precursor Black historians because they did not write about the tragic dimension of Black history in America: Why should Black historians write on the tragedy of Black slave life—or Black history—when white historians do not write on this subject with respect to White history and White life in America. William Dunning and his school of Reconstruction historiography, in a perverse manner, thought it was "tragic" for America that "barbarian freedmen" participated in the reconstructed governments of the south.

Laurence Shore noted that C. Vann Woodward had an appreciation of the tragic situation of some individuals in the South, "bullied about by fate, crushed by outside forces over which they had no control, or victimized by conspiracies of the strong."[36] However, C. Vann Woodward's tragic individuals were all white. Moreover, his sense of the tragic had nothing to do with irony and paradox in southern history, an irony and paradox produced by White racism, even the racism of the victimized Whites in the South, which Shore did not say. These Whites, victimized by more powerful Whites, could have joined forces with Blacks against their common enemy to promote their common interests. But lower-class Whites, owing to their racism, did not see where they had any common interests with Blacks. Tragically, all they could think of was keeping Black people suppressed beneath them, which reduced their clout against upper-class Whites and therefore left upper-class Whites in a position to keep victimizing them. This was a tragic situation of profound character.

A problem that white historians have had since the lay historians of the nineteenth century is that they cannot, will not, and certainly have not dealt with the effect of racism on white people; the effect of racism on the perpetrators of racism—the physical, intellectual, psychological, moral, and spiritual effects throughout the history of America. In 1969 white historian I. A. Newby, in favor of a "new black history" that showed what Whites had "done to Negroes" and what Blacks had "accomplished in America," nevertheless said the following: "Insofar as race is concerned, the white man's problem is not ego weakness and psychological emasculation, but an overriding superiority complex."[37] Newby believed like other white historians, that white people, being racists for centuries in America, have not been affected by their racism in the ways I have indicated.

The truth is that Black people have not faced strong White egos in their historical relations with white people. They have, in fact, faced weak and corrupted egos with intellectual, psychological, moral, and spiritual deformities—even a suppression of imagination—that would not allow Whites to imagine that Blacks were other than what their racism said they were, or that they were capable of doing things other than what Whites believed they were capable of doing. The power of white people, as well as their large capacity for self-deception, another serious consequence of perpetuating racism, have prevented them from seeing the nature of their various serious racist-produced afflictions, which have long been seen by Black people and related to by them.

This has been a tragedy of White history in America. It has been a tragic reality in American history that white historians have not been capable or willing—and it has always been more of the former, which retarded will and interest—to explain to white Americans what their racism has done to them and to this country. Lerone Bennett, Jr. said in the 1960s that the real "social problem" in America was the "White Problem," which white people were not able to see.[38] I would add that the "White Problem" itself has always been a manifestation of the White over Black social structure and social system problem.

It cannot be asked that Black historians focus on the tragic character of Black history as long as white historians will not focus on the tragic character of White history and American history. Precursor Black historians focused on these latter matters to some extent. First-Wave Black historians did so a little more. Second-Wave Black historians demonstrated no interest in the tragic dimension of Black history or White history, making this historical approach seriously inadequate. It actually is going to take Black historians to open up the serious historiographical analysis and explanation of the tragic character of White history in America, and of the larger American history. Third-Wave Black historiography, using Black history as a critical device, would seriously execute this effort. Because of this determination, Third-Wave Black historiography would also deal with the tragic character of Black history. The Black philosopher Samuel Du Bois Cook once asserted why it was necessary to analyze and discuss the tragic side of Black history:

Without a profound sense of tragedy, it is impossible to comprehend, in their fullness and power, the antinomies, the disappointments, the sad and hopeless strivings, the frightening frustrations, ambiguities and contradictions, the gnawing predicaments; in a word, the grim and grinding realities of Negro history. Dissociated from a framework of tragedy, there are, in the stream of Negro history, countless series and concatenations of intelligible events. With a profound sense of tragedy, a deep and intense feeling of the agony of boundless longing without fulfillment, these events are not buried in the already teeming cemetery of meaninglessness. Of the validity of our approach the test is whether it helps to illume the Negro's pilgrimage in the ebb and flow of American history, whether it opens our *eyes* to a realm of meaning and possibility otherwise hidden and obscure. About this, there is little room for doubt; indeed, we are seeking to interpret an embarrassing wealth of obvious historical phenomena.[39]

Second-Wave Black historiography as it is presently rationalized and constituted—seeking essentially divorcement from white people, White history, and the larger American history and their impact on Black history, helping to make it and Black life what they are— is a manifestation of the tragic side of Black history and Black life. A Black historiography is by all means a necessary development in America. But how that historiography is developed—what goes into it to make it what it is—is the great question. The history of Black people has always involved more than just Black people (i.e., Black people interacting historically with Black people). Black people have also interacted with white people and the larger America, which has affected the way Black people have interacted with each other; how Black history, culture, and social life have evolved in America; and how they continue to evolve. Third-Wave Black historiography recognizes this historical complexity, including the tragic dimensions within it, and will write about this complex situation.

Chapter 4

Orthography, History, and Black Ethnicity

Writing about Black identity and Black history, and being accurate about both, requires distinguishing between race and ethnicity. This was not done by precursor Black historians, or by early First-Wave Black historians, and has certainly not been done widely, clearly, or consistently by later First-Wave or Second-Wave Black historians. In the introductory chapter I said that race was biology and that an ethnic group was a subdivision of a race with racial or biological features, but which also exhibited cultural and social characteristics. I intend to expand on this matter in this chapter, as the clarity of these realities are essential for writing Third-Wave Black historiography.

Equally troublesome and inhibiting in dealing with Black identity and Black history are the orthographic or spelling problems that make it difficult to know who Black people are (how they are distinguished from other black people), and thus, whose or which black people's history is being written about under the banner of Black history. Black historians for the most part, and this is also true of other kinds of Black intellectuals for the most part, are utterly careless when it comes to projecting the identity of Black people, invariably eschewing the historical evidence that would be helpful in favor of being able to describe Black people any way they wish or on the basis of some ideological or ahistorical pretext or requirement.

Thus, Blacks are called not only Blacks, but also Africans or African Americans. And if this were not deleterious enough, chaotic spelling is thrown in to augment the muddle. Thus, the Black identity is rendered in writing as Black, black, Blacks, and blacks, making no distinction between adjective or noun, race or ethnicity. The chaotic orthographical spellings of the African description of Blacks, such as Africans, Afrikans, African Americans, Afro-Americans, Afriamericans, Afraamericans, Africo-Americans, or Afrikan Americans just compound an already bad situation. Since Black people are not Africans, these varied African descriptions are not only erroneous but wholly detrimental to establishing and maintaining Black identity, and also to the writing of Black history. But the various spellings and usages of Black are also encumbering and detrimental. On the other hand, this orthographical malaise is not something that Black historians or other Black intellectuals invented. It is something they inherited from American history and culture, which had embedded in them the imprecise manner in which the white settlers of North America used the English language. It took some time for formal grammatical rules to be developed and accepted widely, leaving lots of room for the English and other settlers to spell words phonetically or in ways that would indicate importance or emphasis or whatever was expedient. Blacks had to learn English in America, spoken and written, and the Whites who became their sources of transmission imparted to them what was good and bad about the way they used the language. Before getting into the discussion of orthography and ethnicity in this chapter, I think it apropos to provide some background on the early employment of the English language in North America that carried into the national period and affected the mix of inhabitants.

The English brought their language along with other attributes of their culture and civilization to North America. English became the general language of the colonies and then became the general or national language of the United States, which it still remains. In the seventeenth and eighteenth centuries, when black people from what was understood at the time by some people in Europe and North America to be Africa came to the English colonies and later to the United States, they learned this language, although not very well, as a rule. Some of the black people from what some called Africa learned some English before they came to North America or to the West Indies where the English had colonies. They learned it in Africa to some extent, or in the process of being enslaved and transferred to North America and the West Indies. This was a kind of "pidgin" English.

The English language expressed a strong dichotomization between many thoughts, words, and social realities, and many social or aesthetic symbols. There was a very strong and very rigid dichotomy between the words white and black and the realities to which they referred, and the symbolization of the two words. And such words, realities, and symbols were couched in terms of not just different, but differences that were described as superior and inferior, with the word white, things designated white, and the white symbol being denominated superior and the word black, things designated black, and the black symbol denominated inferior.

In his book, *White Over Black*, Winthrop Jordan remarked about the English before they came to North America: "In England perhaps more than in southern Europe, the concept of blackness was loaded with intense meaning. Long before they found that some men were black, Englishmen found in the idea of blackness a way of expressing some of their most ingrained values. No other color except white conveyed so much emotional impact." Jordan indicated that in the *Oxford English Dictionary* of the fifteenth century the word black meant,

"Deeply stained with dirt, soiled, dirty, foul. . . . Having dark or deadly purposes, malignant; pertaining to or involving death, deadly; baneful, disastrous, sinister. . . . Foul, iniquitous, atrocious, horrible, wicked. . . . Indicating disgrace, censure, liability to punish, etc." Black was an emotionally partisan color, the handmaid and symbol of baseness and evil, a sign of danger and repulsion.[1]

Jordan also said that white and black were sharply dichotomized in the *Oxford English Dictionary*, as they were in thought, speech, and writing in fifteenth-century England: "White and black connoted purity and filthiness, virginity and sin, virtue and baseness, beauty and ugliness, beneficence and evil, God and the Devil." These meanings of white and black in English history and life continued on in the sixteenth and seventeenth centuries and, of course, would be transferred to English colonies in North America and the West Indies.

Centuries prior to the establishment of these colonies, the English language and English culture were characterized by strong and rigid white and black symbolic dichotomization. This was reflected as a linguistic pattern in the English language where the words white and black themselves had opposite meanings and were associated with thoughts and words that in themselves had no color association (e.g., the word innocence would be associated with white and the word guilty with black), and this dichotomization of words would be repeated endlessly in the English language as part of the white–black linguistic pattern found within that language. And, of course, the words white and black were symbolic words, and white and black symbolism were also a part of the white–black linguistic pattern of fifteenth-, sixteenth-, and seventeenth-century English. The white–black dichotomization and linguistic pattern in the English language was also facilitated by the cognitive patterns reflected in that language and facilitated its implementation in speech and writing.

One of the cognitive patterns was the either–or pattern, another was the domination–subordination pattern, and the third was the dualistic cognitive pattern that produced a parallel kind of thinking in which white and black, for instance, or words or phrases with those symbolisms and symbolic meanings, would stand opposite each other as dichotomies that were permanent and not to cross or interact to alter each's reality or meaning. White and black would always stand opposite or parallel to each other, with each always remaining something different from the other. But it was primarily the either–or and domination–subordination cognitive patterns that were most operative in the English language, as they were in English culture and social life, because they were more dynamic in their functioning (i.e., their interactive or action capabilities). Either–or cognition functioning in the English language and the white–black linguistic pattern of that language created a dynamism that allowed the word white to exclude the word black, or white-meaning words or white-meaning phrases to exclude black-meaning words or black-meaning phrases. White symbolism generally excluded black symbolism.

The domination–subordination cognitive pattern created the dynamic that allowed the word white, white-meaning words and white-meaning phrases, and white linguistic symbolism generally to dominate the word black, black-meaning words and black-meaning phrases, and black linguistic symbolism. The domination–subordination or hierarchical cognitive pattern and the either–or exclusionary cognitive pattern that permitted white to dominate black or white to exclude black in the English language also functioned in English culture generally, where these cognitive patterns promoted white and whiteness and black and blackness in domination–subordination or exclusionary ways. God, for instance, was white in the English language and culture, and the Devil was black. God in both mediums dominated the Devil or excluded Satan. Good in the English language dominated or excluded evil, and did the same in the general English culture. By the seventeenth century especially, white people and black people were dichotomized and symbolized in the English language and in the white–black linguistic pattern of that language, and were also dichotomized in English culture.

In all areas—language, linguistic pattern, and English culture—white people were recognized as being not just different from black people but also as superior to them, although at this time it was not necessarily racial superiority, though this was not wholly missing from the thought. Whites were recognized in all three areas to have the power and right both to dominate black people and to exclude them. Before the English came to North America and the West Indies to establish colonies in the seventeenth century, they not only had strong philosophical and linguistic perceptions of white and black as colors, or white and black as symbols, or white and black as word, phrase, or metaphorical meanings; they also had cognitive systems that made this kind of thinking possible.

Thus, it was not just simply that white people were culturally and psychologically predisposed toward white and whiteness and against black and blackness, as Winthrop Jordan said in *White Over Black*, that facilitated their motivation to enslave black people; they had the cognitive patterns that also made it possible for them to do so, and on a continuous basis, as these cognitive patterns (with the dualistic cognitive pattern included) endured on a continuous basis. They were embedded deeply in the English language and the English culture and social life that were planted particularly in England's North American colonies in the seventeenth and eighteenth centuries.

The culture and social life implanted these cognitive patterns in the minds and personalities of the English, associated closely with the words white and black and white and black symbolism, with the color-oriented cognitive patterns reinforcing the color-oriented cognitions and symbolisms of English culture and social life in the colonies, all in an endless pattern of interaction between the minds and personalities of white people and the culture and social life that they continuously produced and that continuously nourished them. In *The Arrogance of Race*, George Frederickson wrote, "The treatment of blacks . . . engendered a cultural and psycho-social racism that . . . took on a life of its own and created a powerful irrational basis for white supremacist attitudes and actions."[2] It is not clear from these remarks that Frederickson saw the minds and personalities of white people as an "irrational basis" for white supremacy/ebonicism; that is, saw White minds and personalities themselves afflicted with racist irrationality and a number of other intellectual, psychological, moral, and spiritual deficiencies, produced by the impact of their racist beliefs and racist behavioral patterns.

The essays of his book did not offer clarification on this matter. There was also no sense in his discussion of the tragic in White history and White life in America, not even in the history and life of southern Whites. He referred to a historian who he credited with having insight for noting how the Ku Klux Klan and other grassroots white supremacist movements and "popular racism" were "infused with moral values."[3] This was actually a false perception.

Racism is an irrational, perverted, and immoral belief system, whether embraced by a few or many. It exhibits these characteristics because it is anti–human being, projecting thoughts, ideas, and images of human beings being "nonhuman" or "subhuman." Racism does not and cannot promote a moral social order, but only an immoral one that racists, of course, like to regard and speak of as being moral. In addition, racist beliefs injected into nonracist beliefs such as liberal, democratic, or Christian beliefs, which the Ku Klux Klan did and which other popular racist movements in the South did, eructs idealism and morality from such beliefs and turns them into racist beliefs covered from view by liberal, democratic, and Christian labels. How racism de-ethnicalizes and abnormalizes nonracist beliefs will be discussed later in this chapter.

The English language, planted in English North America and continuing on as the general language of the new United States, showed another important peculiarity: its special orthographic orientation and problems; namely, the problems of spelling white and black the same way for adjectival and nominative use, spelling whites and blacks uncapitalized when employing the words nominatively or spelling them capitalized when employing them nominatively, or spelling them capitalized when used in an adjectival manner.

This kind of orthographic (spelling) practice in the English language of spelling white and black in arbitrary ways that did not respect the integrity of nominative or adjectival realities was not initially a racist thing, since the English even described their own racial reality in arbitrary nominative and adjectival ways. This loose and illogical orthographic practice was actually and simply endemic to the English language in the seventeenth and eighteenth centuries. These were centuries when the English were still developing their language. Much of the spelling in the English language of the seventeenth and eighteenth centuries was done phonetically, on the basis of how words sounded to those who expressed them in writing or on the basis of the emphasis that one wanted to attach to words, phrases, or ideas.

There was also a general pattern in the seventeenth and eighteenth centuries in English North American colonies and the new United States of spelling words with capital letters that logically, given the thought patterns and perceptions of realities being expressed by the words, should not have been spelled with capital letters. That might also be done because someone wanted to express a certain feeling or emotion or a certain sentiment. The same word might be spelled differently in a written effort, and might even be capitalized and written in the lower case in the same writing. One example from the seventeenth century was the following: "The Word Written and Preacht is the ordinary Medium of Conversion and Sanctification. Now in order to obtaining these Benefits of the Word, it is requisite, that Persons be diligent in *Reading and Hearing*."[4] An individual in Massachusetts wrote in the 1640s, "1. they are all born in Ignorance Rom. 3:7 without the knowledge and fear of god they must have it by doctrine and institution 2ly this ignorance layeth them open to satan to lead them whither he will . . . if you have any Compassion for them take Pains that they may know god."[5] Two colonists, Henry Carpenter and Robert Helmes, wrote at the end of the seventeenth century,

On the 3rd instant in the Evening, Capt. Cope in the *George and Betty* arrived in this Road with 415 Negroes, most women, amongst which [were] about 40 children under the ages of 8 years to our best Judgment, which we told him was contrary to his Charter Party, who answered that they could not buy so many men and women without [also taking] that number of Children, but we believe something else in it which we hope in Little time to discover.[6]

In the eighteenth century these practices in writing English continued. An officer in the First Pennsylvania Regiment described some Black boys waiting on tables in Virginia: "I am surprized this does not hurt the feelings of this fair Sex to see these young boys of about Fourteen and Fifteen years Old to Attend them. These whole nakedness Expos'd and I can Assure you It would Surprize a person to see these d____d black boys how well they are hung."[7] In the early eighteenth century an Anglican clergyman of South Carolina wrote that Yamasees and Greek Indians not wanting war

were against the war all along; But our Military Men are so bent upon Revenge, and so desirous to enrich themselves, by making all the Indians Slaves that fall into their hands, but such as they kill (without making the least distinction between the guilty and the innocent, and without considering the Barbarous usage these poor Savages met from our villainous Traders) that it is in vain to represent to them the Cruelty and injustice of Such a procedure.[8]

Sir William Johnson, a superintendent of Indian affairs in New England in the 1760s, wrote that he "thought it best to advertise them (in newspapers) immediately, but I believe it will be difficult to find the Friends of some of them as they are ignorant of their own Names." The only safe recourse, Johnson felt, was to describe them "more particularly . . . as to their features, Complexion, etc. That by the Publication of Such descriptions their Relations, parents or friends may hereafter know and Claim them."[9]

The English language of the seventeenth and eighteenth centuries was, of course, the same language that Black slaves learned, mainly at the speaking and verbal level and in a rather deficient manner, beyond the deficiencies of most Whites, and which generally launched the development of a Black dialect or speech pattern of English. Those Blacks who learned how to write, as some slaves did and perhaps as more nonslaves did in the seventeenth and eighteenth centuries, learned to write English just like white people in these centuries did, with the same kind of orthographic peculiarities. The Black scientist of the eighteenth century, Benjamin Benneker, wrote the following to an acquaintance, explaining a miscalculation he had made:

I Receiv'd your Letter at the hand of Bell but found nothing Strange to me In the Letter Concerning the Number of Eclipses tho according to authors the Edge of the penumber only touches the Suns Limb in that Eclips that I left out of the Number—which happens April 14th day at 37 minutes past 7 O'Clock in the morning and is the first we shall have, but Since you wrote to me I Drew in the Equations of the Node which will Cause a Small Solar Defet.[10]

A Black slave woman wrote in 1795, "I have been so unhappy at Mrs. Woodbridge that I was obliged to leeve thare by the consent of Mrs. Woodbridge who gave up my Indentures and has often said that had she known that I was so sickly and expencieve she would not have brought me to this Country."[11]

In the nineteenth century the English language developed under more rigid spelling rules and other rules of grammar, owing to the further development of education in the country and efforts to develop the formal or structural aspects of the English language. There were some nonslave Blacks, mainly in the North but also in the South, who had access to this improved formal education and improved English, as reflected in their writings. But Black written expression in the main in the nineteenth century continued to show strong traces of seventeenth- and eighteenth-century written English. This was particularly true among slaves or former slaves who learned to write in some rudimentary manner and wrote words as they sounded, which accounted for their varied spelling. This was also attributable to their lack of formal education.

One Black slave wrote, "Your servant James troubles you with this scrap the object of which is to inform you that your Servant Jim together with his fellow Servants are all well . . . the grand & principal object is to get Master to be so kind as to inquire about my Sister Francis."[12] A former slave wrote, "Master I wish you would send me a present of Some money if you please for Just at this time I am in particular knead of Some. My Mistresses twoo Brothers is dead. Both died the Saim Month."[13] In 1858 a Black slave, Henry, wrote to his master and mistress about a wheat crop: "I did not intend to the faning of it. I left it to Dick lake. of the small Bingham when 100 Bushels an of the white wheat 80 Bushels of Magnolia. . . . I do not wish to keep any more wheat at magnolia than required. . . . 18 hats an 18 blankets for men at magnolia. 13 hats and 13 Blankets for the womens. 9 hats an 9 Blankets for Boys and girles."[14] In 1850, an escaped slave wrote to his former master:

My Dear Mr John Walker
Dear Sir you hav afforded to me murch Plurcher (pleasure) in ancing my letter and dear sir your Letter I recive it on the 28 and was glad to hear that you and all is will and I wish yout [sic] to tell All that wantes to know how I made my ascape that I made it in the knight when the Moon was gon away and thar was no eyes. . . . I am know gitting along and ples to say to my Farther and to my fartherinlaw that I feel happy in my ascape untill I thinkes about my Wife and I hope that you bouth will talk to her and tell Her to be not dischomfierd for I thinks that I shall see you again.[15]

The letter by this escaped slave, Thomas Rightso, shows spelling problems that, of course, stemmed from a lack of formal education. But it also showed the seventeenth- and eighteenth-century patterns of spelling words as one wished to, on the basis of how they sounded and also on the basis of what one wanted to emphasize, or the feelings, moods, or sensitivities that one wanted to express. This was improvisational writing, which the English language of the seventeenth, eighteenth, and nineteenth centuries permitted. It was found in Black and White writing, and even to some extent in the writing of educated Whites and Blacks who were writing the more improved formal English of the nineteenth century.

W.E.B. Du Bois wrote this kind of English, of course, and even the kind of formal English as it was further improved in the nineteenth and into the twentieth century, but he never gave up entirely improvisational writing, or even some of the seventeenth-through nineteenth-century orthographic practices. In *The Souls of Black Folk*, Du Bois wrote, "Patience, Humility, Manners, and Taste . . . all these spring from Knowledge and culture."[16] In "The Revelation of Saint Orgne the Damned," published in 1938, Du Bois wrote phrases like "the evening stars were singing, and he listened to the rhythm of their words: Hear Ye! This is the Freedom of Art which is the Beauty of Life," or "Here roots the rise of the Joy of Living . . . hence rise Love, Friendship . . . and interpreted Truth."[17] In 1958 Du Bois remarked, "This is the great dilemma which faces Africa today, faces one and all: Give up individual rights for the needs of Mother Africa . . . Mother of Men."[18] Two years later, Du Bois wrote, "Perhaps this is insane, but to me it is Reason, Right and Justice."[19]

This kind of improvised writing was to be found less at the end of Du Bois's writing years than at the beginning. But it has to be said that the English language, even in its present formal form, still permits a certain amount of improvised writing. Words and phrases are still capitalized, fillers continue to be permitted such as parenthetical remarks, and emphasis of words or ideas and improvised expression of attitudes, moods, or sentiments still go on, as reflected in italicized words or the use of ellipses to manipulate sentences or paragraphs. Even this book employs seventeenth-, eighteenth-, and nineteenth-century writing practices.

All three groups of Black historians—precursors, First-Wave Black historians, and Second-Wave Black historians—evidence some usage of seventeenth- through nineteenth-century orthographic and other improvisational writing practices in their history writings. Very noticeable is the improvisational orthographic practice of spelling the names of Black people in so many different ways. Precursor historians most often used the name Negro and Colored in their writings, but spelled these words Negro, Negroes, negro, negroes, Colored, and colored, and when using the word Black, it was spelled Black, black, blacks, and Blacks. First-Wave Black historians also used the names Negro and Colored, and invariably spelled them capitalized. But this was not so with the name Black, which was spelled the way precursor historians spelled it. Second-Wave Black historians also show the same flexibility in spelling the name Black, and also flexibility in spelling the name African as meant for Black people, with such names as African Americans, Afro-Americans, Afriamericans, Afra-americans, and Afrikan Americans.

This kind of orthographic and linguistic use of English in no way helps Black people know who they are by name in America. These kinds of practices confuse Black people. This is something that the

White over Black structure and system always encouraged Blacks to do: to confuse themselves, deceive themselves, and demean themselves as part of the structure and system's efforts to maintain Blacks in a controlled, subordinate position in American history and American society. Thus, this was White racism; that is, white supremacy/ebonicism functioning through the structure and system to encourage Blacks to carry out a psychological assault against themselves, to enervate themselves. To the extent that Blacks complied, they helped to construct and maintain the White over Black structure and system, helped to maintain the dominant racist ideology in America and white supremacy/ebonicism, and helped, contradictorily and tragically, to reproduce their subordinate position in American history and society.

There are those who reject the notion of a dominant ideology in a society that pervades its culture and social life and plays a large deterministic role in them. This kind of criticism has primarily been directed toward Marxists, who, following Marx, talked of a dominant "bourgeois" ideology in history and society. Those making the criticism have often been Marxist or Marxist-influenced academics who were seeking to salvage as much of Marx's insights about ideology as they could. Such people held on to the idea that ideology, as Marx had said, was important in history and society, but that there was usually more than one ideology functioning in a historical process or in a society.

Kenneth Thompson, one of these Marxist-influenced critics of the dominant ideology thesis, said, in *Beliefs and Ideology*, that in a given society there were multiple ideologies at any given moment competing for the allegiance of people, making it difficult to impossible for a single, dominant ideology to function.[20] Further proof of this for Thompson was the fact that a country or society was not monolithic in culture, but usually showed a plethora of cultural groups with different ideological approaches, collectively projecting multiple ideologies in a country or society for people to accept. Views similar to these were expressed by Nicholas Abercrombe, Stephen Hill, and Bryan Turner in *The Dominant Ideology*, including the denial of a dominant ideology that helped to form and maintain a dominant culture.[21]

What is interesting about both books mentioned was that neither one of them said anything about racism, white supremacy/ebonicism, or any other form of racism. There was no talk about race or ethnicity or gender in them. In each writing the focus was on social class, but the discussions were not really about social classes; they were about men of social classes. Thus, there was not a class analysis of ideology as both books contended, but rather a gender analysis that was not understood to be so—typical of Marxist or Marxist-influenced analysts. A maleist/sexist racist analysis would have shown that men of all social classes in all the societies analyzed in the two books created and maintained, by maleist/sexist beliefs and power, a male-dominated culture and society, thus also meaning the domination, control, and exploitation of women in the cultures and societies.

White supremacy/ebonicism, in this combined form, has certainly been not only a dominant ideology, but *the* dominant ideology of American history and social life, which is explained generally by the racist-embedded White over Black social structure and social system, the general social structure and social system of America that has reproduced America's racist-interpenetrated history, culture, and society. There are phrases in American history like "white man's society," "white man's rights," "white man's government," "white man's values" or "white man's country" that indicate how dominant White racist ideology (i.e., white supremacy/ebonicism) has been in American history and social life. America, of course, has had other important ideologies in its history that have played prominent, deterministic roles in it, such as its liberal, capitalistic, and Christian ideologies. This represents a multiplicity of ideologies, but multiple ideologies in American history and society have functioned within and on behalf of the White over Black structure and system that has reproduced them, meaning that the combined white supremacist/ebonicistic ideology has interpenetrated these other ideologies, turning them into racist ideologies. This has led to racist practices with nonracist labels when Whites related to Blacks, thus resulting in nonracist ideologies helping to produce and maintain white supremacy/ebonicism and the White over Black social structure and social system.

Du Bois understood the interpenetrating power and reality of White racism in American culture and social institutions. He conveyed an image of racism being *injected* into American culture (i.e., ideals, values, beliefs, and social institutions) to interpenetrate it and make it function in a racist fashion and a racist entity. In 1910, in an essay entitled "The Souls of White Folk," Du Bois wrote,

Worse than this is our moral and religious plight. We profess a religion of high ethical advancement, a spiritual faith, of respect for truth, despising of personal riches, a reverence for humility, and not simply justice to our fellows, but personal sacrifice of our good for theirs. It is a high aim, so high that we ought not utterly to be condemned for not reaching it, so long as we strive bravely toward it. Do we, as a people? On the contrary, we have injected into our creed a gospel of human hatred and prejudice, a despising of our less fortunate fellows . . . which flatly contradicts the Christian ideal . . . there is absolutely no logical method by which the treatment of black folk by white folk in this land can be squared with any reasonable statement or practice of the Christian ideal.[22]

Du Bois was saying that White racism (white supremacy/ebonicism) was injected into Christian beliefs, Christian ideals, and Christian ethics or morality, eructing them of their humanistic, moral, and spiritual content, and investing them with racist hatred, irrationality, pathology, and immorality, turning such beliefs, ideals, and morality into their opposites. Racism, as Du Bois saw it, was injected into all of America's cultural beliefs, values, and ideals—its multiple major ideologies, not only Christianity, but also its liberal, capitalistic, and democratic ideologies—eructing them of their lofty ingredients and investing them with perverted racist afflictions, making them function as racist ideologies with nonracist names.

I wish to conceptualize, as Du Bois did not do, the racist eructing and investment activities he talked about. The eructing activity I wish to call *de-ethicalizing* and the investment activity I wish to call *abnormalizing*. Injected into cultural features, including ideologies, social institutions, and social relations, White racism (i.e., white supremacy/ebonicism) de-ethicalized and abnormalized these societal manifestations, subverting and perverting them and making them function in compulsively irrational, pathological, immoral, and inhumane ways toward Black people. But other things were also part of White racist injection, de-ethicalization, and abnormalization; namely, the either–or, domination–subordination, and dualistic cognitive patterns, and White racist written linguistics and White racist speech. The latter require explanation.

This chapter began by talking about the way the words white and black played a large role in the English language, not only in terms of their meaning and symbolism, but also in terms of the words and phrases that were associated with white and black and their meanings and symbolism. Eventually the English and other white people in the English colonies began devising white supremacist and ebonicist racist beliefs, which white people in America for centuries continued to do. The construction of the combined White racist beliefs were facilitated, as well as implemented socially, particularly by the either–or and domination–subordination cognitive patterns reflected in the English language and English and American cultures, and thus structured into the minds, personalities, and social behavior of Whites.

White people since the seventeenth century have written in racist terms about themselves and Black people, employing the racist linguistics of the English language; that is, racist fantasies, words, phrases, definitions, meanings, expressions, feelings, sentiments, images, and symbolism. White people since the seventeenth century have also spoken with racist speech toward Black people; that is, they have verbally expressed racist fantasies, words, definitions, meanings, expressions, feelings, sentiments, and so on when interacting with Blacks or interacting with each other and talking about Blacks. Of the two, racist speech (i.e., white supremacist/ebonicist speech) has by far been more important in the interaction between Whites and Blacks in America and in the maintaining of racism and the White over Black structure and system: racist speech that has been explicit, and that explicitly promoted and rationalized White racist interaction with Blacks; and implicit racist speech, as when racist code words were expressed verbally, such as various liberal words (liberty, rights, and progress), or various democratic words (equality, equal rights, and equal opportunities), or various Christian words (human dignity, brotherhood, and equality before God).

Injected with White racism and de-ethicalized and abnormalized, these words and other similar ones, expressed explicitly or implicitly in racist speech, did not mean what they appeared to mean, because injected with and impacted by racism, they were no longer general words with general value or meaning. They were racist words, meant for white people and not Black people, or were not meant for Black people the same way they were meant for white people. Blacks knew that when white people said liberty, rights, equality, or equality before God, they knew they were making no reference to them with these words, or were, owing to the racist inundation of the words, making references to Blacks in peculiar ways, such as *Black dignity, Black rights*, and *Black progress*. These were not the same as the general meanings of dignity, rights, and progress, and still less the same, owing to the white supremacist inundation of the words were *White dignity, White rights*, and *White progress*. Wherever Blacks interacted with Whites in America in cultural and social situations, white people related to them verbally, overwhelmingly, with explicit and implicit racist speech. When they wrote about Black people, they employed racist written linguistics, which were also explicit and implicit. This was true when white people spelled the names of Black people in written expression. Historically, white people have referred to Black people, in written expressions, primarily as Negroes, Coloreds or Colored people, or blacks, and sometimes niggers, although that was largely a verbal designation.

Whites (like Blacks), for centuries spelled the names of Black people, Negroes, Colored people, or blacks capitalized or uncapitalized in their writings. This particular practice was not in itself rac-ist, but would become racist when white people spelled Black iden-tities in lower-case letters, because this was their way of showing contempt or disrespect for them. In the early twentieth century, Booker T. Washington, W.E.B. Du Bois, Ida Wells-Barnett, Mary Church Terrell, Kelly Miller, and others carried on a verbal battle with white editors because they would not capitalize Negro or Col-ored in their newspapers or magazines, thinking that Blacks did not have the humanity, stature, or dignity to warrant their identi-ties being capitalized. Even to this day, many white editors insist on spelling Black with a small b even when it is a nominative refer-ence, which is done even more by white writers. There is some rac-ism involved in this activity, when consciously or unconsciously white people do not regard Blacks to be equal to Whites in human-ity or human capability, and this is reflected in deprecated spell-ing. Another reason lower-case spelling occurs when nominative references are made is because it is an emulative activity. White writers copy other white writers in spelling Blacks or Black with lower-case letters when they mean nominative entities. White writ-ers copy Black writers who do this, while Black writers copy Black and white writers who do this. White and Black historians play this copying game, and the playing by both parties denigrates Black people, for racist or nonracist motivations and reasons.

The orthographic problems associated with spelling the name and identity of Black people can be brought to a sudden end. When the reference is to racial attributes (adjectival references), then the word black should be employed. When the reference is a nomina-tive one, referring to Blacks as an ethnic group, an ethnic commu-nity, or as a member of one of these groupings, then the word Black should be capitalized and written as Blacks (Black for the indi-vidual member). If the interest is to refer to the racial characteris-tics of the Black ethnic group or the Black ethnic community, then the spelling should be with a small b, and spelled black ethnic group and black ethnic community, with an individual member of either of these designations being spelled with a small b, as a black mem-ber or a black person as a member of either of these black group-ings. It has to be said that there is more than one black ethnic group and black ethnic community in America, which requires these different lower-case spellings of black. This matter will be discussed fully later.

I wish now to finish my general line of thought by saying that the kind of spelling of the word black should also be done to the spell-ing of the word white as it relates to the name and identity of white people. This has also been a historical orthographic problem that has always directly affected the orthographic difficulties involved in spelling the word black. When the reference is to the racial traits of white people, then the word white should be spelled with a small w. When the reference is to white people as a large ethnic group or a large ethnic community in America (which white people are and have been for centuries in America, an ethnic group of the white race), or as an individual member of either of these groupings, then the appropriate spelling has to be Whites and White. If the interest is to denote the racial characteristics of the White ethnic group or the White ethnic community, then the spelling should be with a small w and spelled white ethnic group and white ethnic community, with an individual member of either of these groupings being spelled with a small w, as a white member, or a white person as a member of either of these designations. The large number of white ethnic groups and white ethnic communities requires these various lower-case spellings of white.

Another major reason for the difficulty of properly naming and identifying Black people in America, and for the continuing orthographic problems involved in doing this, is that it is not widely and as a matter of course understood that Black people are an ethnic group in America, an ethnic group of the black race, along with other black ethnic groups in the country that are much smaller in size. Not knowing that there is a large White ethnic group and large White ethnic community in America is directly related to the lack of understanding that a rather large Black ethnic group, involving millions of people, exists in the United States.

What is widely known in America is that there are a large number of white ethnic groups; that is, ethnic groups of the white race in the country, such as Poles, Germans, Greeks, Jews, Irish, Anglo-Saxons, Italians, Hungarians, Ukrainians, and others. It is also widely accepted that all of these white ethnic groups are spelled with capital letters, and it would be unthinkable that they would be spelled in the lower case. This is the important status that the white race and white ethnic groups have in America, an important status confirmed and reproduced by the White over Black structure and system of the country. That structure and system has never conferred similar status upon or reproduced similar status for the black race and the Black ethnic group in America or for the other black ethnic groups of the country. Indeed, the White over Black structure and social system has always been determined to try to make white and Black people think of Black people as being a race, and being of certain racial features; as being identified by racial traits and not by ethnicity or nationality—or even community. Most Black people in America think of Black people as a race. This is true of all three major groupings of Black historians in this country: precursor historians and First- and Second-Wave Black historians. This will not be true of Third-Wave Black historians who will look upon Black people having a racial, ethnic, community, and national identity; that is, an American identity. Black people, for the most part, during the length of their history in America, have rejected the idea of being a "race," that "race" of "nonhumans" or "subhumans" that white people said they were and tried to make them by implementing racist beliefs and oppressive and cruel racist power and practices.

Over the centuries there were Blacks (there is no way to know how many), who were totally victimized by White oppression and cruelty and who believed themselves to be individual members of the "race" of "inferior" "entities" that white people said Black people were. But most Black people, at no time in American history, not even when Black people were slaves, succumbed totally to the psychological annihilation efforts of white people. A primary reason for this was the ethnic development and ethnic identity of Black people, as well as the American identity that Black people internalized, even when they were publicly denied this identity. These identities, and not just the "positive" Black identity—as Second-Wave Black historians and some of the younger and newer First-Wave Black historians are inclined to say—gave Black people sources of resistance, especially intellectual (including diunital cognition), psychological, moral, and spiritual forms of resistance to the White racist psychological annihilation efforts. Even the black racial identity of Black people could be a source of resistance and inspiration for Black people when they could think positively about it, even though it was not a positiveness that could be readily and easily projected or boasted about publicly.

To deal with race and ethnicity as two different kinds of realities and as two different images and realities of Black people in the United States it is necessary to keep race and racism, as well as race and "race," distinguished in one's mind. Race is biology and racism is a set of abstract fanciful beliefs that produce a "race" or "races," things that really do not exist except in the minds and racist fantasies of racists, but which racists, unfortunately, take to be concrete representations with concrete attributes. The other helpful aid to achieve our objectives would be to turn to race as a geographical reality. Du Bois did this in his historical sociological and sociological writings. He did this very clearly in *The Negro* and in the updated version of that book in the late 1930s, *Black Folk Then and Now*. In *The Negro*, Du Bois said the black race existed all over the African continent. He also said that this race was not monolithic or uniform in its racial characteristics, or even in its cultural or social attributes. He accounted for this by the migration of the race across Africa and by climate, environment, vegetation, biological modifications, and languages and cultural modifications.[23] This was Du Bois saying that a race could undergo internal alteration (i.e., dynamic change and development, variation within the race), even biologically, without amalgamation or the biological mixing with another race and taking on some of its characteristics.

But biological mixing does not have to be very extensive, and it may not produce fundamental biological modifications of the race. The mixing of races could simply lead to the introduction of new traits, and those traits may be added only to a small portion of a race that engaged in biological mixing. The mixing of white people and Black people in America has not altered, in a major way, the racial characteristics of the black race as it exists, for instance, from Africa, to the lower Americas and West Indies, to the United States and Canada. Some of the new features produced by white and black race mixing, such as straight hair, thin noses, or the lightening of the color of the black race, were already present in the black race in Africa and had been present for thousands of years. White racists in America and Europe in the late nineteenth and early twentieth centuries said that all black people looked alike, with what they called "Negroid" features: black in color, kinky hair, broad noses, thick lips, and rounded behinds.

But all black people in Africa did not look this way, as Du Bois noted in *The Negro*, also noting that some black people in Africa had what white people at the time would call "Caucasian" features. These features were produced by internal racial alteration, although Du Bois also said that racial amalgamation in Africa had produced them to some extent as well. Du Bois did not make this observation in his book, but one could observe the white race in Europe today and it would be seen that northern and southern white Europeans look racially different from each other, even though both groups of people are of the white race. In northern Europe the white race is white and pinkish in color (but no one has called the white race the pink race because of this pinkish modification), while white people in southern Europe, living closer to the sun in different climatic, atmospheric, environmental, and dietary conditions, are brownish in color—but still considered to be white people.

Du Bois also noted in *The Negro* that there were cultural and social divisions among the black race in Africa. He used two words, ethnic and tribe, to indicate this variation, although he applied the words somewhat differently. He used the word ethnic specifically in connection with the various people not from the African continent but who became part of Egyptian civilization and contributed culturally and socially—ethnically—to it. The word tribe Du Bois applied widely to the black race in Africa, saying that it was subdivided into many tribes, each tribe with its own language, culture, and social life. Du Bois provided brief discussions of some tribal groups. Today, many scholars would equate tribe with ethnic group, as is done by scholars of African history and life and American Indian history and life. But what Du Bois had recognized was that the black race, extended across the length and width of Africa, was subdivided into ethnic groups. He did not say this, but his understanding of tribe as a racial–cultural–social entity made clear that this was something he discerned, and that it was an understanding that he would not have rejected.

Du Bois actually had a concept of race that was similar to his view of tribe and ethnic group. He rejected the notion of a "pure" race, saying in *The Negro* that a race was varied racially or biologically. He held to this view the remainder of his life: "In this little book, then, we are studying the history of the darker part of the human family, which is separated from the rest of mankind by no absolute physical line, but which nevertheless forms, as a mass, a social group distinct in history, appearance, and to some extent in spiritual gift."[24] A race made history and produced culture, the kind of things that Du Bois said tribes and ethnic groups did. Du Bois's definition of race was largely one of the two general definitions of race that existed in America and Europe throughout most of his lifetime. The second definition left off historical, cultural, or social attributes, and just defined race by biological characteristics. Historian Bernard Lewis wrote in *Race and Slavery in the Middle East* that people who talk or write on race often do not know the history of the concept, and the varied understanding it has had, including the understanding that it was synonymous with nationality, or even a linguistic group such as "a group of peoples speaking related languages." Then Lewis remarked,

As so often happens, social scientists took a word of common but imprecise usage and gave it a precise technical meaning. For the anthropologist, a race was a group of people sharing certain visible and measurable characteristics, such as hair, pigmentation, skull measurements, height, and other physical features. Races thus consisted of such categories as whites, blacks, Mongols, and the like. These might be subdivided—thus, for example, whites could be classified as Nordic, Alpine, or Mediterranean. This kind of race, though obviously overlapping to some extent with ethnic groupings, was independent of ethnic features. Different races could share a culture. Different cultures could divide a race. By the strictly physical definition, even members of the same family, with different genes, could belong to different races.[25]

As things now stood, said Lewis, race had come to mean what it has meant in America for most of this century, a meaning that has spread to other countries:

In current American usage . . . the word "race" is used exclusively to denote such major divisions as white, black, Mongolian, and the like. It is no longer applied to national, ethnic, or cultural entities, such as the English or Irish, the Germans or the Slavs, or even the Japanese, who are now seen as being part of a much larger racial grouping found in East Asia.[26]

Du Bois himself sometimes talked about the "white races," which he did because he saw race as being associated with cultural and social differentiation and felt that this kind of differentiation within a race could be so distinctive that it would split or subdivide a given race, not biologically (or significantly biologically), but culturally, where the subdivisions of a race could be, in a number of ways, culturally and socially different from each other. One could be tempted to talk about different "races," as Du Bois was when he used that phrase or engaged in discussions of "white races," as he did in "The Conservation of Races."[27] In that article Du Bois was actually generally confused in writing about races, as he equated race with ethnic groups and nationalities. But it was only confusing the way he did it, not because race, ethnicity, and nationality did not relate to each other, which he showed more clearly in other writings after the turn of the twentieth century.

Du Bois's definition of race, as he usually described this phenomenon, combined the two definitions of race that have been talked about: the definition that saw race as biological, and the definition that saw race involving biology, history, culture, and social life. Du Bois was interested in showing that race was not simply biology; that it also involved people. An emphasis on the biological or racial characteristics of a race might exclude or minimize the peopleness of a race. People made history and produced a culture and social life. A race made of people made history and produced a culture and social life. In short, for Du Bois, a race never existed independent of people or independent of history, culture, and a social life—any more than people did. But races did exist independently of each other, even if they lived in close proximity to each other, as does the white race, black race, bronze race, red race, and yellow race in America.

Du Bois's definition of race did not clearly distinguish race from what a race did. It seems appropriate to define race in a limited manner; namely, as a group of people with relatively distinctive racial or biological characteristics. It is also necessary to accept the view that a race comprised of people does what people do: It makes history and produces and lives from a culture and social life. A race (of people) spread out over a large geographical area would produce a general culture and social life over that area, as the white race has done in Europe and America, the black race has done in Africa, the red and bronze races have done in the Americas, and the yellow race has done in Asia. To talk about race as Du Bois liked to talk and write about it, it is necessary to have a conceptualization that he did not produce. I propose *racenicity*, a view of race that takes in biology, but also the history and the cultural and social constructions of a race. This does not eliminate or minimize a biological definition of race that would make it possible to distinguish the relative biological differences that produce races and distinguish them from each other. But the concept of racenicity makes it possible to expand the discussion of race without getting into some biological determinism, or a scientistic view of race, or racist fanciful biological determinism.

There are Black historians and other Black intellectuals who talk about race being "socially constructed," and say that produces "race," not an actual biological race. This is their way of saying that race or races do not exist, which is a denial predicated on their belief that a race has to be pure to be a race. Historian Barbara Fields projected this view.[28] Black philosophers Kwame Anthony Appiah and Tommy Lott recently expressed this position.[29] But the fact of the matter is, the notion of a pure race was rejected by physical and social scientists, as opposed to racists and racist pseudoscientists, in the late nineteenth and early twentieth centuries. Du Bois, as seen, argued that a race varied in its internal or racial characteristics. Black historians or other Black intellectuals who argue that a race has to be pure, that the black race has to be biologically pure, are individuals who, in fact, reject the scientific view of race. Black political scientist Adolph Reed, Jr. wrote, "Geneticists recognize that [there is a] range of variation within a given 'racial' population," but he rejected this view nonetheless, motivated by his deep and unslakable view that a race was identified by all of its members having the same exact racial characteristics.[30] This is less a philosophical view than a romantic one. It is also the racist's view of race, which is actually of "race" as the racist projects that quoted word, and which to the racist is pure in either its "superior" or "inferior" "innate" "characteristics" ("attributes" like "race" itself, that do not exist).

Another way to look at biological race in terms of its larger context and discussion, and as history demonstrates, is that races do subdivide into countries and nationalities. The white race exists in a number of different countries in Europe, and each country has a different national identity. This is also true of the black race in Africa, the yellow race in Asia, and the bronze race in the Americas. But a country is not a race, and a national identity is not a racial identity. The latter two realities are not possible without the former reality.

A race can also subdivide into ethnic groups. There is presently considerable debate and confusion as to the definition and reality of ethnic groups. The confusion centers around the questions of whether ethnic group and race are the same (i.e., synonymous), whether a race gives rise to an ethnic group or an ethnic group gives rise to a race or races, whether an ethnic group can exist independent of race, and whether an ethnic group has to be a certain size in order to be recognized as such. Another question that has been a matter of debate is whether ethnic groups are viable entities; that is, do they affect individuals in a thorough and meaningful way, or do individuals identify with their ethnic group and take on its ethnicity only when they wish to or when they find it convenient to do so.

As Mary Waters suggests, these problematic identifications involve present and future generations of long-standing ethnic groups in America, and older generations of groups identify strongly with and are strongly influenced by their ethnic orientation. Waters writes, "Ethnicity has become a subjective identity, invoked at will by the individual. Yet its very subjectivity and voluntary character lead to fundamental questions about its future viability, given increasing intermarriage and the resulting mixed ancestries in people's backgrounds."[31]

It has to be said that ethnicity has always involved subjectivity as well as objectivity, and the two in interaction. An ethnic culture and social life invests members of an ethnic group with ideals, values, beliefs, cognitive systems, and a general psychology that become "inner" realities and "inner" motivations, which are subjective things. Of course, ethnic groups can be weakened by individuals breaking from them, not identifying with them, or identifying or getting involved with them on the basis of convenience. But the viability of an ethnic group is not related to people who leave it, or the size of it. As long as people are a part of an ethnic group and adhere to its ethnicity, then that ethnic group has vitality and is viable. Individuals marrying across ethnic lines does not preclude them honoring aspects of each of their ethnicities in their marriage or family life, which helps to maintain the viability and life of an ethnic group and its ethnicity.

As long as an ethnic group exists, even if it numbers nothing more than several hundred people, a distinctive cultural and social unit exists and would be vibrant and viable, so that a convenient adherence to it would not deprecate it, but would in fact reinforce it, even in this limited way. There is also the reality that some groups come into their ethnicity later than others; that is, they do not become fully conscious of their ethnicity, or consciously seek publicly and socially to exhibit it, until a much later time. This is happening with Black people in America, as their ethnic consciousness and identity continue to grow without as yet a widespread full and formal acceptance of this vibrant and viable reality among themselves. This shows the ability of White racist power to continue to disrupt and interfere with wide Black group acceptance. Generally speaking, oppressed ethnic groups in a society are latent conscious, public practitioners, which, in America, draws in Black people as well as Indians (indigenous) and Asian and Hispanic ethnic groups. The demand for a multicultural approach to higher education suggests that ethnic groups and ethnicity are far from being counted out in the United States.

The central problem with the existence of ethnic groups and ethnicity is the question of an ethnic group's relationship to race. There are people who deny the existence of race and therefore only see the existence of ethnic groups that, in their view, are independent of race. But can an ethnic group be independent of a race? The answer is clearly no. Ethnic groups are of a race; that is, all ethnic groups are racially based. American history and American society amply demonstrate this fact. As seen earlier, the white race in America is comprised of many ethnic groups, to which the Lithuanians, the Russians, the Portuguese, the Swedes, and the Armenians could be added. The red race in America is composed of many ethnic groups, such as the Hopi, the Cherokee, the Sioux, the Penobscots, and the Maliseets. The yellow race in this country exhibits the Chinese, Japanese, Korean, and Vietnamese ethnic groups. The bronze race has a more complicated ethnic subdivision existence in America. This race is joined by other races to comprise Hispanic ethnic groups in America. This grows out of national conditions from other countries.

Take Mexico, for example. That country is comprised of the white race, the red race, and the bronze race as its main racial branches. All these races participate in Mexican history, culture, and social life, and thus take on and assimilate the Mexican historical consciousness, the Mexican national culture and social life, and the Mexican national identity. When Mexicans come to live in America, their national identity becomes an ethnic identity (which is true of all national groups that come to this country, because they come to a country with its own national identity). The ethnic Mexicans in

America would be comprised of at least three racial groupings, and thus this ethnic group would not be singly racially based, but multiracially based.

This would also be true of Puerto Ricans, Cubans, Panamanians, and Columbians living as ethnic groups in the United States, all of which would have the black race added to their racially based ethnicity. In these instances, it can be seen that ethnicity did not create race, and certainly not races. Races joined together to produce specific ethnic groups (that is to say, for the United States), which would be different national groups and national identities in other contexts, predicated upon and produced by racial groups. No one would want to say that one of the white ethnic groups in America produced the white race in the country, which is what one would be saying when they say that race springs from ethnicity. It is clearly the other way around, even when ethnicity is multiracially based.

Sociologist Milton Gordon accepts the idea that an ethnic group is racially (biologically) based, and that it produces and exhibits a culture and social life, or ethnicity.[32] Sociologists Benjamin Ringer and Elinor Rawless recently acceded to this understanding of ethnic group. They also made the valid argument that an ethnic group was not fully internally created or fully autonomous in its development and existence. They argued that ethnic groups in a society were impacted and influenced by other ethnic groups, an impact and influence that helped to constitute them.[33] This same viewpoint was expressed by Stephen Steinberg in his book *The Ethnic Myth*: that it was a myth when it was believed that an ethnic group evolved autonomously and unaffected by other ethnic groups or historical and social factors in a society, and thus also a myth when it was believed that an ethnic group and ethnicity were both static and unchanging realities.[34]

Ringer, Rawless, and Steinberg's comments about the dynamic and multisource construction of an ethnic group and ethnicity are easily accepted, because Black history in America clearly demonstrates that the development of Black people as an ethnic group was not a strictly autonomous thing and involved the impact and blending of diverse historical, cultural, and social impacts and influences. This is something that some Black historians, usually some Second-Wave Black historians with a strong and narrow Black nationalist orientation, sometimes forget or choose to ignore.

On the other hand, Second- and First-Wave Black historians, generally, in each instance, have failed to recognize and promote the historical truth that Black people in the United States are an ethnic group. Both groups of historians, overwhelmingly, like the Black precursor historians before them, regard Blacks as being only a racial group, or they write as if they were. Before black people came to America as slaves, they had belonged to different countries and different ethnic groups within those countries. These national and ethnic identities were destroyed by the slave trade and slavery in America, leaving a black race as a residual reality, with some residual original cultural and social traits to rebuild life upon.

Between the seventeenth, eighteenth, and nineteenth centuries this racial group steadily evolved into an ethnic group, a new ethnic group of the black race that stretched from Africa to the Western Hemisphere. The ethnic character of Black people was revealed when they were juxtaposed to white ethnic groups, and also when other black people came to America in the twentieth century from the West Indies and from the Americas. These new black people were somewhat the same as the indigenous Black people of America, having come originally from the same hemispheric area and having endured a similar history, as well as having some similar original cultural and social traits. But Black people in America developed differently from other black people in the Western Hemisphere or the Western African Extensia. They were a new ethnic group of the black race. The black people who came to America from other places in the Western Hemisphere came from different countries, and came to America with different national identities that had to become ethnic identities in this country. Thus, national identities such as Jamaican, Haitian, Barbadian, or Bahamian became ethnic identities in America. A number of black ethnic groups now existed in America, as did a number of black ethnic communities, with Black people being the largest of these ethnic groups and ethnic communities.

The White racist-inundated White over Black structure and system has historically functioned to lump all black people together as if there were no ethnic distinctions among them, so that all black people in America, whatever their national origins or their ethnic constitutions, could be viewed as a single race of people to be identified by race and racial features and not by histories, cultures, or social existences. Black people in America, as well as other black people in the country, helped to perpetuate this racist denigration and distortion of realities by not clarifying racial and ethnic realities. But it also has to be said that this was probably something that Black people and other black people probably could not have done earlier in their history, or even earlier in this century, because of the pervasive White racist power that precluded such an effort. The historical realities can be clarified now, and Third-Wave Black historiography proposes to do that: to view Black people as a distinctive ethnic group in America and adduce historical evidence to prove it, while acknowledging and insisting upon the reality of several black ethnic groups and black ethnic communities in the country.

Skeptics of a Black ethnic group might point out that all people of that group are not black in color, and thus are not all black people. There is truth in this observation, but some falsity in it as well. What is false about it is the projection of the idea of a pure black race, which has never existed in the world, not even in Africa. In Africa there have always been shades of blackness, including brownish blackness or blackish brownness, or even shades of brownness. An African brownish in color would have kinky hair, a broad nose, and thick lips. On the other hand, an African black in color might have straight hair and a thin nose. An African with kinky hair might have a thin nose and thin lips, as is found among Ethiopians. The variation to be found among the black race in Africa could be seen among the white race in Europe, as was pointed out earlier. Variation within the yellow race of Asia, and the red race that stretches from Canada down through the Americas, could also be noted.

The amalgamation of white and black people in the United States has not destroyed the black race as such, as that race is still overwhelmingly black, blackish brown, or brownish black, as it was before coming to the United States. There are Black people and black people in the United States with yellowish or white skin and with some "Caucasian" features, as there are Black and black people with such skin colors and kinky hair, broad noses, and thick lips. Caucasian racial intrusion into the black race in America and specifically into Black people is not to be denied. But this intrusion does not warrant the conclusion that Black people or the black race do not exist in the United States, any more than black racial intrusion into the white race denies the existence of that race, or into the red race, where there is also some black racial intrusion.

The Black ethnic group in America is not built upon a pure racial foundation, as it had never been, where the black race was monolithic in its racial features. But the black racial stock is the paramount racial stock of the Black ethnic group in America. As discussed previously in describing ethnicity, the latter has always involved more than race. It also involves history, culture, and social life and the psychological and spiritual attributes that flow from them. Thus, to say Black people in America is to say more than race, and this has been true since the initial formation of the Black ethnic group in America that goes back to slavery in the seventeenth century. Black people of light skin color are usually Black ethnically (i.e., historically living among Black people as part of the Black community) and Black culturally and socially, and usually marry within the Black ethnic group, helping to promote it and reproduce it and its ethnicity, which exhibits continuity as well as change. The Black ethnic group is one among many black ethnic groups of the black race from Africa to the Western African Extensia. The Black ethnic group in America, like other black ethnic groups in the geographical area, are a people of black African descent, not Africans. The slave ancestors of all these descendants did not refer to themselves as Africans; that is, they did not have that identity, as the next two chapters will clarify.

Chapter 5

Whites/Europeans and the Origins of the African Identity

It is common to think of the African identity as being indigenous to the continent, having its origins among the millennial black people who have and continue to live there. This is the assumption that Black historians, and other Black intellectuals, for that matter, automatically make. But it is, as it has always been, an erroneous assumption, because the word and identity of African comes from without the continent originally. People outside of Africa, in Europe, Asia, and the Western Hemisphere, for a very lengthy period of time referred to the large island continent as Africa and the people on it as Africans, while most of the black inhabitants were totally ignorant of the two names. Indeed, as strange as it seems, most black Africans did not hear the names and identities of Africa and Africans until after World War II, when they came to them in post-war liberation slogans, such as "Africa for the Africans," "African Liberation," "African nationalism," or "African Unity." There are black Africans today who accept the name and identity of African for themselves, while many others, perhaps even most black Africans, have not done so, preferring other more meaningful identities for themselves, such as family, clan, tribe, or religious identities, or perhaps a national identity. Those black Africans who have accepted an African identity for themselves have accepted it in retrospect, and it constitutes a retrospective identity. There are Black historians and other Black intellectuals in America who call themselves and other Black people and other kinds of black people in the country and without Africans, not knowing that this is a retrospective identity and not a millennial or historically indigenously devised one. This chapter will deal with the origins of the African identity and its retrospective character as it relates generally to black people. The next chapter will deal with this identity as it relates specifically to Black people and the writing of Black history.

What helped to obscure the understanding of the origins and nature of the African identity, and that even blocked the ability to see or to probe this conundrum, was the myriad of names that were used, in addition to Africa and Africans, to refer to the island continent and its inhabitants. From about the sixteenth century on the continent was called Guinea, Negroland, and also Ethiopia. The people on it were called variously Ethiopians, Guineas, Moors, and Negroes. These were all names, like the names Africa and Africans, that came from outside the continent. This means that the black inhabitants not only did not have the words Africa and African in their languages, they did not have the other names in them either, nor any kind of consciousness, commitment, loyalty, or ceremonious relationship with any of these names or identities. Indeed, an irony of what has been for some time referred to as African history is that the people called Africans either had to leave the continent to find out who they were (at least what people were calling them), or people outside the continent, such as Europeans, had to come to the continent to tell them who they were, although this would not be done that often, and would not be said to many Africans, who would be called other names by Europeans, including a myriad of racist epithets.

The ancient Greeks provided the world the names and identities of Ethiopia and Ethiopians, which the Romans and their Christian and German successors in Europe passed on to that continent's history and culture. For many centuries some people in Europe looked upon Ethiopia (sometimes spelled Aethiopia) and Africa to be interchangeable terms, and had the same view about the words Africa and Africans. These interchangeable expressions also passed on to the United States, although they were not used that much by either white or Black people because the reference to Africa and Africans was rarely with these words or, as in the case of Africans, very often with the words Negro and Negroes, and frequently Colored people. But the interchangeability and confusion existed in America and elsewhere, and not just in Europe, because of the way the Greeks devised and employed the terms Ethiopia and Ethiopians, which they and the Romans passed on. The English Egyptologist E. A. Wallis Budge described their usage:

It seems certain that classical historians and geographers called the whole region from India to Egypt, both countries inclusive, by the name of "Ethiopia," and in consequence they regarded all the dark-skinned and black peoples who inhabited it as "Ethiopians." Mention is made of "Eastern" and "Western" Ethiopians, and it is probable that the Easterners were Asiatics, and the Westerners Africans.[1]

Thus, Ethiopia for the Greeks and the Romans was the vast region between India and Egypt, and the Ethiopians were all the black and dark-skinned people there; that is, blackish-brown, brownish-black, and brownish colored people. This ancient understanding of Ethiopia and Ethiopians has been known by Black historians. One of the first to exhibit this understanding was George Washington Williams. In the first volume of his history of Black people in America, he wrote, "The terms 'Ethiopia' was anciently given to all those whose color was darkened by the sun. Herodotus, therefore, distinguishes the Eastern Ethiopians who had straight hair, from the Western Ethiopians who had curly or woolly hair."[2]

Du Bois also knew of the ancient understandings of Ethiopia and Ethiopians and sometimes in his writings one would see him use the words Ethiopia and Africa, or Ethiopians and Africans, interchangeably; not because he did not know they were not sets of interchangeable words in fact, but because he thought the interchangeability of these sets of words was literary, and he used them as literary devices—which also meant that he projected misunderstandings about the words Ethiopia and Ethiopians on occasion. For instance, in his book *Darkwater* he had a chapter entitled, "The Hands of Ethiopia." The chapter was about Africa and European colonizers in Africa. The word Ethiopia appeared in the text only once, when Du Bois wrote, "The hands which Ethiopia shall soon stretch out unto God are not mere hands of helplessness and supplication, but rather are they hands of pain and promise; hard, gnarled, and muscled for the world's real work; they are hands of fellowship for the half-submerged masses of a distempered world."[3] Thus, Ethiopia was Africa, as Du Bois was saying, and "the half-submerged masses" who were the Africans of his textual discussion were also the Ethiopians stretching out their hands.

John Jackson, lay Black historian of ancient Africa and ancient civilizations, has described more precisely the ancient Greek origins of the word Ethiopia and its meaning: "When the Greeks came in contact with the dusky inhabitants of Africa and Asia, they called them the 'burnt-faces.' The Greek word for burnt was *ethios* and the word for face was *ops*. So *ethios* plus *ops* became Ethiopian. The Greeks reasoned that these people developed their dark complexion because they were closer to the sun than were the fairer inhabitants of Europe."[4] Both the Greeks and the Romans associated what they both regarded as African Ethiopians with the color black. This was an understanding that George Washington Williams had: "The word . . . 'Ethiopia' [was] used always to describe a black people."[5] Frank Snowden, Jr., an eminent First-Wave Black historian of ancient civilizations, made the same observation in more recent times, although his views were a modification of those of Williams. He said that the Greeks and the Romans both referred to the African Ethiopians to "illustrate blackness of color." But he also said that the Greeks and Romans saw different shades of blackness among the African Ethiopians, from intensely black, to less black, and even blackish brown.[6]

The Greeks and the Romans, as historiography of the ancient world indicates, with their broad view of Ethiopia, were making reference to a racial group, with biological variations within that group, without being racist in their intentions or observations. This racial group stretched over a wide geographical area from India to northeastern and eastern Africa, where it produced, as the Greeks and Romans said, a general Ethiopian civilization, which both the Greeks and Romans also saw as a subdivided civilization; that is, an Eastern Ethiopian civilization and a Western Ethiopian civilization. There were, as the Greeks and Romans knew, individual countries within each of these subdivided civilizations, which produced them collectively, and which the Greeks and the Romans would sometimes call all by the same name: Ethiopia. But they also called individual countries by other names, names they had for themselves or names they gave countries. One such country, for instance, known as Kemet, the Greeks preferred to call Egypt. That name stuck with that country and passed on into history as the name of it.

South of Kemet/Egypt was Kush, which in time took the name Ethiopia for itself, and in time would be the only country to be called Ethiopia from the original Greek and Roman conception of the Ethiopian civilization. But Ethiopia also acquired another name in history, given to it by Asians and Europeans. That was Abyssinia. The Ethiopians loathed the name Abyssina, but seemed unable to get other people in the world to stop calling their country that, and acquiesced to that identity in their relations with other countries and peoples.[7] This they did until the early 1950s. At that time, a formal, independent nation-state of Ethiopia was established, and the name Abyssinia began to pass from history. Today it is seldom heard.

But the confusion surrounding the names of Ethiopia and Ethiopians throughout millennia helps to explain how the words could be used interchangeably with Africa and Africans, respectively; how they could even lead some individuals to believe that Ethiopia was or might be the original name of Africa, and Ethiopians the original name of Africans. Ethiopia as it related to Africa in ancient Greek and Roman usage (that is, their conception of African Ethiopia), referred to the northeastern and eastern part of Africa. There were some ancient Greek and Roman writers, according to Frank Snowden, Jr., who included some black people of northwest Africa under the name Ethiopian, and these people and this region as part of the general Ethiopian civilization or the African subdivision of that civilization.

A point this discussion makes clear is that Ethiopia and Ethiopians (or even Abyssinia, for that matter), are not names and identities indigenous to what in earlier and later times was known as Africa, or to the millennial black people who primarily lived on that continent in ancient and present times. Only a small number of Africans claim these identities and, of course, they are identities accepted in *retrospect*, meaning that Ethiopia and Ethiopians are *retrospective names and identities* for some Africans—names and identities that came from people outside the continent but which they accepted as their own, as being natural to them, and the way they wanted themselves and their country to be known. In the case of Ethiopians, this was done in ancient times, when they were Kushites, living in Kush, and opted for the name and identity of Ethiopian and the name and identity of Ethiopia for their country.

The Greeks and the Romans provided another name for some of the black people who lived on the land that in time would be called Africa. This was the name Moors, as expressed in the English language. The Greek word for Moors was *Mauri*, and for the Romans (i.e., in Latin) it was *Maurus*. These Greek and Roman words would appear in other European languages besides English at a later time, such as Spanish, French, and Italian, as *Moro, Moir*, and *Mor*, respectively. Black art historian James Brunson and Black historian Runoko Rashidi recently wrote, "During the European Renaissance, explorers, writers and scholars began to apply the term Moor to Blacks in general." They singled out Richard Hakluyt and said that this fifteenth-century English traveler wrote, "In old times the people of Africa were called *aethiops* and *negritae*, which we now call Moores, Moorens, or Negroes."[8] When the Europeans in the fifteenth century and thereafter generalized about the Moors and applied this name to all black people of Africa, they were going way beyond what the Greeks and Romans had done. The Greek *Mauri* and the Roman *Maurus* referred to black people in northwestern Africa (as they had referred to Ethiopians in essentially northeastern and eastern Africa). The Moors of northwestern Africa who were Muslims invaded Spain in the eighth century, and dominated that country and its culture for seven hundred years.

In the late fifteenth century the Moors were finally and fully defeated in Spain by Christians in what was known as the Reconquista, which had taken centuries. Brunson and Rashidi wrote that during the Middle Ages in Europe the Moors of Spain came under European hatred and opprobrium:

During the Middle Ages, because of his dark complexion and Islamic faith the Moor became in Europe a symbol of guile, evil and hate. In medieval literature demonic figures were commonly depicted with black faces. Among Satan's titles in medieval folklore were: "Black Knight," "Black Man," "Black Ethiopian," and "Big Negro." In the *Cantiga* 185 of King Alfonso the Wise of Spain (1254–86), three Moors attacking the Castle of Chincoya are described as "black as Satan." In Cantiga 329, an extremely black man who has stolen objects from a Christian church is identified as a Moor. In the *Poema de Fernan Gonzalez*, devils and Moors are equally described as "carbonientos"—literally the "coal-faced ones."[9]

What can be seen in this passage is a mixture of White racial and White racist thinking in medieval Europe moving into Renaissance Europe, ways of thinking that actually overlap and feed each other and that is seen moving toward being one form of thinking: racist thinking. There are references to the black race in racial terms, and there are the references to the "nonhuman" (Satan) or "subhuman" ("guile, evil and hate"; i.e., "natural") "attributes" of black people. There is even the racist thinking that black people, in their "nature," are ugly, treacherous, dangerous, and thieves. The quoted comments also point to the implied White racial and White racist thinking about the white race and the superior "natural" "attributes" of such people, which would be the implied opposite of the "natural" "guiling," "evil," "hateful," and "thieving" "traits" of black people, that "race" of "nonhumans" or "subhumans."

Often, as historical evidence has shown, particularly from the United States or from European colonies in Africa, Asia, and other parts of the world, white supremacy is asserted as a racist doctrine often by implication, in writing or in speech, by denigrating black people, yellow people, or red or bronze people in racist terms. By the thirteenth century white Europeans were beginning to develop their white supremacist/ebonicistic racist beliefs that would be developed more fully and become more ominous at a later time. The Moors were clearly an object of this racist thinking, as well as a source or motivation for its development. The presence of black slaves in Europe during the Middle Ages and the Renaissance was another source. By the fifteenth century, before the organized and massive slave trade from Africa, there were white people in Europe looking upon the black people in Africa as Moors and, therefore, were looking at them in deprecating racial and racist terms, which the organized and centuries-continuing slave trade would augment further, especially White racist thinking toward black people. The name Moor never achieved much use in Africa, nor was it even known by most black people on that continent.

The name and identity did not survive in a strong manner in Europe, and had almost no existence in America in terms of knowledge of the name or use of it. A primary reason for these realities was the existence and use of the names and identities of Negroes and Colored people, especially the former, for black people, which pushed the name and identity of Moor from public knowledge and use (there were Moors brought to North America as slaves, but the name Moor was not used to describe them in English colonies or later in America). But it has to be said nevertheless that while the name and identity of Moor and the actual Moors existed in Europe and with the racial and racist stigmas attached to both, they were sources of white people feeling as if they were the only people, and as if they were "gods" or "godlike." The defeat of the Moors in Spain at the end of the fifteenth century also contributed to these White racist feelings in Europe.

The name and identity of Negro, which was to be applied to the black people of Africa and the black people who left that continent, especially those who became slaves in the Western African Extensia, did not come from the Greeks and did not derive from the name and identity of Moor. The word and identity of Negro also were not indigenous to Africa and the black people there. The words Negro, Negroes, and Colored people—or even the phrase "Negroland"—all came from the outside of Africa and were then imposed on the people of that continent or those black people who left the continent to live elsewhere. Yet the etymology, the root of the word Negro, has to be traced to Africa. That root word is *Niger*, which was an ancient African word that found its way into Roman Latin. The word itself, in its usage in ancient Africa, had nothing to do with color or race, but was a reference to a river in Africa: the Niger River. Rome brought northern Africa under its domination, which also drew some central Africans into the empire, including those from the area of the Niger River.

These Africans put the word *Niger* into Roman Latin; that is, it was a word that the Romans adopted and made part of their language in the same way that there are French words in English, English words in German, or English and French words in Russian. J. A. Rogers brought clarity to this etymological matter back in the 1950s: "The word comes from the River Niger, and Nigritae means the people from the River Niger. 'Ni' probably means 'great' and Ger, or Geir, is African for river. At first Niger had nothing more to do with black than the waters of the river itself. 'Ater' was the Latin for black."[10] In time in Rome, Niger also became a word that referred to the color black and to a black person, as the Romans made an association with the word and the people who gave it to them. But the word Niger in this new context carried no negative color or racial connotations, as color and race were simply not that important to the Romans, as Frank Snowden, Jr. pointed out in *Before Color Prejudice*, or as Lloyd Thompson has recently pointed out in *Romans and Blacks*.[11] Both authors indicated, however, that the Greeks and Romans had negative views toward the word black, because that word was associated with nighttime and the fears and mysteries of nighttime, which led to evil and unfavorable omens being associated with the word black.

The Christians followed the Greeks and Romans in this kind of thinking, often viewing the Devil as black. All three of these historical groups also looked upon the word white in a positive way, not from any color or racial association, but from the daylight and sunlight themselves, which were felt to be times when human beings were in greater control of their thoughts, fears, and environment. It can be seen, however, that these ancient understandings of white and black in nonracial or nonracist terms could become the basis, or one of the bases, for developing racist views about white and black people, which actually began to occur in Europe during its Middle Ages and Renaissance periods, which was when the black Moors and black slaves became the objects and victims of this emergent racist thinking.

All of this deprecating activity occurred between the thirteenth, fourteenth, and fifteenth centuries. It was not until the sixteenth century that the word Negro began to be used in a frequent manner in European languages, which initially occurred in Spanish and Portuguese, and, it would seem, in the former first. This development was aided by the traditional names for Moors in Spanish and Portuguese, but it was also aided by the serious inauguration of the African slave trade, which had initially taken such slaves to Spain and Portugal and then into the Western Hemisphere.

Historian Jack Forbes has recently thrown much light on the origin of the word Negro and the way it was initially used by both the Spanish and Portuguese. His research indicated that the word actually had its origins in the Latin word *Niger*, but he himself did not seem to know that the etymology of the word was not ancient Rome and Latin, but rather south of the Sahara. Forbes, however, did make the following important observation:

Latin *niger, negri* would seem to be the predecessor of Spanish and Portuguese *negro*, Catalan *negre*, Italian *nero*, French *noir* (black) and *negre* (black or dark person). These terms correspond to Dutch *swert, swart*, German *schwartz*, English "black" ("Swarthy" has come to be the equivalent to "dark" rather than black). As applied to humans these terms do not necessarily imply a true black color but merely a range of dark shades approaching black or reminding one of black. Thus there is a considerable range for interpretation. An early Spanish–French dictionary (1607) translated Spanish *negro* as being equivalent to French "noir," obscur, offisque, brun. "Negro de la Guinea" is equivalent to "un negre, un More." As will be noted in the case of Dutch, the above allows for dark (obscur) and brun to be subsumed under *negro* and uses French *more* (moor) as equivalent to a *negro* from Guinea.[12]

The word negro or its equivalent in other European languages during the centuries of the African slave trade was used primarily as a descriptive adjective to denote a human being that was black or dark in color, or was used as a descriptive adjective to define some negative psychological or social attribute or reality. The Spanish and the Portuguese, when initiating the use of the word negro, employed it primarily as an adjective for the purpose of distinguishing between the black people they knew as Moors and the new black people they were enslaving in Spain and Portugal, who were taken from Africa, which both countries sometimes referred to as Guinea.

This early use of the word negro in the fifteenth and early sixteenth centuries was not really a full recognition of race, but a recognition of color, and it was not a reference to condition, not even slave condition. It would appear that it was in the late sixteenth century, with the further development of the African slave trade that was taking black slaves to the Western Hemisphere, that the Spanish and Portuguese began using the word negro in a harsh manner as a reference to slavery or servile condition. This was a nominative use of the word negro, but it did not refer to color or race, that is, a people of a particular color, or even particularly, or more accurately, exclusively, to black Africans who were being made slaves in larger numbers at this time. Forbes has written that the word negro "lost any mandatory color reference and became a general term of abuse." Speaking specifically about this situation with the Spanish, he wrote, "It is quite obvious, then, that *negro* was not being used in either a color or racial sense (by the latter sixteenth century) but in the sense of slaves or dangerous 'others.'"[13]

The slaves or dangerous others that the Spanish and the Portuguese were referring to at this time were black people as well as the Indians they were enslaving in the Western Hemisphere, who were both called negroes by the Spanish and the Portuguese. Clearly, there was no way to eliminate race and color entirely from the word negro as the Spanish and Portuguese were using the term in the late sixteenth century. It was used as an adjective and noun with respect to enslaved Indians and black Africans, who were not white, which Forbes should have been able to perceive.

But three important points that Forbes did make were that the Spanish and Portuguese, in using the word negro in the late sixteenth century and for years thereafter, used the term with respect to Indians and black people, and not just the latter. The Portuguese even used the word negro to describe Indians in India, as well as Chinese and Japanese. They used the word nigger as an epithet for black Africans, but also for Chinese, Japanese, and Indians of India. In the 1750s Portugal made it illegal to call Indians in Brazil negro or negroes "and other insulting and opprobrious terms."[14] The second point that Forbes made was that when the Spanish and Portuguese used the words negro or negroes in the late sixteenth century and thereafter their reference was primarily toward servile condition and people they regarded as a menace to their imperial position or imperial activities.

The third point that Forbes made in his book was that just when the Spanish and Portuguese were eliminating color and race as the primary reference of the word negro, the English were making color, race, and servile condition all synonymous with the word negro, as well as the word negroes, which was used in an adjectival and nominative sense by the British, even when the spelling of negroes was with a small "n". In addition, the English (and other colonists) used the words negro and negroes in the sixteenth, seventeenth, and eighteenth centuries to describe Indians and black people in their North American colonies. The English were even more elastic with the term than this. Forbes referred to a student of black people in England who had said in a work, "It should be borne in mind that the word *Negro* in this period (1600s) could mean an Asian as well as an African (or other person of African descent)."[15]

In the English colonies in North America in the seventeenth and eighteenth centuries, the word mulatto was a reference, as an adjective or as a noun, to a person who was a mixed black and white person, although the words negro and negroes would also be used to describe mulatto, as well as the word colored by the eighteenth century. In the same colonies of the seventeenth and eighteenth centuries and thereafter the words Negro and Negroes, in upper- or lower-case spellings, the words Colored, Coloreds, or Colored people in similar spellings, the words black or blacks in upper- or lower-case spellings, the word nigger, and later the phrase "people of color"—used in the nineteenth century—all had the meaning of black when referring to black people, with black meaning something negative, denigrative, or threatening.

These meanings were imposed on black people who were regarded by white people as being negative, degraded, and menacing. All these words were used to describe black slaves, especially Negro and Negroes, with the exception of the name "people of color," which was usually a reference in the nineteenth century to northern non-slave Blacks. The latter, as well as nonslave Blacks in the South, were also publicly referred to by all the other names listed, in their various spellings. By the late eighteenth century, Indians ceased to be slaves in North America, and slavery was confined to black people. Thus, the word Negro, capitalized or not, came to be confined to black people, slave or not, and was also made synonymous with slavery (that is, the servile condition of black people) or with the oppressed and outcast condition of nonslave Blacks. The words black and colored, in their upper- and lower-case spellings, came to be synonymous with both conditions of black people in the late eighteenth century and thereafter, and this was also true of the racist epithet, nigger.

As said at the opening of this chapter, the words Africa and African were not indigenous to the continent, although this continues to be the understanding, or more correct, the wide misunderstanding. Historian Ivan Van Sertima has reflected this misunderstanding. He argued that the word Africa was indigenous to the continent, and specifically to the ancient Egyptians. He said the Egyptians had a word, *Afru-ika*, which meant "birthplace," although he did not say that the birthplace was Egypt and that this was what the Egyptians meant by the word.[16] On the contrary, he gave the impression that the Egyptians used the word *Afru-ika* to refer to all of the large island continent of which Egypt was a part, and that it was this continent that was a birthplace. Van Sertima conveyed this general meaning of *Afru-ika* and that it was the original and indigenous name of the large island continent that in time would be translated as Africa to the world in comments he made in the introduction of his *Nile Valley Civilizations*, an issue of the *Jour-*

nal of African Civilizations published in book form when he referrred
to Cheikh Anta Diop's writing in that work dealing with "man's
earliest beginnings in the land the Egyptians called *Afru-ika*."[17]
Egypt itself, as Van Sertima knew, was not the land or birthplace of
"man's earliest beginnings." So he was clearly conveying the impression that the Egyptians had a word, *Afru-ika*, that was a reference
to a large land mass (i.e., a large island continent). The Egyptians
knew that their country was situated on a land mass, but they did
not know that it was situated on a vast island. And it would have
been beyond their knowledge, or the knowledge of any ancient
people, to know that human beings had their "earliest beginnings"
in Africa.

Yosef ben-Jochanan has rejected *Afru-ika*, both as a word and as
the original name for Africa, or as a word that ultimately evolved,
through usage, into the word of Africa. A black historian and anthropologist, he has said of *Afru-ika*: "It is not a word in the Egyptian language that I know, neither in the hieratic (or the demotic)
language that I'm quite familiar with in my research."[18] Ben-
Jochanan has insisted that the appropriate word was *Afriaeka*, and
not *Afru-ika*, and that the latter was a misuse of the word *Afriaeka*
by some scholars. He traced the origins of this confusion to the
early twentieth-century Egyptologist Gerald Massey. In his book,
A Book of the Beginnings, Massey had posited the word *Afru-ika*,
but said it had been an Egyptian word meaning "the inner land,"
"born of," or "birth-place." He did not say the word *Afru-ika* was the
same as the word Africa. He actually said that Africa was derived
from the Egyptian word *Af*, which was a modification of the word
Au. "Both Au and Af signify born of. The name of Africa is derived
from this root of au."[19] But before Massey finished his comments,
he made it appear that *Afru-ika* and Africa were the same words.
Yosef ben-Jochanan insisted that Massey mistook a Greek word
for an Egyptian word and misspelled it to boot:

Afru-ika [not spelled the way Massey spelled it] comes from the Greek
language, "Afrik," and it was the Greek "ae" really and then you had "ika,"
so you had two Greek words that [were] compounded in one word to become "Africa." "Afriaeka" was the Greek way of saying "the land to the
south" and it was to the South of Greece, so they called it Afriaeka and
then it became Africa.[20]

Africa originally was an ancient Greek word, but it was not spelled
the way ben-Jochanan said it was. Moreover, the word was not the
original ancient Greek word for the landmass south of Greece, nor
did it mean "the land to the South." This would not be likely, be-

cause the word south (σουγη) and land (λανδ) are two entirely different words in ancient Greek. Another critical point to make was that the ancient Greeks originally called what they would later call Africa, *Libya* (λιβψα). Indeed, the ancient Greeks thought the world was subdivided into three large landmasses: Europe, Asia, and Libya. In the fifth century B.C., Herodotus wrote in *The Histories*, "Libya, Asia, and Europe: . . . The three continents do, in fact, differ very greatly in size. Europe is as long as the other two put together, and for breadth is not, in my opinion, even to be compared to them. As for Libya, we know that it is washed on all sides by the sea except where it joins Asia."[21] Herodotus was saying that he and other Greeks knew that Libya (later to be called Africa by the Greeks) was an island continent.

But the Greeks used the word Libya in varying ways, in the same way that they used the word Ethiopia in varying ways. On the one hand, the Greeks used the word Libya to refer to the entire island landmass south of Greece. Sometimes it was a reference to land just south of Greece and between Egypt and ancient Carthage. Libya for the Greeks also meant the northern part of what would later be called Africa, which included Carthage. It is not clear when the Greeks began calling Libya Africa. And they may not have been the initial ones to do it.

The Thessurus Graecae Linguae, a dictionary of ancient Greek and Latin, indicated that the word Africa derived from the Greek word *phrike* (φρικη), meaning shuddering. A pun was made upon this word, but it remains unclear who made the pun, the Greeks or the Carthaginians. But at some point, one of these peoples used the word *afrike* (ηφρικη), meaning "without cold, without shuddering."[22] The strongest suggestion is that the Greeks made the pun and devised the word that, in ancient Greek, with the article *he*, became *he afrike*. But the Greeks did not give the name *he afrike* or Africa to the entire continent, which they still called Libya thereafter, but rather employed the word as another way to describe Carthage.

The Carthaginians, it would seem, initially used the word *he afrike*, not to describe their country or empire, but the land around their city of Carthage. At some point the Carthaginians referred to their country or empire itself as *he afrike*, because that is the name they gave to the Romans to describe their country and empire when the Romans conquered Carthage. A dictionary of ancient Latin said the following: "*Africa*, ae, f. (the Romans received this name from the Carthaginians as designating their country, and in this sense, only the Gr. Αφρικη occurs)."[23] This reference indicates that *he afrike* was a Greek word (and, it would seem, devised by the Greeks) that the Carthaginians borrowed and then applied to themselves and their country and empire. Black religious scholar Robert Hood remarked in *Begrimed and Black* that *he afrike* was rendered in the Phoenician language of the Carthaginians as *Aurigha*, pronounced *Afarika*.[24] It is not clear when the Carthaginians gave the word *he afrike* or *Aurigha*, both meaning Africa, to the Romans. The assumption to be made is that the action occurred sometime during the long years that Rome fought Carthage in the protracted Punic Wars of the third and second centuries B.C. After Rome finally defeated Carthage in 146 B.C. in the last of the Punic Wars, it made Carthage a province of the Roman empire that the Romans called Africa.[25] The Romans went beyond that and also called the northern part of the land south of Italy and the Mediterranean Sea Africa. Rome also used to call individual provinces within this broad area Africa, in the same way that the Greeks called individual countries Ethiopia in the general, civilizational area of Ethiopia. The Romans were the ones who popularized the word Africa and made it the word of history to designate a geographical area, using the word to refer to a whole continent or just the northern portion of it. The Romans devised and employed the word *afer* from their own Latin language, which meant African, as a reference to people from Africa. Europeans, following the Romans, would follow upon this legacy.

The Arabs conquered northern Africa, which they then called the Maghrib, in the seventh century. They also referred to this area as the Romans had, as Africa. They took the latter word from Latin, which they rendered in Arabic as *Ifriqiya*. As Bernard Lewis has written, "The term Ifriqiya, an Arab borrowing from the Latin 'Africa,' is used in classical Arabic only of the Maghrib, usually just the eastern Maghrib."[26]

As Lewis also indicated, the Arabs had another name for Africa that applied to a larger area of the island continent that they knew about because of their penetration into it. This was the term *Bilad al-Sudan*. Lewis wrote,

The term Bilad al-Sudan—"land of the blacks"—is applied in classical Arabic usage to the whole of the area of black Africa south of the Sahara, from the Nile to the Atlantic and including such West African black states as Ghana and Songhay. Sometimes it is even extended to the countries of South and Southeast Asia, inhabited by relatively dark-skinned people.[27]

Thus, throughout ancient history, in the B.C. period and then in the early centuries in the A.D. period, right on up to what is called the modern period of European history, there were Whites/Europeans and other people in the world who referred to a land area as Africa and the people there as Africans. But this was not what the indigenous people called the landmass they lived on, or what they called themselves as a people. The indigenous millennial black people had no collective name for the large land area they lived on, nor a collective name for themselves. They were like the Indians in the Western Hemisphere during all the timeframes mentioned: people who were of different tribes or ethnic groups, with different tribal or ethnic names.

The Whites/Europeans gave the Indians their collective name, and also named the landmasses on which they lived: the Americas. Whites/Europeans had done this even earlier with respect to Africa and the black people who lived there. The black people who were known to others in the world as Africans and as living in Africa would find out from these others, particularly the Whites/Europeans, that they were Africans, living in Africa. And not many of them would come into these understandings, because the Whites/Europeans would usually refer to most of these people that they encountered primarily as slaves or near slaves, and for centuries as Negroes, Guineas, or Colored people, or as "pagans," "savages," "barbarians," or just slaves. Those regarded as Africans would know themselves by their tribal (ethnic) name, or by some other cultural identity, such as their religion or language, until they lost consciousness of them.

If any of these people heard themselves called Africans and accepted this name and identity for themselves as if it were their name and identity and the way they should be perceived, then these would be black people accepting an African identity in retrospect; that is, a *retrospective African identity*. This identity would not have much meaning for them, because it would not be an identity of their history, their culture, their language, their clan, or their family, but an identity given to them by their enslavers, or by other people who would dominate, control, and exploit them. Such people would have to grow into an African identity, which would be difficult if not impossible, because that would not be the name that they would usually hear themselves called. They would hear other names much more frequently throughout their entire lives as slaves, or even as nonslaves, in the lower Americas, the Caribbean, and North America.

The very same people in all these areas would have a difficult time accepting the name Africa for their original homeland, which had not had a collective identity when they had lived there. It would not be a name they had ever heard or ever used. If any of the black people now enslaved in the Western Hemisphere or living in the vast area as nonslaves accepted the name Africa as the name of their original homeland, what would be accepted would not likely be an understanding that their original homeland was a continent, because that would not necessarily be the knowledge of the Whites/ Europeans who would tell them that they were from Africa. If they also heard the word Guinea, they would be confused about their new and sudden African identity, if they were referred to as Guineas as well as Africans. And if they were called negroes or Negroes, which would be done more often, they might well be confused as to why they would be called Africans at all.

Black slaves or other black people in America who were still able to hold onto their tribal or ethnic identity, and who did not accept a retrospective African identity, might still accept Africa, in a retrospective manner, as the name of their original homeland. For instance, a black individual regarding himself as a Mendi, and not as an African, wrote a letter to the abolitionist Lewis Tappan to thank him for helping him and other Mendi escape enslavement in America, and for the opportunity to go back to their homeland, which he accepted as being Africa. This individual also thanked, presumably, the Christian God as well: "great God he makes us free and he will Send us to the African country."[28] This individual, as well as others of his near-enslaved group, had no understanding of the Africa they accepted in retrospect, as they referred to it as a country, rather than a continent. The same was true of a former Black slave who had returned to the original homeland, having been born and raised in America as a slave. He wrote to his former mistress who had manumitted him, "People speaking about this country tell them to hush their mouths if they are speaking any thing disrespectful of it. If any man be a lazy man, he will not prosper in any country, but if you work, you will live like a gentleman and Africa is the very country for the coloured man."[29]

This former slave, Abram Blackford, wrote his former mistress from Monrovia, Liberia, where he was living and trying to "do as well as those who had come to this country years before me." Liberia was a country that a number of manumitted slaves would go to in the first half of the nineteenth century. Blackford regarded Liberia as a country, as indicated, which meant that it was not clear in his mind whether Africa was a country or a continent even after he had taken up residence there. Another former slave who had emigrated to Liberia wrote to his former mistress, "I have now been living in Africa for a little more than fives [*sic*] years; you will doubtless allow that to be time sufficient for one to form an opinion. . . . Persons coming to Africa should remember that it is a new country, and everything has to be created."[30]

The fact that these individuals did not know whether Africa was a continent or a country, and the fact that the last two of them emigrated to Africa knowing virtually nothing about it, which could have been said about thousands of other Black slaves who were manumitted and who emigrated to Africa in the first half of the nineteenth century, was a reflection of a lack of an African consciousness, an African identity, and knowledge about Africa among Black slaves.

The same could be said about most nonslave Blacks in America in the first half of the nineteenth century. It might be recalled that it was at this time that some individuals decided to study the history of Black people in America, because they were aware of how little they and other Black people knew about their own history in America, or about what they accepted, in retrospect, as Africa and its history, or about the people they accepted, in retrospect, to be Africans, living in Africa, and from whom they were descendants (based on the acceptance of a retrospective African identity). It was interesting that even George Washington Williams, who studied and wrote about what he called ancient and later African history, referred to Africa as a country rather than as a continent in the first volume of his *History of the Negro Race*: "Africa, the home of the indigenous dark races, in a geographic and ethnographic sense, is the most wonderful country in the world."[31]

When George Washington Williams was writing his history of ancient black people and Black people in America, trying to trace the African ancestral background and black African links with Black Americans and trying to augment the public image of Black people in America, there were individuals in Africa who were seeking to clarify for themselves and others who black Africans were. This was at a time when the Whites/Europeans were moving in for the kill in Africa, to take over the entire African continent. This movement toward and into Africa was rationalized by and facilitated for Whites by their white supremacist/ebonicistic racist beliefs, which publicly portrayed Africa as a blighted or uncivilized continent and the black people of that continent, referred to as Africans, as "uncivilized" or just as often as "savages" or "barbarians." The traditions, customs, and social existence of the people denominated Africans also came under these racist, denigrative descriptions.

One of the black individuals in what was regarded as Africa who sought to counter the White/European racist assault on black Africans, their racial attributes, and their culture and social life was Edward Blyden. He was actually not an African. He was born in St. Thomas in the Virgin Islands, and then later in life went to Liberia, where he became a citizen and lived the remainder of his life. Blyden accepted Africa in a retrospective manner, and accepted a retrospective African identity for black people in Liberia and what he regarded as Africa. He never questioned the names and identities he accepted for the land and its peoples, which was typical behavior in the late nineteenth and early twentieth centuries, as it had been for hundreds of years before.

Blyden was interested in himself and other black people in Africa knowing what it meant to be African. He was urgent in his interests, because of the way he saw White/European racism, colonialism, and imperialism assaulting African history, culture, and social life, and the way White racist colonists were bringing in Western European cultural and social traits that were destroying, suppressing, or altering traditional African cultures and social lives. These White/European forces, in their entirety, as Blyden saw it, were devaluing the black race, and black African people, as well as the traditional African culture and social life.[32] As Abiola Irele has written,

For the originality of Blyden resided in the simple fact that he conceived Africa as an autonomous entity, one might say, as a category *sui generis*. Blyden posed Africa, and this for the first time, as the immediate reference for the black man. It was no longer a question of acclimatizing European ideas and values to African conditions, but rather of starting from a recognition of the African personality and the validity, on its own terms, of the culture and way of life which underlay and molded that personality.[33]

Blyden had a great fear of White/European scientific and technological development, and also the industrial capability and development of such people. He felt the moral and spiritual qualities of Whites/Europeans lagged far behind their materialistic capabilities and interests. He felt that the European world (including America) was on a path of great internal conflict and collision that would see great destruction brought to it. He did not want the same for black Africans and Africa, and consequently spoke against the continent and its black people following in the scientific, technological, and industrial path of Whites/Europeans, and advocated resistance to their rigorous and full implementation in Africa. Blyden regarded black Africans to be a moral and spiritual people, which were the primary characteristics of the "African personality," and were all products of the moral and spiritual African cultural and social life. Blyden was fully aware of the White racist attack against the black race and black people, the scientistic writings and pronouncements on race, and he countered it in his own writings. He was a strong advocate of the black race, arguing that it was not inferior to the white race. He praised the racial features of black people, and specifically black Africans. In his view, it was not a difference in intelligence between the white and black races that accounted for their different kinds of development and their different ways of life. For him, it was a matter of applying intelligence differently. He also believed that black people applied intelligence differently to their history and way of life because of their moral superiority to white people, which history (not race) had bestowed upon them.[34] There were aspects of black African life that Blyden felt that black Africans had to protect from the White/European assault and preserve for themselves: the sacred features of that life, the communal and collectivist orientations of it, the individual's harmonious relationship with the community or the whole, the interconnectedness of the people, as well as the individual and collective interconnectedness with nature and the cosmos.

Blyden's thinking had an impact on a number of black African (accepted in retrospect) intellectuals. One of them whom he influenced in the early years of his intellectual life was Leopold Senghor, who would, in 1960, become president of the newly independent country of Senegal, a former French colony. Senghor was a philosopher and a poet as well as a head of state, and was a strong advocate of *Négritude*, which was the basis of his philosophy and poetry, and what informed and guided his political leadership of Senegal. Senghor was such a champion of Négritude that it was thought for some time that he was the progenitor of it. But that accolade goes to Aimé Césaire, a West Indian from Martinique, who was himself influenced by Blyden, but also by what was called the "Harlem Renaissance" of the 1920s, an aesthetic cultural outpouring by Blacks in the United States that had as its aesthetic symbol the "New Negro."

In the 1920s there were Black intellectuals seeking to clarify who Black people were and trying to reunite Black people culturally—at least in the area of art—with Africa and black Africans.[35] There were also political movements seeking to reforge and promote links between Black people and Africa, such as W.E.B. Du Bois's Pan-African Movement and Marcus Garvey's African Redemption, or Back-to-Africa Movement. Césaire was living in France at that time, as was Leopold Senghor, when Blackness and blackness were being publicly exalted in America, and he was strongly motivated by the development. He devised the concept and viewpoint of Négritude from what he observed and felt, and also from the hopes he had for black people to have a better future in Africa and elsewhere. As Césaire described it, "Négritude is the simple recognition of the fact of being black, and the acceptance of this fact, of our destiny as black people, of our history, and our culture."[36]

For Césaire, Négritude focused on race and less on culture and social life, feeling that the strong White racist assault on the black race—on black people, their physical and psychological attributes, and their very being—had to be addressed with urgency and with decisiveness. Admittedly for Césaire, his Négritude rhetoric, as it was more that than a fully developed racial philosophy, was romantic and even mystical thinking about the black race and black people, from Africa to the Western Hemisphere. While Blyden had been more interested in countering the White/European attack against African culture and preserving the best of it, Césaire, influenced by Blyden, nevertheless concentrated his thinking on race, to counter the White/European racist damage done to the thinking of black people about their color and other racial features, and viewing Négritude as a method to help repair this damage by providing black people with the intellectual and psychological means to focus consciously and positively on their color and race.

This was also the great interest of Leopold Senghor. He took Césaire's concept and viewpoint of Négritude and worked it into an elaborate racial philosophy. It was a racial philosophy and not a racist philosophy, because Senghor was not trying to create abstract, fanciful, and mystical nonexistent "superior" and "inferior" "races." He was seeking to speak to the general existence and unity of the black race and black people on this planet. Senghor felt that Négritude spoke to the inner life or the inner existence of black people wherever they resided in the world, an inner feeling that was itself timeless and even outside the historical process. It was, as Senghor saw it, the "collective soul" of the black race and black people.[37] As Abiola Irele has written,

The point of departure of Senghor's Negritude is the fact that for him, black people all over the world form a community of experience, due to their peculiar relationship with the world. Thus, Senghor's Negritude defines itself in its immediate aspects, as a preoccupation with the fact of racial belonging, and as an effort to clarify its particular significance. It is this aspect that he refers to as the "subjective Negritude"—the assumption of one's blackness as the external mark of an original and fundamental identity.[38]

Edward Blyden would have taken exception to Senghor's extreme romanticism and mysticism about race, and such a focus on race to the tune of racial values—black racial values—constituting traditional black African values. These racial values equaled the "spirit" or "soul" of black Africans and determined their traditional cultural and social life and what was also transferred to black people wherever they were on the planet as the basis and determiner of their culture and social life. Blyden had no interest in racial determinism, and looked upon culture, social life, and values to be historically produced. He was more interested in preserving traditions, customs, and traditional values. Senghor saw black African values transcending time and place, and as being the basis for new traditions and life for the black race and black people in Africa and elsewhere in the world. Senghor's philosophy of Négritude has also been described by some as his philosophy of "Pan-Negroism."

Kwame Nkrumah was a contemporary of Senghor's and also a head of state, of Ghana. He was also a political philosopher, and was concerned about the politics and political destiny of Africa. He was interested in a unified Africa and was an advocate of "Pan-Africanism," which called for newly independent African countries to unite across Africa to establish continental as well as national political, economic, and other institutions. Pan-Africanism was not "Pan-Negroism" (or the Négritude of Leopold Senghor), of which Nkrumah was critical, seeing it as romantic thinking, focused too much on abstract matters. Nkrumah, as an advocate of Pan-Africanism, was interested in concrete ways to unify black people and black countries in Africa. Showing the influence of Edward Blyden on his thinking, he was also interested in having traditional aspects of black African life, the same kind of things that Blyden had identified, be a part of the future independent black African countries. He felt they would function to unite black Africans and black African countries. These traditional aspects of black African life had helped to form and perpetuate the "African Personality," and would continue to do so in the future.

Nkrumah took his concept of the "African Personality" from Edward Blyden, and argued that it, rather than "Pan-Negroism" or Négritude, would play a constructive role in uniting black Africans and helping to build strong, independent black African countries. Nkrumah was a strong state socialist, and wanted independent black African countries to be socialistic. He felt that Africa's traditional communalism could help foster this kind of construction in individual countries and across the African continent, producing a socialism in black African countries that combined state socialism as practiced in Western Europe with ancient African communalism.[39]

Blyden, Senghor, Nkrumah, and others were Africancentric thinkers, seeking to look at Africa and Africans and the African way of life (all accepted in retrospect) from the viewpoint of black Africans, not the Whites, in Africa, Europe, or America, who denigrated all of these realities in a white supremacist/ebonicistic racist manner. These three thinkers and others have tried to define who black Africans were in terms of race, culture, and social life, and also spoke to some extent about the destiny of black Africans, the black African way of life, and the destiny of black Africa. None of these three thinkers, or others who could be mentioned, such as contemporary black African thinkers like Wole Soyinka, Camara Laye, Gabriel Okara, J.F.A. Ajayi, Theophile Obenga, and Chinua Achebe, raised any questions about the origins of the African identity they accepted for themselves and for black African people, or about the name of Africa, all of which they accepted in retrospect for themselves and for others on the continent.

The truth is that the mass of black people on the continent do not readily accept or identify with the African name and identity, or even with the name Africa itself for their broad homeland. It has only been since World War II that the mass of black people in what is understood by many in the world to be Africa have heard themselves described as Africans, that this was their identity, and that Africa was their continental home. The initial instructors in this understanding, as Ali Mazrui wrote three decades ago, were the white European colonizers: "In colonial schools young Bakongo, Taita and Ewe suddenly learned that the rest of the world had a collective name for the inhabitants of the landmass of which their area formed a part."[40] In the 1950s and 1960s, independence leaders used phrases like "African nationalism," "African unity," and "Africa belongs to the Africans" to tell the descendants of millennial black people that they were Africans and that Africa was the name of their continental homeland.

Trying to convince the black people of what they are told is Africa, and that they are Africans, has not been an easy matter, or even particularly successful. Other than the lack of knowledge (historical, cultural, and familial) or familiarity with it and its sudden introduction and imposition, the ethnic identities of the people in what is regarded as Africa stand as a strong barrier to assimilating and accepting a continental identity. There are also the various national identities, which are given more emphasis than the continental identity and impede assimilation and acceptance. In a publication of 1991, *The Black Think Tank*, a letter carried the title, "Africans Do Not Want to Be Africans." The writer of the letter remarked,

Whatever it is, my mind keeps getting preoccupied with one topic: "The problem of the African being." Or put less philosophically, the problem of being African.

We both know the problems and have discussed them often. So that it is not really the topic this time. The real discovery is that the problem of the African is that he *cannot* and does *not* wish to be African. Examples abound to support the above theory. So I skip that issue also. The real issue therefore is, why can he not and why does he not wish to be an African?

The reasons are historical and these historical reasons led to psychological ones. Though I could name many, I will dwell on one this time. The destruction of our culture.[41]

The destruction of culture and social life are not as much a problem in the situation as the writer suggests. What he has failed to consider is that the people of the island continent simply do not think of themselves as Africans and have no ancestral or historical reason to do so. This means that they do not think of an African culture or social life being destroyed, or these destructions being the source of the destruction of an African identity. Indeed, the destruction of an African identity would not mean anything to most of them anyway. They would ask, What is an African? What does it mean to be an African? What's an African culture anyway? These would not be idle questions, because they are the same questions that present-day black African intellectuals are actually asking. Their actions reflect the fact that it is not widely or generally understood on the island continent among the black people there what an African is or what African culture and social life is. That matter becomes further confused when one thinks of white people who live on the island continent and are therefore Africans living there, at least the white Arabs who live there and the white people who have accepted the rule of black people, as in Zimbabwe or Kenya.

Black African intellectuals are primarily concerned with trying to define black Africans and what is literally black African culture and social life. The Nigerian writer Chinua Achebe has written, "It is, of course, true that the African identity is still in the making. There isn't a final identity that is African."[42] The African philosopher Kwame Anthony Appiah has written that the problem of defining who the black African is, or the reality of black African culture and social life, is complicated and hindered by the existence of individuals trying to accomplish this task who are from different ethnic groups or different black African countries, and who let these identities influence their conceptions about what is a black African, a black African culture and social life, or a black African "worldview," which they usually refer to (ignoring white people on the continent) as African, African culture and social life, and as an African worldview:

For African writers the answer is not easy. They are Asante, Yoruba, Kikuyu, but what does this mean? They are Ghanaian, Nigerian, Kenyan, but does this yet mean anything? They are black, and what is the worth of the black person? . . . So . . . the African asks always not "who am I?" but "who are we?" and "my" problem is not mine alone but "ours."[43]

Kwame Anthony Appiah also wrote, "The reason that Africa cannot take an African cultural or political or intellectual life for granted is that there is no such thing: there are only so many traditions with their complex relationships—and, as often, their lack of any relationship—to each other."[44]

Appiah and other black African intellectuals have taken for granted an African identity in retrospect for themselves and other black people on the island continent, and have accepted, in retrospect, the name Africa for this continent for themselves and other black people living there—all done without questioning or analysis. What they have taken on as their task, based on their presumptions, is defining terms and realities they presume to be legitimate. But what is also clear is that even if they were successful in doing that, which could take many years—perhaps even many decades—there would still be the problem of the mass of black people accepting the constructions they made. Identities cannot be fashioned by intellectuals alone. They also have to be constructed by the people who have to assimilate and accept them and who have to live them and propagate them.

What this entire discussion makes clear is that the people on the island continent, who the world has for a long time called Africans and their homeland Africa, have not accepted, in a wide and meaningful manner, these designations for themselves and as the actual realities with which they live and want other people to understand. This is something that Black intellectuals in America seem not to know or to have ignored, although it seems more the former than the latter. Neither First-Wave nor Second-Wave Black historians exhibit knowledge of these realities. This raises serious questions about the sanguinity with which individuals from these two groups of historians insist that Black people in America are African Americans, or even Afro-Americans. It raises serious questions about Black historians or other Black intellectuals trying to define who Africans are or what constitutes African culture and social life (meaning black Africans and black African culture and social life), or what constitutes an "African worldview."

Molefi Kete Asante has brought forth a conception and theory of what he calls Afrocentricity that are picking up acceptance among some Black and black intellectuals in America, including some First- and Second-Wave Black historians. Not a historian, but a communication specialist and the founder and former chair of the Afro-American studies program at Temple University, Asante has provided the following definition of his concept of Afrocentricity: "Afrocentricity . . . means, literally, placing African ideals at the center of any analysis that involved African culture and behavior."[45] Asante has also written that "African American culture and history represent developments in African culture and history, inseparable from place and time."[46] The certainty that Asante has about African ideals stands in contrast to the lack of certainty to be found among many black African intellectuals. This also raises questions about placing "African ideals" in the center of an analysis of what Asante terms African culture and behavior, especially when his reference is to Black American culture and behavior. As the second quotation from Asante indicated, he saw no *spatial* separation between what he called African history and culture and Black American history and culture, which he called African American history and culture.

As argued in this book, Black people are not Africans, but rather people of black African descent (predicated on the retrospective African identity). But clearly, time and spatial separation occurred between Black people in America and their ancestors and the original land from whence they had come, which would include historical, cultural, social, and psychological separations (i.e., changes). Certainly, over two hundred years of slavery in America makes that point. But so does what some people, including some Black historians, call the *African Holocaust*.

Asante's conception and theory of Afrocentricity reflects no sense of the tragic or tragedies in what he calls African history or in what I call Black history in America. A concept of African Holocaust (based on a retrospective African identity) speaks to these misfortunes in both instances, and requires seeing a serious modification of the African time–spatial reality. The African Holocaust is a primary reason why Black history cannot be considered African history or any of the derivative descriptions, and why Black people cannot be designated Africans or any of the derivations, and why Black culture and social life cannot be regarded as African, African American, or Afro-American culture and social life.

A major consequence of the African Holocaust, and a consequence that continues today, was the separation of black people on the African continent from black people in the Americas, Canada, and the West Indies in the Western Hemisphere. Another major consequence of the African Holocaust that also continues to this day was the destruction, suppression, and distortion of the knowledge of Africa, black Africans, and black people from Africa, and the role all these elements played in world history and in helping to construct cultures and civilizations of the world. Those who oppose the development of an Africancentric Perspective, a perspective that will provide its view of Africa, black Africans, and black people in Africa and in the world, would be perpetuating the African Holocaust and its effects. They would also be perpetuating in a more restricted manner the African–Black Holocaust.

The African Holocaust was brought to North America (as it was to other parts of the Western Hemisphere, which cannot be the subject of this book), and it affected the history and development of Black people in North America, particularly in what became the United States, which was where the transplanted Africans went and where their descendants for the most part lived. Africans and their descendants in English colonies, and then in the United States, produced Black people and Black history, a history that had, and that continues to have, a holocaustic dimension, and that grew out of the African Holocaust and that is still affected by it, which I call the African–Black Holocaust, which would be an intellectual and analytical interest of a Third-Wave Black historiography. The latter would accept the relevance of an Africancentric Perspective to look at the African Holocaust generally, as it affected all areas of the Western Hemisphere generally, and would employ that perspective to look at the history of Black people in the United States up to the point where it would be clear that this perspective would only be able to cast partial light on the history of Black people in America and their continuing holocaustic experience there. The major light on both realities would have to be provided by the Blackcentric Perspective that is presently undergoing development.

Third-Wave Black historiography, as said in the introductory chapter of this book, would use both Africancentric and Blackcentric perspectives, in interaction (i.e., in a holistic manner), to try to understand Black history in America. Molefi Asante's Afrocentric Perspective, in particular (but any Afrocentric Perspective along his lines), would not be of much benefit, because Afrocentric or Afrocentricity themselves are illogical concepts when it is considered that they are concepts that refer to African history and culture and African people, and thus should not be concepts containing the phrase "Afro." Another serious drawback of Asante's concepts and the theoretical views produced by them is that they recognize no serious breaks in African history and culture and in African people, and seek to maintain the notion that an African identity is applicable wherever black people are found in the world, and that all cultures and social lives of black people on this planet are African cultures and social lives, even if other identities have been chosen by people, and even if other kinds of cultural and social attributes, distinctly different from an African endowment, are part of the existing culture and social reality or if the non-African attributes are the dominant feature of the mixture.

A final weakness of Asante's conception and theory is that they do not allow for any, or at least do not evidence much interest in or accord much legitimacy to, historical uniqueness, and thus historical difference and variation. Black history in America is a unique form of history, which means that Black people themselves are a unique group of human beings. These realities have to be recognized, respected, accepted, and explained, and not be suppressed or obscured by some overarching conception or theory that seeks only or essentially generality and the suppression or devaluation of uniqueness and difference. An Africancentric Perspective (and not an Afrocentric Perspective) could speak to, with historical evidentiary support, the generality of the African Presence in the world. But that Presence underwent modification in time and in places in the world (uniqueness and difference).

Third-Wave Black historiography would accept and work with the concept of African Presence and the generality and uniqueness of it, which it would do by employing diunital cognition and the concepts of Africancentricity and Blackcentricity in diunital interaction. There is also the White over Black hierarchical social structure and social system, conceptualization, and reality that have to be considered, which play a very large role in the unique history and unique development of Black people in America. Actually, Africancentric and Blackcentric perspectives have to be worked through this general analytical framework, which is the way a Third-Wave Black historiography would have it and which becomes the way for Third-Wave Black historians to see the limits of an Africancentric Perspective to analyze Black history in America and the reasons why the Blackcentric Perspective has to be given more credence. The Africancentric and Blackcentric perspectives, in interaction, and working through the general White over Black structure and system analytical framework, will be the approach taken to look at the way that Black people have related to Africa and the African identity in their history, both of which have always been retrospective acceptances, even when Black people did not know this.

Chapter 6

Blacks and the Retrospective African Identity

The discussion of the last chapter made it clear that the black people who came to North America, initially to the English colonies and then to America in the seventeenth, eighteenth, and nineteenth centuries, did not call themselves Africans and did not call their homeland Africa. That means, contrary to what many Black or other historians say, that they did not come to the English colonies and then to America knowing themselves to be and thinking of themselves as *Africans*, or as having an *African consciousness* or *African ethnic identities*, or with notions of *Pan-Africanism*, or *Pan-Negroism*, or *black nationalism*, or even with Africancentric and still less Afrocentric perspectives. These are identities, concepts, and ideologies that individuals have imposed on people and historical realities, in the case of most of these constructions in the twentieth century, with some of these constructions being the products of the 1960s and thereafter.

Some of the younger or more recent First-Wave Black historians and a number of Second-Wave Black historians like imposing virtually all of these constructions (Pan-Negroism being the exception) on Black history in America from the seventeenth century to the present day. There are white as well as other historians in

America and outside of America who do the same thing, apparently taking their cue from Black historians. The result of all of this, of course, is considerable romantization, and even worse than that, considerable falsification of Black history in America.

Yet this assertion cannot be presented too critically, because there is a certain innocence in all of this. Black and white historians of the past, as well as of today, as well as other historians of these times, inside or outside of America, have been told—one way or another—that there is a large island continent known as Africa, that the black people who live on that continent are Africans, and that the black people who were transplanted to the Western Hemisphere as slaves in the sixteenth through the nineteenth centuries were Africans. There has been a widespread acceptance, outside of Africa, of African identities and what are called African realities, which has been acceptance in retrospect but not with a knowledge or understanding that this was the case. Nor was there the knowledge and understanding that the people on that island continent, over millennia, did not call the island continent Africa, and did not even know they lived on a continent; and that most of the people living on that continent today do not think of themselves as Africans, and do not think much of the name Africa itself. The people that the world knows as Africans are only now, after millennia, giving thought to calling themselves Africans; that is, considering a retrospective African identity.

So Black and white historians and other people, inside and outside of America, past and present, cannot be blamed for calling Africa Africa, Africans Africans, and black people who came to the Western Hemisphere over a period of several centuries as slaves, Africans. But where criticism is valid is if such people continue to use names and identities in a retrospective manner without knowing, or without caring, about what they are doing. This becomes an especially salient criticism of historians, because they are required by professional standards to adhere to historical evidence to write history and to make historical interpretations.

To say that black slaves knew that they came from Africa is false. To say that black slaves called themselves Africans is false. To say that black people being transplanted to the Western Hemisphere as slaves developed an African consciousness, or a Pan-African consciousness in the process of the transplanting, is false. Historical evidence would not, as it does not, bear this out. These latter viewpoints are purely ideological, and as such are a romanticization and falsification of the history of black people moving into the Western Hemisphere as slaves, and also a romantization and falsification of Black history when the scholarship takes a turn toward North America and follows this early history.

The origins of the names and identity of Africa and Africans cannot be left out of the knowledge of historians writing about Africa or the African Presence in the world in any of its manifestations. Nor can the fact that such historians have accepted a retrospective identity of Africa and Africans. All of this becomes particularly true when the subject is the history of Black people in America and their culture and social life in the country. Of the presently estimated 12 or 13 million black people who came to the Western Hemisphere as slaves, only between 350,000 and 400,000 came to North America over the 350-year history of the African slave trade and the African Holocaust.[1] That means that most Black people who have ever lived in the United States were born here, and continue to be born here in a historical, cultural, social, psychological, and even, in many respects, physical environment very different from such realities on the African continent.

It has been shown by a number of studies, such as Melville Herskovits's study, *The Myth of the Negro Past*, that the black people of the lower Americas and West Indies kept more of what can be called an African heritage, accepted in retrospect, than Black people kept in the United States.[2] Thus, it is considerably suspect and imbalanced for Black historians or other Black intellectuals to be so concerned to prove the retention of what are called *Africanisms* in Black history and Black cultural and social life. This is not to deny the retentions or to speak against seeking to understand their extent and their past and continuing impact on Black people and even on white people and America, as John Edward Philips recently did.[3] Second-Wave Black historiography especially seeks to do this, and this would also be a quest of Third-Wave Black historiography. But this becomes an abuse and misuse of the Africancentric Perspective, because it ignores or denies the origins as well as the reality of the Blackcentric Perspective, which throws more light on the history, culture, and social life of Black people in America, as well as on their uniqueness and difference as a people in America and among other black people in the Western African Extensia.

John Henrik Clarke viewed African history and Black history in the United States, as well as the history, culture, and social life of all black people in the Western African Extensia, from an Africancentric Perspective. I wish to present a lengthy quotation from Clarke, and then provide some critical comments about it from a Third-Wave Black historiographical perspective, involving use of the Africancentric and Blackcentric perspectives in diunital interaction:

The Africans who came to the United States as slaves started their attempts to reclaim their lost African heritage soon after they arrived in this country. They were searching for the lost identity that the slave system had destroyed.

The Afro-American connection with Africa is not new. In fact, this connection was never completely broken. "Africa-consciousness," in varying degrees, good and bad, has always been a part of the psyche of the African people, in forced exile in South America, the Caribbean Islands, and in the United States. There has always been a conflict within the Black American's "Africa-consciousness." This conflict was created early and was extended beyond all reasonable proportions by the mass media of the twentieth century through jungle movies, elementary textbooks on geography and history, and travel books written to glorify all people of European extraction—in essence, white people. These distorted images have created both a rejection of Africa and a deep longing for the Africa of our imagination, the Africa that was our home.

Contrary to a still prevailing opinion, most of the literate Africans in forced exile have always had a positive image of Africa. They have rejected the image of Africa as a backward and barbarous land. To the extent that the information was available, the early black writers and thinkers made every attempt to locate Africa on the map of human geography. They soon discovered that Africa and her people had a history older than the history of their oppressors. They also learned how and why the Europeans came to Africa in the first place, and the circumstances, in Africa and Europe, that set the slave trade in motion. They learned why the Christian church had to read the Africans out of . . . human history.[4]

There is much that one can agree with in Clarke's comments, but there are some remarks that necessitate critical commentary and even rebuttal. Clarke's Africancentric Perspective was possible because of his acceptance of a retrospective African identity, which was not something that he understood or perceived he had done, and as has been seen, is not unusual behavior in this matter. But Clarke's Africancentric Perspective falls down, or shows uncertainty, because he does not describe black people from Africa to the Western African Extensia consistently as Africans.

Black Americans, for instance, are described in several ways, as Africans, Afro-Americans, Black Americans, and black people. If Black people are not just and simply Africans, then it would mean that Clarke was, in fact, recognizing the limitation of his Africancentric Perspective without being aware of it and without having some other kind of perspective, such as a Blackcentric Perspective, that induced him to call Black people something other than Africans. Clarke, like so many Black historians and other kinds of Black and black intellectuals in America, seemed not to know that Afro-

American is strictly a fictitious name. Africans in Africa and Africans anywhere in the world would not be "Afros." It might be recalled that in the 1960s an "Afro" was a hairstyle!

Clarke made a reference to the "Africa-consciousness" of Black people in America (to stay with this group of black people in the Western African Extensia). This was not the same as saying "African consciousness." But either one of these positions would be false, because the black people who came to North America did not even know the names Africa or African, and thus could not have had any consciousnesses about either one of these specific names and identities. Clarke failed to recognize this in his book on the African Holocaust, published in 1992. His actual discussions rended any contention of an "African consciousness" among transplanted enslaved black people in the Western Hemisphere. Indeed, Clarke wrote in his small publication that the African Holocaust produced "something called a Negro" in this area of the world.[5]

Clearly, this reality, lasting for several centuries and involving a lengthy and even permanent physical separation of black people in Africa from Black people in North America and the placing of Black people in another and very different historical context and a very different cultural and social context, which required Black people to make an imperative cultural, social, psychological (including cognitive), and spiritual adaptation and reconstruction, could have destroyed or, at least, seriously undermined and weakened an African consciousness or an Africa-consciousness among Black people if such thoughts had existed in their minds. The African Holocaust was a massive, tragic affair. The African–Black Holocaust—to which Clarke also made no reference—was also a tragic situation. These tragic situations have to be recognized and have to become part of any historical analysis of Black people in America. An Africancentric Perspective could well recognize and accept the African Holocaust and its consequences on Black Americans and their history and development in America, even if Clarke's did not. But that concept and conceptual analysis would have to make room for a Blackcentric conceptual analysis to take the holocaustic experience of Black people in America to a deeper and more comprehensive historical analysis, informed, where relevant, by an Africancentric Perspective and evaluation.

Calling black people in the Western African Extensia "forced exiles" was a rather misleading thing for Clarke to do. Others in Black history in America had done the same thing, such as bishop Alexander Crummell. Exiles are people who are usually driven from their homes and homeland, but have some thoughts or prospects of returning to them. There were some black people in the Western

African Extensia who returned to Africa, not as exiles, but as former slaves or as people who escaped falling into slavery in that Extensia. In North America there were individual efforts to help some black people to return to Africa, such as the efforts of Paul Coffe in the late eighteenth and early nineteenth centuries. In 1817 the American Colonization Society launched a program that continued over a number of years that involved manumitting Black slaves and aiding them to get back to Africa, principally to the West coast of Africa. Something like eight thousand Black people were shipped to West Africa, most to the new Liberian Republic, established in West Africa by former Black slaves.[6] Between 1860 and 1962 over two thousand Blacks emigrated to Haiti.[7] In the late nineteenth century Bishop Henry McNeil Turner tried to persuade Black people to go live in Africa. Only a few did, and a number of them returned to the United States after failing to succeed at building a new life on the continent. In the early twentieth century Chief Sam helped some Black people to go to Africa, but not very many. Marcus Garvey's African Redemption program called for Black and black people in the United States, and black people, especially in the West Indies, to go to Africa. But this program had virtually no success in terms of actual emigration.

Black people in the Western African Extensia were cut off from Africa by the white people who owned, dominated, controlled, and exploited them. They had not been driven out of Africa in the sixteenth century and thereafter. They had been captured and bought and sold and taken out of the continent, and transplanted or "resettled" by the millions, in another part of the world. The concept and image of exile in no way conveys the horrendous ordeal that black people underwent moving from one continental area to other physical settings in the world. Africans—accepted as a retrospective identity—were made victims of a holocaustic experience that involved the reality, consciously determined by their enslavers and oppressors, of continuous, forced physical separation between black people in Africa and black people in the Western Hemisphere.

This is what an Africancentric Perspective conveys about the situation of Black people in the United States. But when one focuses analytically on this reality, an Africancentric Perspective loses analytical power and requires a Blackcentric Perspective to step in and carry on with the analysis. As said earlier, most Black people who have ever lived in the United States were born here, and did not come from Africa. Thus, most Black people were not part of the African Holocaust in a direct manner, although several hundred thousand were, bringing that Holocaust to North America and creating an African–Black Holocaust from it. With most Black people being born and raised in North America, this meant that most Black people were not part of what John Henrik Clarke called "forced" exiles, meaning black slaves forcefully "exiled" to the Western Hemisphere, although Black people were forcefully kept from Africa, which was the situation of all Black slaves in America until slavery was abolished in the 1860s, which released 4 million people from the historical institution. At the time there were half a million nonslave Blacks in the country, most in the northern part of the country.

Most of these Blacks, throughout their history in America, did not consider themselves African exiles in America, as most of them did not consider themselves Africans. They considered themselves Americans even if white people did not, and had no wish to go to Africa. This was particularly true of such people between the late eighteenth century and the first half of the nineteenth century, when they made efforts to dig into America, physically, culturally, and socially, to make it their country and their home. This action helped to give rise to the American Colonization Society, which had a fear of nonslave Blacks, and wanted them out of the country.

Clarke contended that the black people who came to North America as slaves engaged in a search for a "lost identity that the slave system had destroyed." This was not so. These people had no single identity to lose or to regain, which meant they had no African identity to lose. Black slaves in America lost numerous ethnic identities over the course of their enslavement in the country. These slaves did not seek "to reclaim their lost African heritage." They did not regard themselves as African, or their culture and social life as African; thus, they had no "African heritage" to lose and no such heritage to reclaim. What the Black slaves in America endeavored to do was to hold onto as much of their cultural and social attributes as they could, which, in their minds, were their tribal (ethnic), clan, family, or village traits.

There were some northern Blacks in the first half of the nineteenth century who made an effort to reclaim African history. This was not done for the Black slaves in the South, at least not as a conscious and deliberate activity. They did it for themselves and other nonslave Blacks in the North. Specifically, and as we saw earlier, it was individuals from the emerging Black middle class in the region who became the precursor Black historians, and who, through their published writings and public talks, inculcated an interest in African history and Africa's relationship to world history. John Henrik Clarke remarked that most "literate Africans in forced exile" in the Western Hemisphere rejected the idea that Africa was a backward and barbarous land. Focusing on this matter with respect to Black people in the United States, who Clarke was also talking about, it has to be said that this remark was in great error. "Backward" and "barbarous" was precisely how many if not most literate Black people thought of Africa from the late eighteenth century to the 1960s, and even beyond; that is, they had some nonracial racist views about Africa and the black people there. Richard Allen, who was a founder of the Free African Society of Philadelphia in 1786, and then later the African Methodist Episcopal Church (AME), thought black Africans were pagans in religious beliefs and wished them to become Christians. He further regarded them as being "barbarians" and "uncivilized," and thought and hoped that Christian churches and Christianity in Africa would help modernize and civilize such people.

Alexander Crummell was another Black clergyman who thought black Africans were "heathens," "savages," and "uncivilized," and Africa a blighted continent. Crummell lived in Africa off and on for twenty years, trying to take civilization to the "natives." He even supported European colonialism in Africa, because he thought this might be a civilizing agency there. Reverend Henry Highland Garnet, feeling that black Africans were "backward," "uncivilized," and "primitive," helped to establish the African Civilization Society, of which he became president. "According to a printed circular, its primary aim was the 'Evangelization and Civilization of Africa, and the descendants of African ancestors wherever dispersed.'"[8] There were a number of Black clergymen, diplomats, and intellectuals in the nineteenth century who thought of Africa and Africans as backward and needing "enlightenment" and "civilizing," and who thought white Europeans would be able to help contribute to these conditions because of what was regarded as their advanced civilized attributes.

W.E.B. Du Bois, at least for a number of years, thought that black Africans were backward and even "savage." In 1903, in a review of Joseph Tillinghast's book, *The Negro in Africa and America*, he said the black Africans were "savages and barbarous people" and lived under "primitive social conditions."[9] In 1920, in *Darkwater*, Du Bois was of the strong view that black Africa was in need of modernization, although he felt that some of traditional African culture and social life should be retained for the present and future. But "deleterious customs and unsanitary usages," as well as traditionalisms that interfered with modern, civilized development, had to go.[10] In 1937, Carter Woodson wrote, "Negroes themselves accept as a compliment the theory of a complete cultural break with Africa, for above all things they do not care to be known as resembling in any way those terrible Africans!"[11]

In the 1940s and 1950s educated Black middle-class people often derided Africa and its black peoples. The popular Black magazines,

Ebony and the *Negro Digest*, reflected this reality. A writer for the former magazine recorded the views that a Black doctor, living in Africa, had of Africans: "He laughingly admits that all of them, probably because of their recent savage ancestry, love to operate or 'cut' at the slightest provocation or without any at all."[12] Writer Hugh Smyth said in *Ebony* magazine that black Africans needed to "learn something about the nature of civilization."[13] In 1951 a writer in the *Negro Digest* wrote, "The astonishing background to all of this is the dark backdrop of a continent of people confined in a prison of their own making from almost the dawn of time until about 60 years ago. . . . Channels of contact had been open for hundreds of years. But the Africans had no use for progress of any kind."[14] Even when educated or "literate" Black people criticized Whites/Europeans for their abuse of Africa and black Africans, there was still a tendency to be supportive of a White/European presence in Africa because of their modernizing and "civilizing" influence there, and a readiness to criticize black Africans for failing to aid themselves in their own development, or to do so with consistent zeal.

However, in the 1960s and 1970s, with the establishment of independent black African countries and the Black liberation movement in America, and talk of reforging connections between black Africans and Black Americans, "literate" Blacks dropped off in their negative criticism of Africa and the black people there. A different kind of writing appeared that moved away from any racist comments and tended to ignore or downplay the tragic history and tragic and debilitating characteristics of black African life. A good deal of romantic thinking and writing was done about Africa and the black people there, even by Black historians.

There has been and continues to be romantic writing about Black history and Black people in America as well. A manifestation of this historiographical romanticism found among First- and Second-Wave Black historians refers to Black people in America as Africans and derivative depictions. This occurs not only because of the presumption made about an African identity being indigenous to Africa and Africans, and this identity being transferred to the Western Hemisphere by incoming black slaves. Also, there is a widespread refusal in both schools of Black historiography to read and analyze the documents on this matter, and therefore to accept historical evidence about it. The words Africa and African seldom appear in Black historical documents, whether Black slave documents, such as letters or folklore materials, or the documents of nonslave Blacks, such as letters, individual writings, or organizational reports. The Black people who referred to Africa and Africans in their written efforts were people who knew about the existence of Africa and Africans, which they, like other people in America who knew the same—white people—accepted the names in retrospect with no thoughts or questions about what they were doing.

In Black written documents the name African or Africans usually appeared as references to black people in Africa, or to people who were known to be from Africa and who were therefore Africans. Seldom were Black people referred to as Africans in Black written documents (which would also include written songs), and when they were it would be common to see them also referred to, in the same writing, as Negroes or Colored people, or blacks, usually in lower-case spelling, or simply as slaves, which would stand for their name and identity. For instance, David Walker was one who accepted Africa and African as retrospective identities, and talked about Africa and Africans in his pamphlet, *David Walker's Appeal*.[15] He indicated that Africans were brought to America as slaves, and his reference to Africans in America in his pamphlet, which he did not do very often, was usually a reference to slaves he regarded as Africans. On occasion, Walker referred to nonslave Blacks in America as Africans, but the references he most often used with respect to such people, as well as to Black slaves, was blacks, coloured people, coloured man, or man of colour, as he spelled these words.

Maria Stewart, in a collection of her political writings of the early 1830s, seldom referred to Black people by any kind of racial or ethnic identity. Twice in her writings she referred to Black people as Africans, and just a few more times than that she referred to them as colored people. A poem printed with her collection of writings was called "The Negro's Complaint," not "The African's Complaint." On a few occasions, Mary Stewart used the phrases "daughters of Africa," "sons of Africa," and "daughters and sons of Africa." These were not references to Black people being Africans, but rather people who were of black African descent; that is, descendants of black Africans who had come to America.[16] David Walker used the phrase "sons of Africa" in the same way in his pamphlet. William Cooper Nell generally made a distinction between Black people and Africans in his book, *The Colored Patriots of the American Revolution*. Africans were people who lived on the African continent or who came to America as slaves. Indigenous Black people, those Blacks born in America, Nell usually called colored, colored people, negro, negroes, or black—all usually spelled in the lower case—and Nell felt these were people of black African descent. He called Phillis Wheatly an African, but also called her a "negress." He wrote that Benjamin Benneker was born of an African father and a mother who had been born to an African slave woman, but Nell called Benneker a "negro."

Frederick Douglass knew of Africa and Africans and accepted these names and identities in retrospect. They appeared sparingly in his autobiography, *My Bondage and My Freedom*. When he used the word African, it was usually a reference to black people in Africa, or a black person in America that Douglass considered still to be an African. He wrote in his book, "I found Sandy an old advisor. He was not only a religious man, but he professed to believe in a system for which I have no name. He was a genuine African, and had inherited some of the so-called magic powers, said to be possessed by African . . . nations."[17] Frederick Douglass actually thought of black Africans in Africa as savages, living in "savage tribes."[18] He felt African slaves underwent the process of civilization in America, and felt this was even more true of the descendants of such slaves. Douglass, as *My Bondage and My Freedom* indicates, felt that Black people were not Africans, but people of black African descent, who he described in his autobiography repeatedly as black, black people, Negro, or colored people (in lower-case spelling), and often simply as slave or slaves.

The word African appeared only a handful of times in Frederick Douglass's *The Life and Times of Frederick Douglass*. Douglass primarily used the word to refer to the black African descent of Black people in America, such as when he used the phrase "African race" (which he also called the colored race) or "African blood." On one occasion he described Samuel Ringold Ward as being of "unmixed African descent." On another occasion he said that Dr. James McCune Smith and all Black people were of African descent: "Educated in Scotland, and breathing the free air of that country, he came back to his native land with ideas of liberty which placed him in advance of most of his fellow citizens of black African descent."[19] In his second autobiography, Douglass used the words Negro, colored, colored people, colored man, slave, slaves, and black often to describe Black people in America. John Russwurm, a contemporary of Frederick Douglass (for a while), who edited the first Black newspaper, *Freedom's Journal*, considered himself an African, and eventually emigrated to Africa.

Martin Delaney, another contemporary of Douglass for many years, considered himself an African and gave his children African names. But the report that he submitted to the emigration convention of Black people in Cleveland in 1854 was entitled, "Report on the Political Destiny of the Colored Race on the American Continent."[20] The report did not have the phrase "African Race." The title of the book that Delaney would become noted for, and which some Second-Wave Black historians assert established him as an early "Father" of Black nationalism and as an early writer on "Pan-

Africanism," was entitled, *The Condition, Elevation, Emigration, and Destiny of the Colored People of the United States Politically Considered.*[21] The title of Delaney's book did not have the phrase "African People" in it. In his book, Delaney had a chapter, "Claims of Colored Men as Citizens of the United States," in which he talked mainly about Africans and Africa in history, and about how Africans were brought to the Western Hemisphere as slaves. In that chapter he referred to Black people as being "men of African descent." Delaney usually described Black people as colored people in his book, and sometimes as colored persons, blacks, black, and negroes, all in lower-case spellings. While Delaney considered himself and his family Africans, he did not consider Black people in America to be Africans, which was a strange viewpoint.

At a much earlier time, between the latter half of the eighteen and early nineteenth centuries, Black people had put the name African in some of their institutions, such as the New York African Free School (1787), the Pennsylvania Society for the Abolition of Slavery, the Relief of Free Negroes Unlawfully Held in Bondage, and for Improving the African Race (1787), the Bethel African Methodist Episcopal Church (1799), the African Baptist Church (1809), and the African Church of Charleston (1818). There were other Black institutions, churches, mutual aid societies, and cultural societies that had the name African in their titles in the early nineteenth century, and even well into it. But this was rather peculiar behavior on the part of Black people, mainly northern Black people. While they put the name African into the names of their institutions, they did not, as a rule, regard themselves to be Africans, or African Americans, for that matter. They usually referred to themselves as Negroes, Colored people, Negro Americans, or Colored Americans.

Between the 1830s and 1850s, on an intermittent basis, northern Blacks especially, but also some Southern nonslave Blacks, participated in a convention movement that gave such Blacks a public forum to engage in political protests and to express their political prescriptions for America. The state conventions, which really comprised this movement, were known by various names: the State Convention of Colored Citizens of New York, the State Convention of the Colored Freemen of Pennsylvania, the State Convention of the Coloured Men of New Jersey, or the Maryland Free Colored People's Convention. Sometimes a state convention went by two names, as did the one in California, which was called the State Convention of the Colored People of California and the California State Convention of Colored Citizens. The published reports of these various state conventions seldom used the words African or Africans.[22] This meant that the Black men of these conventions did not think of themselves as Africans, although they did think of themselves as people of black African descent. The state conventions rejected the American Colonization Society, because the Black men of them did not see themselves or other Black people as Africans, and did not regard Africa as their home or the home of other Black people. The State Convention of Colored People of New York expressed this sentiment in a typical manner in 1851:

Ought we not the more so when colored men turn "pliant minions," and insufferable dupes, at the bidding of a class of men who professedly are our friends, yet whose very system of philanthropy, were it possible to be put into operation successfully, would, our peace and harmony and felicity destroy; particularly ought we record our dissent, firm and utter condemnation, having not a particle of sympathy with the spirit and letters of a colored man, recently published in the *New York Tribune*, in favor of "African Colonization," based upon spasmodic ebullition, a seeming panic and phrenzy of despair of the colored people ever securing their legitimate rights of enfranchisement, immunities, &c., in this country.[23]

The Black men of the state convention movement, as well as the Black men of the Black antislavery and Black abolition societies, who often overlapped in membership, were members of the emerging Black middle class. Such people not only thought of themselves and other Black people (except for some black slaves, i.e., those smuggled into America from Africa) as not being Africans, but they were also anxious to have Black people not refer to themselves as Africans. In their minds, this would fuel the White thinking about colonization and their efforts to get nonslave Blacks and manumitted slaves to leave America. Whites generally did not regard Blacks as citizens of America and thus as Americans, and did not want them to be in America, certainly not with power and rights in the country. This thinking of Whites, racist and anti-American and therefore tragic, was aided by Black people calling themselves Africans, which translated, in the racist minds of white people, as not only naturally inferior people, but also as foreigners—unassimilable foreigners—in America. Indeed, in the decades before the war between the United States and the Southern Confederacy, the name of African was taken out of a number of Black institutions.[24] This was not a traumatic activity, as the name African was not rooted in the consciousness or being of Blacks in the North and South anyway.

Thus, the question becomes, Why did some nonslave Blacks in the late eighteenth and early nineteenth centuries opt for an African identity at all? Why would they do this when they usually thought of and described themselves as Negroes, Colored people, or blacks? The explanations are political and psychological. White people in the late eighteenth and early nineteenth centuries were engaging in strong public racism. This was true in the North and in the South. In the North, White racism took on an especially viru-lent form, because white people from the 1770s on ended the Afri-can slave trade to the region and embarked on a program of gradual release of Black people from slavery that saw the last Black slave released from slavery in 1829 in the state of New York.

But Whites in the North in the late eighteenth and early nine-teenth centuries were racists, and they had the White over Black structure and system of the region to use against nonslave Blacks to keep them subordinate and exploitable. If Blacks were not going to be slaves in the North, they were not going to be free either, and have the political and civil rights and the opportunities that white people had. Confronted by this racism and having no intention as far as most in the North were concerned to leave the United States, the despised and unwanted Black people began digging themselves in culturally and socially in the North to try to develop some kind of power against a larger hostile population. That hostility and fear eventually led to Whites seeking to get rid of nonslave Blacks, and Blacks, in turn, between the 1830s and 1860s, organizing to exer-cise power in America in their own behalf, through organization and protest, to try to end racism, to demand the end of slavery, and to fight against efforts to remove them from America.

In the 1850s there was a heated debate among some northern Blacks about Blacks staying in the United States or emigrating to Canada or elsewhere, even to Africa. In that decade nearly twenty thousand Blacks emigrated to Canada to establish a larger Black ethnic group there. But the debate among Black middle-class ele-ments in the North was not over whether Black people in America were Blacks, Negroes, Coloreds, or Africans. There was general agreement that they were not Africans, but, as most thought, Col-ored people or Negroes of black African descent. The debate was over the question of where Blacks would likely have the best chance for development and for a future. The prevailing view was that the best chance for either was in the United States. Black men ulti-mately fought or served in the mid-century war, thinking that par-ticipating in the war to save and restore the United States as a single country would help them to achieve long-sought-for objec-tives. Even Martin Delaney, who wanted to emigrate to Africa and wanted some Blacks to go with him, fought to save and restore the United States, hoping this would aid Blacks in the country.

But Blacks in the North still had their problems. No matter how hard they tried to be Americans, no matter how many sacrifices they made—no matter how much they tried to emulate Whites in certain forms of behavior, thinking of it less as White behavior than as American behavior that was incumbent upon all Americans—Whites, functioning as racists, and employing the White over Black structure and system, denied Blacks full inclusion and full freedom in America. They publicly denigrated Black people, saying that God created them apart from white people, in a separate act of creation, and also called them "savages" and other kinds of names that spoke to their "nonhuman" or "subhuman" status. Out of desperation and/or anger, and as a defense against White racist inundations against their character, dignity, and being, some Blacks reached for and accepted an African identity for themselves.

This would also help to explain, at least to some extent, why the word African was put into the names of Black institutions: to give the institutions instant status, more status than they thought the words Colored or Negro conveyed. These Blacks also felt defiant taking the name African for themselves or their institutions, knowing how Whites usually denigrated the name. Precursor Black historians aided these defiant and compensatory efforts before the mid-nineteenth century and thereafter by their praise of African civilizations. The people the precursor historians helped overlooked the fact that the historians did not refer to Blacks as Africans, except sometimes in a literary manner, to make a telling point. Invariably, they referred to Blacks in America as Negroes, Colored people, or blacks, all of whom were of black African descent.

The slave narratives, which were really narratives of former slaves, would not have been much help to those Blacks claiming an African identity for themselves or their institutions. The words African and Africans seldom appear in them, and they are also bereft of positive discussions about Africa. In more recent times, Black and white historians have put out edited collections of slave documents, letters, or recorded verbal testimony. The words African and Africans seldom appear in these documents, such as the documents put together by B. A. Botkin in *Lay My Burden Down*, Julius Lester's *To Be a Slave*, and Norman Yetman's *Life Under the Peculiar Institution*.[25] The word African appeared only once in Robert Starobin's collection of antebellum Black slave letters, *Blacks In Bondage: Letters of American Slaves*, and the word Africa only a few times.[26] African appeared twice and Africa twice in Charles Blockson's edited slave documents, *The Underground Railroad: First-Person Narratives of Escapes to Freedom in the North*.[27]

The infrequent reference to the names African and Africans in Black documents speaks loudly to the fact that Black people, as a people, did not regard themselves as Africans or African Americans in their history in America. Those Black historians and other Black intellectuals or political activists who insist on referring to Black people of the past by these names and/or who insist that Black people of today go by these names are simply being unhistorical and romantic.

The words black, blacks, Black, and Blacks frequently appear in Black historical documents. But the reality of Black history and the larger American history was that the words Negro and Colored also meant black or Black. The English had taken the Spanish and Portuguese word *negro* and made it synonymous with their word black, and spelled the word negro in a lower or upper case, using it as an adjective with both spellings or as a noun with both spellings. The word black and its varied spellings, logically, should have appeared more often in Black and other American historical documents, given what both Negro and Colored meant. But white people preferred to use the words Negro and Colored to describe Black people, which became a cultural practice with them; this was also true of Black people, who preferred to use the words Negro and Colored to describe themselves, which became a cultural practice with them. These were preferences and practices created by and perpetrated in America by the White over Black structure and system, which made this peculiar linguistic usage available to white and Black people and offered each group of people a psychological advantage in using Negro and Colored the way they did. This is an important thing to discuss, because it also makes it possible to better and more fully understand the historical use that Black people made of the words Negro and Colored, in which neither First- or Second-Wave Black historians show an interest.

The word black (and thus, also, Black) was simply a taboo word in America, a word for the most part to be avoided in usage. There was a fear of the word black and the meanings of that word, which were all negative and of a foreboding or threatening kind. The English had brought the word black to North America with its negative meanings and the fears associated with it, which were passed on to the Americans who developed from them and from other Europeans. For the English, and then for white Americans, the word black was the primary word to express extreme negativity or great loss, or to castigate, to scorn, or to denounce a situation or a person. White people, first in the English colonies and then in America, became afraid of black and blackness—that is, all the various negative and threatening meanings of the word black—which all got locked into the physical being and presence of black people who lived in the English colonies and then in America among Whites, as their opposite in color and race and as their social opposites.

Black people and the negative meanings of black became synonymous in the minds of white people, which made white people
want to avoid the word black and its meanings, and black people as
well, who, in their racist minds, embodied those meanings and thus
threatened the mind and psychology, that is, the mental state and
the mental health of white people. It was all a social and psychological reality and a social and psychological threat that white people
created for themselves by their own tragic racist thinking, beliefs,
and social behavior. But they were realities and threats that white
people blamed Black people for, and for which they in one way or
another punished them. White people had to relate to Black people
on a daily basis in the English colonies and then in America, either
directly interacting with them or indirectly; that is, hearing about
them or having thoughts about them. So white people had to have
a way to relate to Black people that was psychologically "safe" and
not a threat to their own psychological well-being. The words Negro and Colored provided that "safe" way to relate to Black people.
They meant black and Black, but those realities could be avoided
in the minds of Whites, or did not have to be a part or a strong part
of their consciousness when they related to Blacks, employing the
names Negro or Colored, or these names with lower-case letters.

Black people grew up in America as slaves and nonslaves, and as
part of the White over Black structure and system of the country
that promoted and reproduced White racism and the meaning of
the word black and all the fears or threats associated with it. Black
people grew up knowing that white people feared them and that
they were a threat to white people, not because of anything they
said or did necessarily, but simply because of who they were in the
minds of white people. Black people learned that the word black
not only meant extremely negative things, but that black and blackness were not something that could be flaunted publicly, which was
translated by Blacks to mean that they could not publicly favorably allude to their black racial characteristics or their Black (ethnic) cultural and social traits.

These were difficult times for Black people, because, after all,
they were black and Black, and it would be natural and quite human to express these things. But this was precisely what white
people did not want Black people to think—that they were human,
and that they had a right to publicly express their humanity in all
its blackness and Blackness. But Black people had no choice but to
be who they were, black people and Black people. They had to figure out a way to be black and Black without being offensive or threatening to Whites and without incurring the rebuke or the wrath of
Whites. The words Negro and Colored helped to offer these protec-

tions, as well as to facilitate Black interaction with white people, and even to enable Blacks to publicly project their Black humanity in America.

This was the social value and accepted identities of Negro and Colored; the socially "safe" (or safest way) to interact with white people. The words and identities of Negro and Colored were also psychologically "safe" for Black people. These were words and identities that enabled them to avoid being psychologically threatened by their own blackness and Blackness. These words enabled them to not always think and feel negatively about themselves, which white people wanted them to do, and which they mobilized American society and civilization, with the aid of the White over Black structure and system, to try to get them to do. But that same structure and system, and therefore that same American society and civilization, had a reprieve built into them, a safety mechanism, when it came to thinking about Black people and relating to them. This reprieve or safety mechanism were the words Negro and Colored, which was a reprieve and safety mechanism put in America by white people for white people. Black people learned to use the reprieve and safety mechanism themselves and for themselves, even if they were not intended for them. But their persistent use of them, meaning their persistent public use of the names and identities of Negro and Colored, which were much less threatening to Whites and their domination and control of America, brought an acceptance of this public practice and became a feature of the White over Black structure and system.

In addition to the social and psychological uses that Black people made of the names and identities of Negro and Colored, there were also political uses of them that became a feature of the White over Black structure and system—always under scrutiny and attenuated, of course—and that were also reproduced by the structure and system. The words Negro and Colored made it possible for Black people, over centuries, to speak positively about their individual or group attainments in America. They allowed them the opportunity to express their desires and aspirations publicly. These were the names and identities that went into Black organizations and institutions that gave them some public prestige and acceptability, and which took some of the fear out of the minds of white people as they observed and contemplated these organizations and institutions. White people perceived these organizations as being forms of power, which they would have been afraid of had they had the name Black in them as it would have been perceived as Black Power, and thus as something threatening and less tolerable, or intolerable, to Whites.

Over the centuries Blacks were able to protest publicly against racism, slavery, and racist segregation, referring to themselves as Negroes and Colored people and referring to their protest as Negro and Colored protest, as opposed to Black protest, which would have met with greater White resistance. Over the centuries, Blacks publicly demanded American citizenship, rights, equality, and opportunities for development under the names and identities of Negroes and Colored people, which facilitated their efforts and even legitimized them to some extent in the eyes of white people. The progress that Black people have made in America over the centuries of living here was aided by the Negro and Colored names and identities, and would have been less over this time span if the effort to make progress publicly had been done by using the Black name and identity.

But yet, the Afrocentrist Molefi Asante has excoriated the word Negro as a historical name and identity for black and Black people, basing his excoriation on what he felt was the negative way that Whites/Europeans and Whites/Americans used the word Negro, without giving any thought to the way any black people might have used the word and name, including Black people in the United States. A number of First- and Second-Wave Black historians have shown that they would agree with the following remarks made by Asante in *The Afrocentric Idea*:

They [Whites/Europeans and Whites/Americans] would usually call it "Negro Culture," or speak of "the African slave in the New World," or "Negro Emancipation." The fact that the spatial referent is Africa is ignored and *Negro* becomes a crypto-term that is used to designate our degradation. In this way the Eurocentric writer ties the African to Negro a false concept and a false history, separate from any particular spatial reality. *Negro* did not exist prior to slavery; both the term and its application were products of the social and economic context of the slave trade. Consequently, the attachment of the term *Negro* to African meant a negation of history and culture.[28]

Whites/Europeans and Whites/Americans did use the word Negro in a denigrating manner, over centuries. But as it was pointed out in the previous chapter, the word Negro, in its historical usage, was not always associated strongly and negatively with race or with racism. In America, where it (and the word Colored) was associated with race and racism in a strong manner, the word was also used somewhat positively by Whites, as detailed already, which also made it possible for Blacks to use it somewhat positively and to try to invest it with even more positive value. The words Negro and Colored facilitated some effective communication and social interaction between Whites and Blacks that redounded to the benefit of Black people. Precursor Black historians aided these efforts, at least from the side of a Black response and Black motivation, by their rather positive histories of Black people in America, which they wrote primarily under the names of Negroes and Colored people. First-Wave Black historians, before the more recent joiners to the ranks, followed their predecessors in writing Negro and Colored history and doing so essentially in a positive manner, seeing no devaluation of Black people or their history by using the names Negro and Colored.

That means that precursor and generations of First-Wave Black historians did not view or use the name Negro (or Colored) as a "crypto-term." They gave this term a meaning, and a rather positive one. When they called African culture "Negro culture," there was no derision in their usage; nor when they referred to Black culture itself as "Negro culture." They did not ignore an African time–spatial referent, or the African Extensia, they just simply recognized how this time–spatial referent had undergone modification in the world, especially in the Western African Extensia, where African people became people of black African descent, and African culture and social life (also accepted in retrospect) became Black and other kinds of cultures and social lives.

Asante's comment that "Negro did not exist prior to slavery" was his way of saying that Whites/Europeans gave black people and Black people the name Negro, and that it was not a name of their own construction. But it also has to be said, as it was in the previous chapter, that even the name African was given to black people and Black people, if the latter chose to use it. Asante, as well as some First- and Second-Wave Black historians, do not want to give full credence or are unable to give full credence to the creative adaptive capacity and responses of Black people in their history in America. One of these creative adaptive responses was to use the words and identities of Negro and Colored in ways that they would benefit themselves, as well as America, for that matter. Blacks over their history in America also understood and used the words nigger and slave differently than white people.

Talking about Black literary writers, or writers of Black prose, from the eighteenth century to present times, Houston Baker remarked, "One might argue, therefore, that black Americans preserved their own concepts of experience despite the pressures of acculturation. One might additionally argue that blacks were able, as a result, to introduce into the total Sinnfeld [area of 'sense' or meaning of words] new dimensions of experience."[29] Baker was talking about Blacks who could be referred to as Black middle-class people, primarily from the northern part of the United States. But Black slaves initiated the activity of Black people in America describing the same reality differently than Whites, which not only their different experience but the development of their diunital cognition, with its flexible usage, made it possible for them to do.

When Black slaves stole from their white masters, they did not see their behavior as criminal or immoral, but as a means of getting some due, some justice out of a system of slavery and injustice. When they ran away from slave plantations or farms, they did not see this as a violation of rules or trust, or as dishonorable behavior. They saw it as resistance to oppression, or as an expression of defiance or independence, or as a desire to be released from the institution of slavery.

It was not until the post–World War I period, nearly three centuries after they were made slaves in America, that Black people finally projected their blackness and Blackness publicly. A number of things went into this historical, moral, and spiritual triumph. One thing was the regeneration of Black people in the South that occurred under the leadership of Booker T. Washington and his plethora of southern Black leaders, a regeneration of psychology that had many Blacks, just "up from slavery," thinking of themselves as being "new" people, to match what they heard to be the "New South," and saw considerable material progress of Black people that also helped to generate this new feeling of self and positive group feeling. Washington's National Negro Business League, stretching across the South and the North and promoting Black middle-class development and Black economic and other material progress, were important factors, as well as Washington using his vast *Tuskegee Machine*, which included the National Negro Business League, national Black churches, Black fraternities and lodges, and the Black press, to unite the two regional communities into a single Black community in America; a national Black community.

There was the urbanization of Black people in this period, in the South and in the North, which was often done against White racist intimidation and violence and with many acts of defiance and courage, which were also important contributors. The urbanization of Black people in the North as well as in the ghettoizing of Blacks in northern cities, paradoxically gave Blacks a feeling of greater unity and greater community, and emboldened them in their desires, aspirations, and demands against White racist power in America. Between the late nineteenth and early twentieth centuries, Black people produced more educated people among themselves than they ever had in America. A substantial number of college- and university-educated and professional Black people appeared in this period of

Black history, particularly in the South, from the Black colleges and universities, but also in the North, from the White-dominated public and private institutions of higher education.

The educated Black people helped to enlarge the growing Black middle class, and helped to develop it and Black middle-class leadership, making both more articulate and demanding. They also increased the social and organizational skills of the Black middle class and Black middle-class leadership, and, as a consequence of these augmentations, helping to produce better functioning community organizations and institutions. Black artists, writers, musicians, singers, humorists, and dancers appeared between the late nineteenth and early twentieth centuries, producing a flowering of Black aesthetic culture in the 1920s and somewhat in the 1930s, known as the "Harlem Renaissance," but which should have been known and described as the "Black Renaissance," because there were Black aesthetic cultural outbursts in a number of American cities in the North and in the South.

All of this was *Black* cultural and social development, but was usually described publicly and privately as Negro and Colored development. This was so until Marcus Garvey and his African Redemption Movement hit the American scene. Garvey and his movement projected black and blackness publicly and in a vainglorious manner, defying all historical inhibitions and taboos against Black people. Garvey and his movement even publicly insisted that God, Mary, and Jesus were all black. Garvey's movement collapsed by the end of the 1920s, when Garvey himself was deported from the United States to Jamaica, from whence he had come in 1916. But during the 1920s Garvey inspired the indigenous Black middle class and the writers, artists, musicians, and other aesthetic elements of that class (as well as those elements of the Black lower class) publicly and vociferously to promote Blackness and blackness. Carter Woodson headed up First-Wave Black historians who helped to promote this Blackness and blackness with their historical studies of Black people that emphasized their achievements in America and their contributions to the country.

The public projection of Blackness and blackness lasted for about two decades and then receded as a vital, public happening. It was not until the 1960s that Blacks publicly projected their Blackness and blackness again, doing so within Black America, as Marcus Garvey and his movement had done, but having more public outlets in America: radio, television, movies, theater, and colleges and universities (Black and White dominated) than Garvey had to chant the beauty, power, and resourcefulness of the black race and Black people. A part of the public projection of blackness and Blackness that was not a part of the earlier period was the development and implementation of direct Black political power. At the turn of the twentieth century, and owing to racist repression, Black people ceased sending Black elected officials to the national government. It was not until 1929 that another Black person was elected to the House of Representatives, Oscar De Priest, from Chicago. Blacks as voters switched from the Republican Party to the Democratic Party in the 1930s and stayed with the latter, which enabled them to apply pressure to it and gain some appointments and help from it in the national and some state and local governments.

In the 1950s Blacks launched their liberation movement (leading from political efforts of the 1940s), which saw Blacks elected to the national government and state governments, to city councils in the 1960s, and to the surprise of Black and white people in America, even to mayoral offices. In the 1970s many more Black mayors were elected, and some to important cities. Black Power did not mean simply the development and organization of power among Black people to be used within Black America and as a pressure force against White people and America as it had primarily meant in the 1920s. In the 1960s and 1970s it meant that, but also the use of Black Power directly in America's political institutions, which sparked Blacks to exercise Black Power in societal economic, educational, and cultural institutions. The exercise of this kind of Black Power in America continues.

As said at the outset of this discussion about public black and Black projections, the immediate origins for this development have to be seen in the late nineteenth century, particularly in the South. These were the years when the mass of Black people were emerging from the historical institution of slavery. They had to throw off a slave mentality and develop not only a nonslave one, but the mentality of people who wished to be free in America. The former slaves also had to start thinking directly and positively about their blackness and Blackness. If they left slavery behind they would be Black people. What did it mean to be Black? What were Black people capable of doing? White people in the South, and also in the North, said they were not capable of doing any more than when they were slaves, as they were still the same naturally inferior people.

Indeed, in the late nineteenth century, white people resenting and fearing Blacks who were declared no longer slaves and who would be trying to integrate fully into American society, returned millions of them to another form of slavery, principally through indebtedness, sharecropping, political disenfranchisement, rigid segregation, and a relentless barbarous outpouring of racist slander, intimidation, and violence. The racist slander said that Black people were not human beings, but were apelike or some sort of brute animals. At the same time this was being said of them, it was also said that they were regressing to a state of savagery. Since the seventeenth century, white people had assaulted the racial traits of Black people, especially their color and their general humanity, even denying this humanity. Throughout their history in America, Black people had to protect themselves against this racist assault, which their Black culture and social life and the avoidance of direct contact with white people as much as possible helped them to do. But another thing that Black people had to do to combat this racist assault was to think differently about themselves than did Whites.

This they did, but they thought of themselves in a different way as Negroes and Colored people, and not necessarily or strongly as black or Black people. It was really the blackness and Blackness of Black people that white people disliked or hated, assaulted, and sought severely to impair in the minds, spirit, and psychology of Black people. Had white people mainly referred to Black people as black, with its very negative meanings, over a period of centuries, then the damage to the minds, spirit, and psychology of Black people would have been very bad, perhaps even intellectually, psychologically, and spiritually destructive, and thus very physically destructive to Black people.

The development and interposition of a Black ethnicity that was not publicly lauded and defended as black and Black would not have been able to function as an effective counter to such an assault. White people mitigated their assault against the blackness and Blackness of Black people by calling them Negroes and Colored people, and did this only because they were not anxious to have their own minds always focusing on the color and meaning of black the way they understood and feared it. In publicly and positively promoting their Negro and Colored identities throughout the nineteenth century and during the first half of the twentieth century, Black people only indirectly focused on their blackness and Blackness, and only indirectly did repairs on the intellect, morality, psychology, and spirituality associated with this reparation.

Booker T. Washington was fully aware of the reparation that Black people had to do for themselves. His primary concern was the reparation they had to do to their slave mentality, how they had to change that and develop a nonslave mentality. He used to say as virtually an aphorism that Black people had learned to work for others but had not learned to work for themselves. They had learned to take direction from others but had not learned to give themselves direction. They had learned to be submissive but had not learned to be independent. Washington argued that "the greatest injury that slavery did to my people was to deprive them of that sense of self-independence, habit of economy, and executive power, which are the glory and destruction of the Anglo-Saxon race."[30] These were attributes that Black people had to develop not only as nonslaves, but as people seeking to be full individuals, a distinctive and developed group, and full Americans. These were attributes that had to be developed as black people and Black people.

Washington was able to encourage a reparation (i.e., an intellectual, psychological, moral, and spiritual repairment of blackness and Blackness in a direct fashion) only in a minor way, because the word black was very taboo in the late nineteenth and very early twentieth centuries. Washington preached to Black people that they had to be positive about their Negro identity and about being Negroes in a strong, resolute manner, despite the opprobrium that white people imposed upon them, which was considerable during Washington's long leadership of Black people. A typical comment that expressed his concern that Black people strengthen their Negro identity, which to Washington was the same as their racial identity (because he thought of Black people as the Negro race in America) and which would indirectly help to repair the damage to their thoughts about and feelings of blackness and Blackness, was the following: "It is with a race as it is with an individual: it must respect itself if it would win the respect of others. There must be a certain amount of unity about a race, there must be a great pride about a race, there must be a great deal of faith on the part of the race in itself."[31] Another typical remark was, "Where you find a race that is ashamed of itself, that is apologising for itself, there you will find a weak, vacillating race. Let us no longer have to apologise for our race in these and other matters."[32]

Washington preached this race (not racist) doctrine, which was also the doctrine of a Negro identity, for more than thirty years, twenty of which when he was the leader of the more than 10 million Black people in America. This helped to repair the damages done to blackness and Blackness thought, morality, and psychology, and the spirituality of Black people. World War I, with Black people fighting for America, and also killing white people, also contributed to this development. So did the Harlem (or Black) Renaissance, even though the symbol of that aesthetic cultural outburst or movement was the "New Negro," not the "New Black."

Marcus Garvey, a professed disciple of Booker T. Washington, promoted like the latter, and publicly, a strong Negro identity for Black and black people in the United States. But Garvey also publicly and vigorously promoted the black identity of black and Black people in the United States more than anyone in the Black past had done. The 1960s and 1970s represented a continuation of this effort, but even more rigorously, because Black people in these decades really went to work on black and Black identity reparations, using not only Black America to carry out the program but the larger American society itself, as it was believed that forcing white people to think differently and even positively about blackness and Blackness, which would mean them rejecting a centuries-old way of looking at black and blackness, would only aid Black people in doing repairs to their blackness and Blackness.

This reparation process, so needed by Black people (and by white people as well, who had to learn to think differently about blackness) was interrupted and undermined by some Black middle-class people who insisted, in the latter 1970s and throughout the 1980s, that Black people had to think of themselves as Africans, Afro-Americans, or African Americans. Some First-Wave and especially Second-Wave Black historians participated in this disruption process, jettisoning the Black consciousness and Black identity they had prior to the late 1970s, but not entirely, because these same people still described themselves and other Black people as black or Black people. This showed confusion on their part without them understanding that this confusion was a reflection of the damage done to their own intellects, morality, psychology, and spirituality by White racism, the general White over Black structure and system, and the African–Black Holocaust working through it.

Such people disclosed several things: Deep down they accepted the White racist view of black and Blackness, which means that deep down they were ashamed of their blackness and Blackness and wanted to escape them. They also disclosed that they thought of Black people in America as a racial group and not as an ethnic group, or at least not very strongly as an ethnic group. They rejected being known by a racial identity, thinking that it was less than a national or ethnic or even a continental identity. Actually, they had continental (North American) and national (American) identities, but this seemed to be of no importance, or only of minor importance to them. The African identity seemed to be very important to them, even though it was not that important to the people who were supposed to be Africans and who they regarded as Africans.

But such people were not even consistent in calling themselves Africans or African Americans and the rest of Blacks in America the same. They also seemed to be unaware that the Afro-American identity was totally fictional. They reflected desperation in wanting a positive identity for themselves and for Black people. These people were primarily Black middle-class people, and they were reminiscent of individuals of the emerging Black middle class of the late eighteenth and early nineteenth centuries, who, seeking in an immediate way a gratifying and soothing identity and one presumably of status, chose to call themselves Africans (although not African Americans). In these days they did not call themselves Afro-Americans either. The term used in the early nineteenth century was either Afri-American or "Africo-American," or "Africo-Americans."[33] The name and identity of Afro-American seems to have been a late nineteenth-century development, which did not make it any less fictional than the Afri-American or Africo-American identities of the earlier period, or the singular "Afric" identity, which some Black people called themselves and other Black people at this time.[34]

At the time that the Afro-American identity emerged and was used, finding itself in the name of the Afro-American League, the Afro-American Council, or the Afro-American Industrial Insurance Society and other institutions, the word Negro appeared in many more institutions, such as the National Negro Business League, the National League on Urban Conditions Among Negroes (the Urban League), the National Negro American Bankers' Association, the National Negro Suffrage League, the American Negro Academy, the Negro Farmers Conferences, and the Negro Legal Aid Society of the United States. It is to be noted that Marcus Garvey called his organization the Universal Negro Improvement Association. When Black people had a chance to accept the name Afro-American in the 1960s and 1970s, they rejected it. They also rejected numerous other false identities for themselves. Surveys taken in the 1990s and discussed in the introductory chapter of this book showed that Black people today, even educated Black people, overwhelmingly wish to be called black and Black people.

It is curious that Black people who insist on calling Blacks in America African Americans, which includes Black historians, always use the full description and identity. They say "African American" or "African Americans." Jews, Poles, Greeks, or Irish usually do not use the full identity to describe themselves in America. They usually just say Jews, Poles, Greeks, and Irish. So why do Black middle-class people, and it is mainly them, say African American or African Americans? For the simple reason that if they just said African, this would produce great confusion. There are black Africans in this country who know themselves to be Africans and who know how Black people in America are not Africans, but rather people of black African descent.

The black Africans in America are either indifferent to black people calling themselves Africans or African Americans, or are willing to indulge this romantic thinking. But it is not just idle or romantic behavior. It interrupts and undermines the effort on the part of Black people to do realistic thinking about themselves and their history in America, and about their future in the country, specifically the kind of effort they have to exert in America for full inclusion and full freedom. It also deters Black people from the reparation efforts they must make on their blackness and Blackness, and also undermines efforts that have already been made and that keep being made.

To be Black in America means to be a people, an ethnic group that is basically black but that also exhibits some white racial characteristics, that combines European American and what could be described in retrospect as African cultural and social traits in a dynamic synthetic mixture that ever grows. Black ethnicity is a central concern of Third-Wave Black historiography. This will be the subject of the next chapter, along with highlights of some of the other specific concerns of this historiography.

Chapter 7

Third-Wave
Black Historiography I

I have spoken sparsely thus far in this book about Third-Wave Black historiography and my desire to make this a new way of writing Black history. In this chapter and the next I shall endeavor to provide a general view of its philosophical and methodological orientations. Precursor Black historians and First- and Second-Wave Black historians have all helped to establish Black history as a respectable, professional project, and as a recognized and accepted subdivision of the American history profession. The subject matter is being deepened and expanded by the Black female historians who have become part of the Second-Wave group, and who are diligently providing testimony of the role and contributions of Black women to Black history. The 1980s and especially the 1990s marked the full entry of Black women historians into the Second-Wave ranks, such as Darlene Clark Hines, Nell Irvin Painter, Elizabeth Higginbotham, Bettey Gardner, Deborah White, and Rosalyn Terborg-Penn. In the late 1980s Darlene Clark Hines was appealing to Black male and other historians in America to take Black women's history into serious account and to recognize its vital part "within women's and Afro-American history."[1] But she and other Black women historians were not waiting for an acquiescence by other historians. They were publishing books, such as Hine's *Hine Sight: Black Women and the Reconstruction of American History*, Higginbotham's *Righteous Discontent: The Women's Movement in the Black Baptist Church, 1880–1920*, and White's *Too Heavy a Load*, to make their case, knowing that this was the best argument they could make for their position.[2]

But while Black women historians have expanded and deepened the knowledge and understanding of Black history, they have not made the discipline more critical in its analytical capacity than what previously existed. The newer historians are just as careless as the old in using words like black, Black, African, African American, or Afro-American with respect to Black identity, and thus continue to exhibit confusion about what constitutes Black history. A number of the Black women historians regard themselves as Black nationalist historians and, like their Black male counterparts in the Second Wave, exhibit strong ideological and even romantic orientations in their historical writings. Most Black women historians, like their Black male counterparts, do not have a sophisticated or developed racist analysis, and like their male counterparts seem not to know about the White over Black structure and system that has and continues to be the centerpiece of American history and society and greatly affects Black history and life and the relationships of Black people to white people and other Americans and to American history and society. In short, the newer historians in the Second-Wave ranks, like those long in it, exhibit the lack of a developed and critical sociology to write Black history or Black women's history.

Du Bois developed a critical sociology to write Black history based on a developed racist analysis and his broad White over Black analytical framework. These were dimensions of his historical sociology, which were guided by his philosophical view that history was the broad context in which human beings were born, lived, and died, and that it provided them with basic knowledge to understand themselves, their lives, their relations with other people, and their relationships to their own society, and also knowledge and understanding of their conflicts or struggles, even their struggles for freedom.

I am a Du Boisian scholar, and specifically a Du Boisian historical sociologist. I have imbibed Du Bois's philosophy for writing historical sociology, as well as his basic analytical methodology, while adding to this contingent, as demonstrated in this chapter. I see this new historiography as being necessary to write a more critical Black history, to avoid the numerous confusions that still plague Second-Wave Black historiography, and as a means to investigate and disclose more of the complex reality of Black history. Third-Wave Black historiography readily makes use of what remains relevant in precursor Black history, and also draws extensively on the production of First- and Second-Wave Black historiography. But Third-Wave Black historiography is not like the other two forms, including the writings of Black women historians, of canonical historical writing. Historical sociology is a different form of historical writing that contains a larger capacity for critical historical analysis.

Recently, the French scholar Paul Veyne explained the difference between history and sociology:

The fact is that the difference between sociology and history is not material but merely formal. They both seek to explain the same events in the same way, but whereas sociology deals with generalities (concepts, types, regularities, principles) that serve to explain an event, history is concerned with the event itself, which it explains by means of generalities that are the concern of sociology. In other words, one and the same event, described and explained in the same way, will be, for the historian, his actual subject, whereas, for a sociologist, it will be merely an example that serves to illustrate some pattern, concept or ideal type (or will have served to discover or construct this).[3]

Dennis Smith has recently supplied a definition of historical sociology:

To oversimplify, historical sociology is the study of the past to find out how societies work and change. Some sociologists are "non-historical": empirically, they neglect the past; conceptually, they consider neither the time dimension of social life, nor the historicity of social structure. Similarly, some historians are "non-sociological": empirically, they neglect the way processes and structures vary between societies; conceptually, they consider neither the general properties of processes and structures, nor their relationships to acts and events. By contrast, historical sociology is carried out by historians and sociologists who investigate the mutual interpenetration of past and present, events and processes, acting and structuration. They try to marry conceptual clarification, comparative generalization and empirical exploration.[4]

Historical sociology was a rather popular academic discipline in the early part of this century, but then it declined. It was resurrected in the 1960s and has been developing steadily ever since. Dennis Smith holds out great hope for historical sociology as a mode of explanation: "At its best, historical sociology is rational, critical and imaginative. It looks for mechanisms through which societies change or reproduce themselves. It seeks the hidden structures which frustrate some human aspirations while making others realizable." Historical sociology would also make it possible "to explore the social preconditions and consequences of attempts to implement or impede such values as freedom, equality and justice." Summing it up, Smith said, "Through their work, historical sociologists have the chance to give their fellow citizens knowledge and skills which may help them to assess competing views about what is 'possible' or 'impossible.' In brief, historical sociology can be a positive force for democratic citizenship."[5]

I accept these possibilities of historical sociology, and this is why I propose it as the form of historical writing for Third-Wave Black historiography. My interest in doing this does not stem from theory alone, but also from W.E.B. Du Bois, who was a historical sociologist and wrote historical sociology. His contemporaries of the late nineteenth and early twentieth centuries, Max Weber and Emile Durkheim, did the same. All three of these men were following the path of Karl Marx, who had earlier written historical sociology. Weber and Durkheim were fully aware of this, and their own writings were conscious criticisms of some of Karl Marx's descriptions and analyses. All three of these Europeans were concerned with Europe's transition from a traditional village and small-town society to an industrial and urban society. They sought to explain this transition, its problems, and its prospects for human freedom and development; that is, the transition from traditional society to contemporary society and what the latter held out for the good and free life.

Du Bois was interested in the same transition from traditional to contemporary society, but in a significantly different way. His focus was primarily on one society: America. While white scholars and other kinds of white intellectuals, and also white politicians, liked to talk about American history being progressive and American society being open and always changing, Du Bois viewed all these perceptions with a critical eye and saw them all as attenuated and even functioning in a manner opposite of what was persistently and popularly said of them. Du Bois also saw a traditionalism that ran very deep and wide and continuously in American history and American society; namely, the White over Black hierarchical social structure and social system that traditionally and continuously reproduced American history, culture, society, and civilization. It ultimately changed America from a village and small-town orientation and focus to an urban and national focus. Throughout this transition from traditionalism to contemporary America, the White over Black structure and system functioned, and it functioned to maintain and perpetuate the traditional White over Black social relationship, which was not totally traditional and conservative in itself.

The White over Black structure and system made American contemporary development available to white people to augment their power, their social position, their wealth, their opportunities, and their lives in America, while it denied these advances to Black people, for the most part, and maintained them in a traditional mold of existence that involved being dominated, controlled, exploited, and violently abused, and even denied elementary human status. Du Bois actually welcomed the transition from a rural America to an urban America, and was not as upset by this development as the German sociologist Tönnies was, or as the French sociologist Durkheim was, or even as much as Max Weber was, who saw contemporary society turning from rationality toward irrationality and the suppressing of human freedom and development. Du Bois looked at the situation that Max Weber looked at from an entirely different point of view. Du Bois saw Western or European contemporary life growing up with irrationality and being inundated by it; namely, racist irrationality and the irrationality of enslaving human beings, which Western ideals and values condemned as being irrational and inhumane. Du Bois made this observation in a succinct manner in his historical sociological study, *The Negro*:

These were not days of decadence, but a period that gave the world Shakespeare, Martin Luther, and Raphael, Haroun-al-Raschid and Abraham Lincoln. It was the day of the greatest expansion of two of the world's most pretentious religions and of the beginnings of the modern organization of industry. In the midst of that advance and uplift this slave trade and slavery spread more human misery, inculcated more disrespect for and neglect of humanity, a greater callousness to suffering, and more petty, cruel, human hatred than can well be calculated. We may excuse and palliate it, and write history so as to let men forget it; it remains the most inexcusable and despicable blot on modern human history.[6]

Du Bois was not only saying that racism and slavery and the irrational and severe deprecating of human beings and humanity got locked into contemporary Western and/or European development. He was also saying, without having the conceptualization for it, that the African Holocaust and the African–Black Holocaust described in this book got locked into this development. Whites/Europeans and Western history and civilization were strongly impacted by all of these negative and contradictory features, the impact being the rooting of Whites/Europeans and Western history and civilization in the gross abuse of human beings and not the lofty ideals and values hoisted high and praised. These ideals and values were inundated with racism and its afflictions and were de-ethicalized and abnormalized, as they were used, contradictorily, to promote the enslavement of people and their holocaustic experience and also to rationalize and justify the inhumanity.

Long before Marx, Weber, or Durkheim and other European thinkers took up the analysis of Europe and the Western world's transition from traditional to contemporary society and its consequences for people, there had been a centuries-long transition of disrupting and destroying traditional life and using modernizing forces against human beings. Neither Marx, Weber, nor Durkheim had much to say about this earlier human catastrophe, which was continuing in their day. Du Bois made this subject matter for his historical and sociological analyses. Beyond that, Du Bois looked upon the transition of America from a rural and agrarian society to an industrial and urban society with great satisfaction, because he saw it as a transition that could help Black people break away or, at least, over a period of time, severely mitigate the racism and oppression they lived under, and to help them to develop and become full and free people in America.

Du Bois consciously used his sociological and historical sociological writings, as Dennis Smith said, to provide people with "knowledge" to help them understand the world in which they lived and the ways they contributed to it. But the white people in America who should have been listening intently to Du Bois essentially turned a deaf ear toward him. Even white sociologists tried not to acknowledge him. Histories or summaries of the rise and establishment of sociology as an academic discipline in America, by contemporaries of Du Bois or by writers following his death in 1963, would not even mention his name, even though he had been the progenitor of scientific sociology in the country. Of course, that could well have been the reason why he and his work were not acknowledged in such accounts. Not even his *Black Reconstruction*, with which many historians, especially white historians, had great difficulty, was mentioned.

This book, like its predecessor, *The Negro*, upon which it was partially based, was a historical sociological study. That kind of historical writing was waning in America in the 1930s. This might have been a reason for a negative reaction to it, or its grand narrative style, or its efforts at synthetic interpretation, which were also aspects of historical writing no longer appreciated by a profession that had become so narrowly professional and had accepted and legitimized the narrowly conceived and written monograph as the model of historical writing. But the content of Du Bois's magnum study was also bothersome to some historians. There was even an effort to go back to the Dunning School of Reconstruction historiography and to ridicule Black participation in it. But Du Bois had made his case too strongly, logically, and truthfully for such a regression, even though he had been denied access to documentation in southern White libraries, and even to the libraries themselves to write his book!

Du Bois's thoughts on Western or European contemporary society have yet to be written in a full manner. But the comments in the earlier quotation are part of that thought, which included thoughts about how Western or European history, in efforts to modernize and develop, separated morality from rationality and, on a much larger scale, morality from social behavior. Philosopher Ross Poole has recently written,

The modern world calls into existence certain conceptions of morality, but also destroys the grounds for taking them seriously. . . . The modern world . . . provides no good reason for believing in its own principles and values. Modernity has called into play a dominant conception of what it is to have reason to act; this conception has the consequence that the dictates of morality have little purchase on the motivation of those to whom they are addressed.[7]

Western or European modernizing efforts, as Poole saw it (as others have seen it), occurred during the seventeenth and eighteenth centuries, which historians have called the Age of Reason and the Age of Enlightenment, respectively.

These two centuries were also the centuries when Whites/Europeans developed white supremacy/ebonicism (as well as white supremacy/redicism), and made the African slave trade the biggest business in Western civilization, which also continued on into the nineteenth century, and which was rationalized and justified during all the centuries by white supremacy/ebonicism. But what Poole could not see in 1991, and what Du Bois saw in 1915 and even before, was that the rationality of contemporary European history and life was connected to and rooted in racist irrationality, pathology, and immorality, and in anti-humanism and anti-humanity. This was the "grounds" that destroyed the validity of European or Western morality, where the latter was immediately separated from rationality and from social life when white people interacted with black people (or red people), and which remained a continuous "grounds" to continue to impact and subvert the rationality that white people employed toward each other, diminishing its morality and the morality of their social interaction, and that had white people, initially and especially in the nineteenth and twentieth centuries, treating other white people as if they were black people (or red people). White people used contemporary society against other white people; in short, white people treated other white people as if they were "niggers" or "savages."

Poole had no conception of the link between the failure of rationality and morality in white people's interaction with black people (and red people) and the failure of rationality and morality in white people's interaction with each other. And he had not seen that this had also been true of Marx, Durkheim, and Weber. That Du Bois understood these matters can be gleaned from his sociology and historical sociology and other kinds of writings. In *The World and Africa*, for instance, published in 1946, another writing in historical sociology, Du Bois wrote, "There was no Nazi atrocity—concentration camps, wholesale maiming and murder, defilement of women or ghastly blasphemy of childhood—which the Christian civilization of Europe had not long been practicing against colored folk in all parts of the world in the name of and for the defense of a Superior Race born to rule the world."[8] Du Bois saw linkages, not only in terms of de-ethicalized and abnormalized thinking, but also de-ethicalized and abnormalized social practices. He felt that America was a primary place where de-ethicalized and abnormalized rationality (i.e., the separation of morality from rationality and the separation of morality from social behavior) took place, because of its strong racist orientation and its long enslavement and gross exploitation of a group of people, which became a role model for other white people to emulate. Du Bois argued they did this in their colonial possessions, which, as he said, was later emulated by Nazi Germany.

For Black people in America, as Du Bois saw it, the shift from a rural and agrarian to an industrial and urban environment would still have them facing the White over Black structure and system in both parts of America on a daily basis and with their de-ethicalized and abnormalized afflictive capacities. But he also felt that Black people had a better chance of combating this structure and system and its abnormalities and achieving more for themselves in America in an industrial and urban environment. He dedicated all of his scholarship, particularly his sociological and historical sociological writings, to trying to help Black people achieve these goals. As John Hope Franklin once wrote, "Du Bois saw no real conflict between history and advocacy. His decision to study history . . . was for the purpose of finding the truth about the past in order to discover lessons that would help . . . society . . . solve the great problems that [it] confronted. It was a waste, he felt, to discover those truths and fail to apply them."[9]

Thus, Du Bois and his sociological and historical sociological writings were a reason for my turn to historical sociology as the academic discipline to produce a Third-Wave Black historiography, with no small interest in carrying on and expanding a legacy left by Du Bois. But there was also the motivation that came from the theoretical conceptualizations of historical sociology, including those revealed in the quoted thoughts of Paul Veyne and Dennis Smith. However, I think Paul Veyne's distinction between sociology and history is not totally accurate. Historians also engage in comparative writing, as do sociologists, or at least they can, and writing in that vein can choose historical examples to clarify or validate a conceptualization, or to be able to devise conceptualizations for future comparative historical writing, or even for the usual form of historical writing. Sociologists and other social scientists are not the only ones interested in theories to understand subject matter.

There are some historians, though admittedly not many, who seek to devise historical theories on, say, revolution, civil wars, intellectuals, modernization, or economic development that can be used by other comparative historians, or even by regular historians. Theories of history devised by historians using a comparative approach (i.e., comparing one period of a given history with another, or comparisons of two different people's history, using historical examples to help devise the theories) I call *intrinsic theory*. Historians could also borrow concepts and theories from other academic knowledge areas, such as philosophy, psychology, sociology, or political science, and use them to engage in historical research and writing to understand and explain historical periods, processes, or events. Theories that historians use that come from outside the discipline I call *extrinsic theory*. Both forms of theory can be used together by historians as explanatory devices, and historians might well want to use historical evidence to clarify or to validate extrinsic theories, to affirm their usefulness for historical writing, or to pronounce on their inadequacy or uselessness for the same. Third-Wave Black historiography would make use of intrinsic and extrinsic theories to try to bring forth more knowledge and understanding about Black history in America.

Such theories would be used to augment the critical and analytical capacity of the Du Boisian sociology, which forms the sociological basis from which Third-Wave Black historians would research and write their historical sociology. At the center of a Du Boisian sociology is the racist-inundated White over Black social structure and social system, and all the concepts, processes, patterns, and so on associated with it. Intrinsic and extrinsic theories could help understand the general social structure and social system and the concepts, processes, and patterns that are produced by it, and that in turn help the general structure and system to function and to carry out its reproductive or repressive activities.

The historical sociological methodology of Third-Wave Black historiography would be augmented in its analytical and critical capacity, and as a mode of critical explanation, by several methodological attributes that would be integral parts of the methodology. These heuristic features are (1) *critical reasoning logic*, (2) *concept integrity*, and (3) *premise, definition of words, and image critique*. When researching historical documents, Third-Wave Black historians would determine if there were a logical and apropos use of words and descriptions. They would determine if ideas were stated clearly and thoroughly, and if they were related logically to their descriptional and situational contexts. They would check expressed statements for contradictory thinking, arguments, images, or exaggerations. They would determine if the facts or evidence of historical documents support the thinking, ideas, arguments, and images projected from it. This same kind of rigorous logic would be applied to the evaluation of a historian's scholarship on a subject; in short, historical essays, monographs, or textbooks. With respect to both academic efforts, critical reasoning logic would function like a surgeon's scalpel, penetrating and cutting into historical documents and professional uses and interpretations of them to lay bare their value, their purpose, their correctness, or their usefulness.

Third-Wave Black historians would also employ concept integrity to write their own historical works or to evaluate the historical works of others, or to evaluate how historical figures used concepts. A concept must have the strictest meaning possible, and must be employed in this fashion. It cannot be used interchangeably with another concept or other concepts as if they all mean the same thing. Even when a concept changes in use and meaning, it has to change along conceptual lines, continuing to refer to the reality to which it has always referred, even though the reality itself had changed, which called for the alteration of the concept. For example, liberalism as a concept must always mean liberalism, no matter what time (i.e., what period or "age") it is used in history. Liberalism cannot at any time in history mean socialism or democracy, or be used interchangeably with them. Liberalism is different from socialism and democracy, referring to realities that are different from socialist or democratic realities. If liberalism as a concept and social reality help to give rise to democracy or socialism, then it would be said of liberalism that it had receded in history, conceptually and practically, and no longer had any use, meaning, or reality, and had been replaced by the concept and reality of democracy or socialism.

Third-Wave Black historiography would be conducted on the assumption that virtually all, if not all, documentary evidence that historians examine in their research efforts are predicated upon and reflect expressed or implied value assumptions, understandings of words, and images. These are the "givens" to be found in historical documents. Third-Wave Black historians would conduct research looking for and examining these givens in documents. They would do the same when evaluating scholarly writings on historical subjects, which would also be based on the authors's expressed or implied value premises or assumptions, understandings of words, and projected images. Premises, words, or even images projected in documents or in the scholarship can be inadequate, exaggerated, or even wrong. All three of these features of documents or scholarship can be deliberately misapplied or falsified. A critical evaluation of expressed or implied assumptions, understandings of words, and images in documents or scholarship can change the way such things are to be read or interpreted, and what their meanings might be other than what was projected. This kind of evaluation would provide more insight into the interests, intentions, or prejudices of those making documents and of the historians in their research and written efforts. Third-Wave Black historiography would seek to be clear about its own research and writing assumptions, its word definitions, and the images it projected.

The three methodological devices just discussed, which would be part of the general historical sociological methodology of Third-Wave Black historiography, would enable this methodology and historiography to concentrate more critical attention on the language that historical actors and historians use to describe intentions, situations, events, or other kinds of realities. Human beings can be very loose in the use of language, and thus in the way they describe or define the reality they observe or in which they participate. Human beings can use words or concepts or definitions or descriptions in such a loose or sloppy manner that they have no relationship to the matters they are endeavoring to talk or write about, or to the situations or events that they are describing. A point that has been made in this book is that the words African, African American, Afro-American, Black, Negro, and Colored have been misunderstood and misused by historical actors, as well as by historians. The same has been true with respect to the concept of Black nationalism, which has also been spelled black nationalism, and which will be discussed in this chapter.

Getting at the way words are used by historical actors or by historians helps to establish what is and what is not, and helps to make for a more critical analysis of documents or scholarship. Du Bois always felt that understanding Black history and Black life, or American history and American society, was only partly a matter of theory, concepts, or evidence. What was equally critical was the gap that existed between what Black people said and what Black people did, what white people said and what white people did, and what America was purported to be and the way it actually functioned. Penetrating these gaps in terms of the reasons for them, their constitutions, and the ways they functioned made it possible to engage in a "deeper," more critical analysis of historical or social phenomena.

Third-Wave Black historiography would seek to understand these gaps through its historical sociological methodology to produce a more critical evaluation of Black history, but also White history and American history. Indeed, as Third-Wave Black historiography would have it, conceptually, and as a stated and/or implied premise or assumption, Black history could not be understood in its deepest possible manner by just focusing on the gap between what Black people said and did. That would also require knowing fully the gap in White historical behavior and the gap between America's ideals and its actual practices, both of which relate directly to Black history and Black people and the deepest possible understanding of both.

This brings us to what I call the Blackcentric Perspective, which would also be an integral part of a Third-Wave Black historiography as a philosophical guideline for it, as well as part of the methodology of this historiography. The Blackcentric Perspective posits the view that there are Black people in America who have a distinctive history, culture, and social life, and that it is important, and even critical, to understand Black people and their history and existence in America in the most critical, comprehensive, and deepest manner. Thus, the Blackcentric Perspective becomes a drive or stimulus to seek to understand the gaps in Black history, White history, and the larger American history, and to relate to them so that more is perceived and understood about these histories and Black people.

This comprehensive and deep interest is not what a simple Black Perspective, a concept often used by Black and white historians, would have as objectives. A Black Perspective, as it is normally employed by American historians, is usually employed as an ideological concept of limited content, and limited only to Black history and Black people. Marxist historian Eugene Genovese wrote that there is no such thing as a Black Perspective on Black history:

There is no such thing as a black ideology or a black point of view. Rather there are various black-nationalist biases, from left-wing versions . . . to right-wing versions. . . . There are also authentic sections of the black community that retain conservative, liberal or radical integrationist and anti-integrationist positions. Both integrationist and separatist tendencies can be militant or moderate radical or conservative.[10]

Genovese, as his comments showed, was looking at Black history from an either–or cognitive orientation, where he could see only one strand of Black thought at a time, and where he could see only one side of Black history at a time. The severe limitation of either–or cognition is that it makes it impossible to see two things at the same time in the same space; that is, separate and integrated thinking simultaneously and interactively, or the separate and integrated sides of Black history functioning simultaneously and interactively. This represents a failure to see Black history as a whole, as well as the movements of Black history. A Black nationalist thinker, thinking diunitally, could also simultaneously be an exponent of integration.

This was true of Marcus Garvey, who historians, white or Black, often refer to as a Black nationalist or black nationalist. Actually, both descriptions would be correct in Garvey's case, because he was both a Black nationalist, promoting that line of thought among Black people in America, as well as a black nationalist, promoting that kind of thought among black people in America, the West Indies, and Africa. But Garvey was not only a separationist (as opposed to a separatist, in the sense of seeking isolation or withdrawal); he was also an integrationist, because he was also an internationalist. Garvey wanted independent black African countries established in Africa, but he also wanted those countries to integrate (i.e., to participate in the international arena of nation-states) in a state of equality with other nation-states. Marcus Garvey was even an advocate of Blacks and other black people integrating into American life as a prelude to final withdrawal.

Du Bois has been mistakenly called a Black nationalist or a cultural nationalist. He was neither during his lifetime. Du Bois was always, throughout his life, interested in and an advocate of Black people developing their separate life in America, and also integrating into the culture and institutions of the country. Adam Clayton Powell, Jr. has been considered a Black nationalist by some historians and political scientists because he was an advocate of Black Power and Black political, economic, and social development in America. But Powell, who himself participated in the national Congress as a very powerful politician for many years, was also a strong advocate of Blacks fully integrating into American society and achieving their full rights therein.

Black history, as a history, has never been an either–or history, where Black people did this but not that: where they protested but did not construct socially and culturally, where they endeavored to build a Black economy but did not seek to integrate into the American economy, where they engaged in social and cultural construction but showed no interest in political power and participating in American politics. It could be said that Black thinkers or Black leaders or Black people as a people, at a given point in time, might have put more emphasis on their separate existence than their integrated existence in America or vice versa, which would be decisions made owing to given circumstances; that is, the particular functioning of the White over Black structure and system and the way it was affecting the lives of Black people. But Black people have never promoted one side of their history to the exclusion of the other. They have never sought not to promote the wholeness of their history, which involved the interaction of the separate and integrated sides of their history, with each side contributing to the formation, the development, and the functioning of the other. And more than that, Black people might promote the separate part of their history in a radical manner while simultaneously promoting the integrated side in a moderate manner. This was the diunital ideological thinking that Booker T. Washington engaged in to lead Black people, and the way he guided their historical development between 1895 and 1915.

During the 1930s Black leaders and Black people were strong public advocates of Black political power and Black participation in America's political, economic, and educational institutions, while privately (that is, away from the public view) and without much fanfare they continued the construction and development of their separate Black existence, which, of course, was their separate Black ethnic existence. In the 1960s and 1970s Black thinkers, Black leaders, and Black people promoted Black consciousness in a strong public manner, and just as strongly advocated Black rights and full Black participation in the larger American society, which resulted in more Blacks becoming elected officials, more Blacks integrating the management levels of America's economic corporations, and more Blacks becoming students, faculty, and administrators in public colleges and universities.

As said earlier in this book, Black historians have to avoid employing either–or or domination–subordination cognition when researching and writing Black history, and have to employ Black Cognition as much as possible, which is diunital cognition, because Black people have primarily made history in America following this kind of cognition and logic. As also said earlier, Black historians have to avoid looking at Black history in the simplistic terms in which white historians like to look at their history, the larger American history, and Black history: in left–right terms, radical–conservative terms, liberal–conservative terms, or moderate–conservative terms. Black history is too complicated and too important to Black people, white people, and this country itself to be analyzed and described in those limited ways. When Black historians do use any political terms, they should use them as they relate to Black history and the complicated character of Black history.

Third-Wave Black historiography would employee diunital cognition to research and write Black history and would be critical of political terms and cautious, as well as realistic, in using them to explain Black political or historical behavior, which might well find these terms being employed in different ways than white historians would employ them in their writings. Third-Wave Black historiography would also always have the *wholeness* of Black history as its focus: the separate and integrated side of that history, in diunital interaction, that produces the whole history. These approaches are all part of or attributes of the Blackcentric Perspective on Black history. A Black Perspective is a limited concept, as it has neither the analytical capacity or the reach that a Blackcentric Perspective would have, as that perspective would seek to reach into White history and the larger American history to try to understand Black history. Indeed, as said before, it would be necessary to understand White history and the larger American history to understand Black history itself, especially in a "deeper" manner.

The effort to understand Black history in a whole and deeper manner would also have to go beyond a Blackcentric Perspective and the historical and geographical confines of America itself. There has to be a turning to African history and Africa, and a drawing on those realities and sources of information to help in these historiographical efforts. This means that Third-Wave Black historiography would not only function from a Blackcentric philosophical orientation, but would also employ as part of its general historiographical approach the following four concepts and content areas as they logically and realistically apply: the retrospective African identity, the Africancentric Perspective, the Western African Extensia, and the African Holocaust.

Third-Wave Black historiography has to accept and will accept the retrospective African identity, but will do so in a special manner consistent with historical reality and practicality. As said in these pages, since ancient times there have been people calling an island continent Africa and its inhabitants Africans, even when the inhabitants did not call their homeland Africa or themselves Africans. So historical records do reflect the names and identities of Africa and Africans. Historical records also indicate that the people who the world called Africans did not know themselves by that name, did not call themselves by that name, and rarely employed that word. Only now and with any seriousness are the people long known in history as Africans endeavoring to accept the name African for themselves; that is, accepting an identity for themselves in retrospect. Most Black people throughout their history in America did not think of themselves as Africans and did not describe themselves as such. Only a few Black people, compared to the vast number that did not, ever called themselves Africans or some very fictionalized derivative name, such as Africs or Africo-Americans or Afro-Americans.

Third-Wave Black historiography would work out the following solution to this African identity problem that it has to relate to and resolve for itself. It would accept the retrospective African identity and would call the island continent, past and present, Africa and the inhabitants of the continent, past and present, Africans. It would accept the idea that the black people who came to the Western Hemisphere as slaves were Africans, but that they lost their African identity, any collective African consciousness, or any African perspective or worldview and became people of black African descent. In Third-Wave Black historiography, this would be attributed to the three and a half centuries of the African Holocaust. The latter was a prolonged and massive disruptive and destructive event in the lives of Africans and the Africans who became slaves in the Western Hemisphere, and it continues in ways to this day. The African Holocaust transferred millions of people to another part of the world, extending the African Presence in the world, specifically to the Western African Extensia. The former had long ago reached the Western Hemisphere; that is to say, there had been an African Presence in the Western Hemisphere thousands of years before there had been an African Holocaust that transferred millions of people to the area. That means that the Western African Extensia existed thousands of years before the African Holocaust, which the latter augmented, as it did the general African Presence or the general African Extensia.

Thus, Third-Wave Black historiography cannot avoid employing an Africancentric Perspective, because dealing with all these things African requires that. The Africancentric Perspective is needed to show how the African Holocaust occurred and how it came to North America, transferring hundreds of thousands of Africans to the area as slaves. The African Holocaust became the African–Black Holocaust in North America, as the Blackcentric Perspective and Third-Wave Black historiography would have it, which continues to this day. This perspective and this historiography also accept the reality of Black people in America having three ancestral groups: original black Africans, original Black descendants, and a White European–American ancestry. African slaves gave birth to Black slaves, destroying African slaves and African people in the process and creating Black people, Black slaves, and the beginning of the Black ethnic group in America. The Blackcentric Perspective and Third-Wave Black historiography would employ the Africancentric Perspective to be able to discuss and analyze the African culture and social life that African slaves brought to North America and the way they used them to adapt to their new environment and to develop their new cultural and social life here.

But the Africanness or "Africanity" of Black slaves can only explain the development of Black ethnicity and a Black culture and social life in America up to a point, the point where White European–American cultural and social traits or ancestry have to be worked in and be made part of the general explanation. Thus, Third-Wave Black historiography stresses that Africancentric and Blackcentric perspectives have to be used simultaneously and interactively, in a diunital manner, to explain the initial construction and development of Black culture and social life in America, or, as it could also be said, Black ethnicity: Blacks as a new and distinctive ethnic group in America, even distinctive from other black ethnic groups in the Western African Extensia or Africa.

There were Africans who did not wish to be part of the Black ethnic group evolving in America, or America itself, and succeeded in returning to their original homeland, which they heard in America was called Africa. This occurred in the latter half of the eighteenth century and in the first half of the nineteenth century. In the latter time period there were Black people born and raised in America who wanted to and did go to Africa to live. These manifestations of African and Black emigration from America, which was not always to Africa, has induced some First- and Second-Wave Black historians to write about a "Black nationalist" past or tradition among Black people in America. Some Second-Wave Black historians even write about an "African nationalist" past or tradition among Blacks in the country. There are some white historians who also write at least about Black nationalism in Black history.

Third-Wave Black historiography would reject the idea of "African nationalism" as a tradition or traditional response in Black history. When a people do not consider themselves Africans, how can they have an African nationalist past or tradition? Or a "Pan-African" past or tradition? Did Black people have a Black nationalist past or tradition? Third-Wave Black historiography would accept the concept of Black nationalism and the phenomenon of Black nationalism in Black history; that is, there has been Black political behavior that could be described appropriately as Black nationalist behavior. To understand nationalism in Black history it is initially necessary to understand what nationalism itself means. Nationalism is a political ideology that refers to a nation-state or country, and that might even be used to help construct a nation-state or country.

There have been Black people in Black history who have advocated the construction of a Black country inside or outside of America, or who have emigrated to a black country to live as citizens or to help build a strong black country. Black historians who regard themselves as Black nationalist historians, or Black historians who are significantly influenced by a Black nationalist ideology have written of Black nationalism in the manner just described. But these groups of historians (as well as white historians who write of Black nationalism in Black history) do not often or consistently write of Black nationalism in this manner. Most of their writing on the concept is a violation of the concept, and most of their writing on the historical phenomenon is not about that phenomenon at all. Instead, it is usually about ethnicity or community, Black ethnicity and the Black community.

It is possible to see discussions of actual nationalistic phenomena and ethnic and community phenomena in the same work as if all the matters were nationalistic phenomena. Language and descriptive devices, such as words, concepts, rhetoric, comparative statements, comparative discussions, quotations, and images would be employed to create these understandings, which would actually be confused understandings and misunderstandings. Unless Black or white historians are prepared to say, with evidence to support their contentions, that Black people were seeking to use Black Power and Black ethnicity and the Black community as devices and bases to establish a Black country within continental America or outside the country on some other landmass, or as means to encourage or to support Black people emigrating from the United States to live in a black country, then they should cease describing historical and present-day everyday Black ethnic and community behavior as nationalistic activity or as nationalistic phenomena. Third-Wave Black historiography would maintain a separation between Black nationalist and Black ethnic and Black community realities. It would also be critical of historians who did not.

There are Black historians who, while they are not interested in Black people trying to establish a Black country within or without America, or large numbers of Black people emigrating to a black country (or even some other country that would fall within a Black nationalist description), they were interested in Black people being more defiant of white people and White power, and in Black people acting politically, culturally, and socially more independently and autonomously in America. They probe the Black past in America to find evidence of these kinds of values and Black responses. But these kinds of values and responses would not necessarily be Black nationalist values and responses, and should not necessarily be described as such. They might well be only ethnic and community values and responses, relating to Black people trying to build a stronger Black ethnicity and a Black ethnic community in America, even a more politically, culturally, and socially independent and autonomous Black ethnicity and Black ethnic community in the country.

A Black nationalist orientation, ideological and rhetorical as it is, could seriously restrict or retard research in Black history and result in seriously flawed discussions of aspects of it or the history generally. It could result in writing a strongly romanticized account of some aspects of Black history, and thus not augmenting the understanding of this general history in America, but detracting from it.

It seems to me that two prominent studies by two Black nationalist Black historians, Sterling Stuckey and V. P. Franklin, show the negative effects that a strong Black nationalist orientation can have on historical scholarship, and how it can result in strong romanticized historical writing that distorts Black history and suppresses knowledge of it. The two books in question, Sterling Stuckey's *Slave Culture* and V. P. Franklin's *Black Self-Determination*, have been received favorably by Black and white historians.[11] Of course, the two books are not without their merits, but the serious flaws of them seriously undermine the merits of the works.

Stuckey and Franklin were both interested in clarifying the legitimacy of looking to Black slave culture and social life to find the inauguration of a Black nationalist past and tradition in Black history. Stuckey even argued that this past and tradition had its genesis in the African slave trade itself. But each of these books was not really about Black nationalism, but rather mainly about Black ethnicity and the Black community. Stuckey's book could even be regarded as a work that focused on the origins of Black ethnicity and the Black community and intellectual attempts to promote them in America, even though this was not Stuckey's conception of what he had done. His actual discussions, and not his Black nationalist assumptions and rhetoric, legitimate this interpretation.

But it was not totally clear what kind of nationalism Stuckey sought to write about in his book, because he provided a confused view of his intentions. It was not clear whether he was writing about African nationalism or Black nationalism. This was all further confused in his book because he called Black people both Africans and Black people, and also used the phrase "black nationalism." The very title of Stuckey's book reflects this confused presentation. The full title is *Slave Culture: Nationalist Theory & the Foundations of Black America.* This title suggested that Stuckey was writing about Black ethnicity and the Black nationalism that grew out of this ethnic history. But Stuckey also said that his book was about the origins of African ethnicity in America, and thus of African nationalism. But that would suggest that the subtitle of his book should have been *African Nationalist Theory & the Foundation of African America.* Stuckey also referred to Black people as Negroes in his book and employed the phrase "Negro Nationality."

But it was Stuckey's fundamental contention that the black people who came to America as slaves were Africans, and that they came to America with an African identity, African consciousness, and an African viewpoint. This was the contention that Stuckey felt he proved, and it was the foundation on which he wrote his study. But these were not contentions or a foundation that were supported by historical evidence or that could be supported by such evidence. Stuckey, in writing this book, accepted, not on the basis of evidence but on the basis of common practice, a retrospective African identity for what he called Africans in Africa and Africans in America, as slaves and nonslaves. The "African nationalism" and the "Pan-Africanism" that he said African slaves forged initially during the slave trade, in transit to America during the horrendous "Middle Passage," and in the early stages of being enslaved in the new land, were not predicated on historical evidence, but on a historical writing practice. The "African ethnicity" that Stuckey said began to evolve among slaves at the initial stages of their enslavement in America was not an identity that historical evidence supported, but was established by a writing practice. Needless to say, Stuckey's Black nationalist orientation also figured strongly in the projection of these identities and concepts. He wrote in the first chapter of his book,

The . . . slaves . . . responded to cultural challenges before them. That consideration led to the inescapable conclusion that the nationalism of the slave community was essentially African nationalism, consisting of values that bound slaves together and sustained them under brutal conditions of oppression. Their very effort to bridge ethnic differences and to form themselves into a single people to meet the challenge of a common foe proceeded from an impulse that was Pan-African.[12]

The historical truth is the black people who came to America as slaves did not call themselves Africans and thus did not have an

African identity or an African consciousness, did not promote African nationalism or Pan-Africanism, and did not develop an African ethnicity during initial stages of enslavement in America. Stuckey did not find historical evidence for these contentions. He accepted a retrospective African identity that made this kind of writing and this kind of "proof" possible, without knowing that this was what he had done and without qualifying how he was using the identities and concepts; that is, what had made it possible for him to do so, since he had not relied on historical evidence to do so. The Black slave community had no nationalist orientation, African or otherwise, throughout the entire history of Black slavery in America.

For Stuckey to have been able to prove that, he would have had to make the argument, supported by evidence, that the Black slave community sought to free itself from bondage in America so that it could establish a country within or without America, or that this community sought or made an effort *en toto* or partially to emigrate to a black country. Nothing like this ever happened during the 230 years that Blacks were initially slaves in America. And it has to be said that the establishment of a Black slave community and a Black ethnicity, as I would say, was not primarily a matter of conscious decision or conscious free choice, as Stuckey implied in his comments referring to Black slaves as Africans. The African slave trade, the enslavement of Africans in America, and the dictatorial White over Black structure and system that emerged during these years, of which Black slavery was a part, played the primary role in establishing these realities, even stimulating the kind of thinking and cultural and social adaptations that initially African and then Black slaves made to their new oppressive and exploitative environment. Stuckey's comments were considerably ideological and romantic, and many of his discussions continued that way throughout his book.

What helped to enable Stuckey to talk as he did about African ethnicity and African nationalism being planted during Black slavery in America as the foundation of Black life in the country—in addition to his Black nationalist thinking and assumptions, and the historical common practice of accepting an African identity in retrospect—was his failure to recognize or give credence to what I and other Black historians call the African Holocaust. Leaving this horrendous reality out of his discussions made it possible for him to say things he would not have been able to say had he drawn this reality into his discussions. Stuckey indicated no sense of the tragic dimension of early Black history in America, which was produced by the African Holocaust and locked into Black history and the larger American history by the White over Black structure and system. He did not even see tragedy in the iniquitous Middle Passage that took Africans to the Western Hemisphere. In his book he wrote,

During the process of their becoming a single people, Yorubas, Akans, Ibos, Angolans, and others were present on slave ships to America and experienced a common horror. . . . As such slave ships were the first real incubators of the slave unity across cultural lines, cruelly revealing irreducible links from one ethnic group to the other, fostering resistance thousands of miles before the shores of the new land appeared on the horizon—before there was mention of natural rights in North America.[13]

The African slave trade went on for three and a half centuries. Taking all phases of the trade: the capture, the warehousing, the inspections, the Middle Passage, the inspection and selling in the Western Hemisphere, and the "breaking-in" period, millions of Africans lost their lives. The African slave trade was a long period of disruption of histories and the disruption and destruction of peoples, cultures, social lives, ethnic groups, loyalties, and ancestral connections. These were the overwhelming consequences of the African slave trade, which were dimensions of the African Holocaust, not the establishment of links between African ethnic groups, slave unity, a "Pan-African consciousness," or an emerging response or tradition of resistance. African slaves in large numbers underwent intellectual confusion, psychological dislocation and disorientation, mental anguish, and a sudden and prolonged fear of life itself.

Having come from histories and ways of life that had affirmed their humanity and had provided them opportunities to participate in this affirmation, they were now faced with the destruction of or severe threat to this humanity, with no respect for ways they wanted to redeem their humanity or even many opportunities to do so. The Africans that came to North America as slaves between the seventeenth and nineteenth centuries underwent these horrendous realities, and more that could be said of the African Holocaust. Thus, Stuckey was engaged in ideological and romantic writing—even painting an idyllic picture when he projected an image of African slaves "networking," developing an aggressive Pan-African consciousness and a rebellious spirit—as if, in the face of all the horrendous things happening to them, they had such a surplus of physical, psychological, mental, and spiritual energy and direction to do what Stuckey said they did, which his writing and imaging projected as essentially their main behavior on slave ships and when they were immediately plunged into slavery in North America.

The White over Black structure and system was being planted in North America simultaneously with the planting of African, and its prodigy, Black slavery, and helping to plant both. The White over Black structure and system, with the new African and Black slavery as part of it, functioned to convert the African Holocaust into the African–Black Holocaust. The latter was locked in American and Black history by the structure and system, reproducing and perpetuating it in both of these histories. In neither of these histories was the name and identity of African permitted to be accorded to Black people as their acceptable name and identity. The White over Black structure and system and the African–Black Holocaust that it perpetuated in America made white people and Black people primarily think of Black people as a race of people to be identified by their color and not by history, culture, and social attributes. The White over Black structure and system and the African–Black Holocaust prevented Black people from having or developing an African identity, an African consciousness, an African ethnicity, or an African nationalism—even a public Black identity, Black consciousness, Black ethnicity, and Black nationalism—before the twentieth century, which Black people actually foisted upon white people and America, with Black ethnicity still to be a concept and reality widely assimilated, understood, and accepted by Black people.

Stuckey recognized and acknowledged the destruction of what he called African cultural and social traits (which can be accepted as those things, accepting the retrospective African identity). He even recognized and acknowledged that traits that survived underwent a transformation, taking much of their original substance and meaning from them. But Stuckey did not accord much importance to the destruction, as the focus in his book was on African cultural and social retentions that, in his view, enabled Black slaves to remain Africans on a "profound level." For Stuckey to say that Black slaves remained Africans on a "profound level" was a clear indication that he accorded no reality to an African Holocaust (or an African–Black Holocaust), and rejected this tragic reality of Black history.

For certain, one of the things that African slaves or Black slaves would have had to retain in America to think of themselves as Africans on a profound level was African drums. These were essentially taken from African and Black slaves, as Stuckey himself admitted. He wrote, "The drums were rarely available to slaves." Drums were considered a menace to the institution of slavery, and were kept from the slaves. The slaves turned to hand-clapping and foot-stomping and other devices to get the rhythm, percussion sound, and beat. But what Stuckey did was to minimize how important drums were to African culture and social life and what their loss would mean to Africans in America. African musician Francis Bebey has described what the drums mean to present-day West and Central African life, which is what they would have meant to this life in the seventeenth, eighteenth, and nineteenth centuries when West and Central Africans came to America as slaves. "It is scarcely necessary to emphasize the importance of drums in African music. . . . The drum is, without question, the instrument that best expresses the inner feelings of black Africa."[14]

Drums were also used "to communicate a piece of news or to send a message from one village to another." Drums were used in "ceremonies to mark important stages in a man's life." They were used to imitate the sounds of animals that were worshipped, or that were part of rituals and ceremonies. Drums were primary musical instruments for court life and ceremonies. And finally, drums pervaded "the spiritual and mystical aspects of African life."[15] Since African culture and social life were inundated with religion, preventing each of these areas from subdividing into sacred and secular spheres, the religious drums had extraordinary importance, an importance that was lost to African and Black slaves in America and that hand-clapping, foot-stomping, banjo playing, or fiddlin' could not restore.

But what the African Holocaust and the African–Black Holocaust really say was that there was an overwhelming loss of original African (accepted in retrospect) culture and social life for African and Black slaves that would have made it extremely difficult for Black slaves to have held onto an African identity, if they had originally had one; and would have made it impossible for them to have remained Africans on a "profound level." Sterling Stuckey provided no sense of the horrendous loss of culture and social life. He focused on attributes that remained, which he admitted remained as truncated or transformed realities, such as the ring shout, as if what was left or retained after awesome destruction constituted all that there had once been.

Other Black historians (and white historians, too, for that matter), have ignored or downplayed the horrendous destruction of African cultural and social traits to concentrate on what is frequently described as surviving "Africanisms," and for the same reasons: to prove that Black people are Africans, African Americans, or Afro-Americans, with a nationalist past or tradition and a legitimate right to project and hold onto these identities in America. But the loss of African culture and social life was too enormous for that to be a legitimate historiographical conclusion. During the seventeenth, eighteenth, and nineteenth centuries religious beliefs, religious cults, religious rituals and ceremonies, and ancestral beliefs and ceremonies were lost to Black slaves. Philosophies and artistic and magical practices were lost. Political, judicial, and legal thinking, institutions, rituals, and ceremonies were lost, as well as national or ethnic unifying loyalties and rituals and ceremonies. Languages were destroyed. The drums were essentially lost with the large number of events, rituals, and ceremonies associated with them, including the ceremonies involved in naming drums.

Ceremonies and music associated with ethnic or village diplomacy or national diplomacy were lost. The various rites of passage (for boys and girls), the rituals and ceremonies surrounding birth and death, as well as those surrounding the birth and death of animals, were lost. The warrior cultures, military institutions, secret societies, as well as economic institutions and the cultural and social practices that regulated them, including religious practices, were destroyed. Courtship, other kinds of pre-marriage cultural and social practices, and marriage practices passed away. Patrilineal and matrilineal lines of descent or inheritance and the many rituals and ceremonies involved in them went down. Medicine man functions and medical and culinary practices were lost. The roving griots and the tribal memory historians were lost. Circumcisions, scarring and painting the body, and the rituals and ceremonies that pertained to those activities, as well as the practices of identifying with totems and worshipping animals, died. The hunting culture, including making weapons, initiation practices, training activities, and hunting itself, was lost. There were cultural and social traits that survived in slavery in diminished and fragmented forms, and were separated from larger cultural and social complexes that had invested them with importance and meaning.

Stuckey made a distinction in his study between black slaves who were brought to America and slaves that were born in the country, but he did not see any great significance in that distinction. He did not see where African slaves gave way to Black slaves, and that there were, as I said earlier, Black slaves who were the immediate descendants of African slaves, and who, therefore, were the second ancestral group of Black people. This ancestral group and its descendants, rather than the original Africans (including the ones who kept coming into the country as smuggled slaves), played a much larger role in constructing Black ethnicity and building Black culture and social life.

In time, most incoming Africans were shaped into Black people, and it was the latter who really had a history in America that carries on to this day. What Stuckey failed to see, and the failure that marks other Black and white historians, was that Black slaves thought of themselves—always deeply so, even when they did not make it constant thought or project it publicly—as black people. In Africa, before they became slaves in the Western African Extensia, they thought of themselves as black people, and this was the only collective identity that they really had. It was not a conscious identity, as it did not have to be, because they did not see that many white people who contrasted racially with them to produce a consciousness of being black. But when black people in Africa encountered white people, primarily as enslavers, they became conscious of their blackness, especially since the enslavers were so cruel toward them. The Portuguese and the Spanish called the Africans negro or negroes, uncapitalized, rather than African, as a rule. These were not "crypto-terms" to the Africans, nor were they offensive terms toward them. Negro or negroes meant black or dark, which was the understanding that Africans had of themselves. The word black was in their languages, such as *tuntum* in Fanti, *tuntimi* in Asante, *yibc* in Ewe, *ojii* in Igbo, and *dudu* in Yoruba (as told to me by a Nigerian colleague, Samuel Andoh).

In the sixteenth century the Portuguese and the Spanish began to use the words negro and negroes in derogatory ways, partially as assaults against racial characteristics, but mainly as synonymous with servile condition. The English carried this derision to a great extreme, making black synonymous with evil, baseness, ugliness, savagery, criminality, "nonhumanness," and "subhumanness," putting Black slaves on the defensive about their skin color and other black racial characteristics. As said earlier, Whites used the words Negro and Colored most often to refer to Black people, which was also the ways that Black people usually referred to themselves, even Black slaves. But white people and Black people also used the words black, blacks, or Black to describe Black people, even if they were not used as often as the other terms.

This can be seen by perusing the following collections of Black slave documents: *Lay My Burden Down, To Be a Slave, Puttin' On Ole Massa, Life Under the "Peculiar Institution," Blacks in Bondage, Slave Testimony*, and *The Underground Railroad.*[16] In a document in *Slave Testimony*, a slave wrote, "About three or four days after the 4th of July, a black boy, James Bayard . . . and soon after, Ephraim Lawrence, a black boy . . . were brought to the garret, and then a black [nominative], Henry, a young man grown, was brought there."[17] Another slave used the description "blacks" nominatively: "He met Hunn at the kitchen door, and asked for the blacks."[18] Thomas Jefferson, speaking nominatively but spelling in lower case, wrote of "a black, after hard labor through the day."[19] In Africa and America, black people knew themselves to be black. The black Africans knew this before they became slaves in the Western Hemisphere, and afterward. The Africans who came to North America knew this, as did the Black people who emerged from them. But it was difficult for Black people here to develop a strong Black consciousness, and even more difficult to project it and a strong Black identity publicly, a consciousness and identity as black people and as Black people that was always, for the most part, suppressed in their history, and American history, until the twentieth century.

Stuckey sought to use some Black intellectuals in Black history, such as David Walker, William Highland Garnett, W.E.B. Du Bois, and Paul Robeson, to show how African ethnicity and African nationalism, planted in America by what he called African slaves, was promoted by such individuals in their Black political thought. It is not possible in this critique of Stuckey's book to deal with all of these intellectuals. But I do wish to consider three briefly: Walker, Du Bois, and Robeson. What is really ironic here, and a reflection of Stuckey's own confused thinking about the national past or national tradition in Black history, is that these three men whom he selected to help him make his arguments actually contradicted them.

Stuckey alluded to Walker being the "father of black nationalist theory in America," but in the same chapter said, contradictorily, that Walker thought it unthinkable that Blacks "should leave America to satisfy those interested in colonizing them in Africa or elsewhere."[20] It was not simply that Walker did not want to satisfy the white people of the American Colonization Society. He genuinely believed that the home and country of Black people was America, and that Blacks should become full, free members of the country, all of which Stuckey said in his chapter. Walker was even interested in Black slaves engaging in rebellion to end slavery and to gain full inclusion in America. Walker focused his political thinking on the separate life of Black people in America, even linking Black people with African history and Africa, not out of any sense of "Pan-Africanism," but out of the sense that Black people in America had to know about their African past as a means to enhance their self- and group images, one of the primary reasons that precursor Black historians turned to African history and Africa.

Walker also focused his political thinking on the integration side of Black history, reflected in his desire to see Blacks remain in America and become full, free citizens of the country. In typical and erroneous fashion, Stuckey sometimes equated Walker's racial thought with an implication of ethnic thought; that is, his thinking and writing about race, and sometimes ethnicity, with nationalism, and specifically Black nationalism, which he also denied was nationalistic thinking.

Stuckey said that Du Bois was a Black nationalist. Du Bois was never a Black nationalist at any time in his life, although he could well visualize how some Blacks might want to go to an African country to live: to get out of an oppressive America, or for some other personal reason. David Walker had a similar attitude about this kind of individualistic action. For much of his life, as Stuckey said, Du Bois was a Pan-Africanist, but a Pan-Africanist who did not combine Black nationalism with Pan-Africanism as Marcus Garvey did. Du Bois saw Black nationalism in America, and black nationalism generally in the Western Hemisphere, as means to organize or induce many Blacks and many black people to emigrate to Africa. Du Bois sometimes used the phrase a "Negro Nation." He did so in a famous article in the mid-1930s, "A Negro Nation Within the Nation."[21]

In that article he talked about Black people developing their separate life in America in the strongest possible manner, particularly the economic side of that life, which would be done through producer and consumer cooperatives, the economic base upon which a Black separate life would be constructed and strengthened. This was Du Bois's theory of the Black Cooperative Commonwealth, which he wrote and talked about in the 1930s and 1940s. But Du Bois never at any time regarded this as nationalist thinking, and not even Black nationalist thinking. Nation for him meant racial group or racial community in both instances, in the sense of racethnicity—that combination of race and ethnicity—he essentially used to exhort Black people to develop their separate life. Du Bois also used the word nation as a literary device. Stuckey was aware that Du Bois did not regard his Black Cooperative Commonwealth thinking as Black nationalist thinking. Du Bois the historian was fully cognizant of how southern Whites had not been able to establish a permanent separate country within continental America, and saw this as no kind of possibility for Black people, who did not have the armies that southern white people had had. And Du Bois was totally against Black people, in any sizable numbers, emigrating from the United States.

Commenting on Du Bois's article and the political program presented there and during the 1930s and 1940s, Stuckey, incredibly, said the following: "Despite a curious disclaimer that he was advocating black nationalism, Du Bois drafted a prospectus for a self-contained black community in America . . . as he considered the feasibility of black nationalism in America on a programmatic basis."[22] Du Bois considered no such feasibility. What he did in his political thinking, which Stuckey had not done in his, or in his scholarship, was to distinguish between community and nationality or community and country. Blacks formed a community in America, not a country within it. Du Bois wanted that community developed to its fullest in the country and also with some autonomy, and also wanted a Black community strong enough to help Blacks integrate fully into American life.

Paul Robeson denied that Black people had an African identity in America, or any national identity for that matter. It was Stuckey's contention that Black people had an African identity before they came to America, that they held onto it in the country, even as slaves, and that they continued to promote that identity and African nationalism throughout their history. This was not Robeson's view, which Stuckey explained, but which he also curiously and contradictorily praised. He provided an extended discussion of Paul Robeson's article "I Want to Be African." Stuckey said Robeson had said that Black people in America were a tragic people because they had no nationality. Although Blacks might want to claim an African identity, "You cannot assume a nationality as you would a new suit of clothes." Stuckey described Robeson as being courageous and insightful for saying that the assumption of an "African nationality" by Black people in America was "an extremely complicated matter." Prior to 1934, Stuckey asserted, "No nationalist theoretician had noted the extent of the difficulty of assuming an African nationality. Nor . . . of getting his people . . . to ground themselves in African values." In Stuckey's mind, Robeson thereby "introduced a consideration not easily ignored, that consciousness of kind was needed to realize nationalism in a meaningful sense. Afro-Americans must open themselves to African influences and create self-propelled movements rooted in part in their African heritage."[23]

Stuckey conveyed the clear idea that he endorsed Paul Robeson's thinking in his article, and that Robeson had charted the way for Blacks to develop an African nationality and a "genuine" Afro-American nationhood. A few lines down the historian said Blacks would have to achieve and "secure the benefits of a nation in the absence of nationhood in the literal sense." Here Stuckey was contradicting his whole study. He was admitting that Black people were not seeking to establish a country within or without America (i.e., "nationhood in the literal sense"). Nation in the absence of a country, and a nation being synonymous with a country, could only mean ethnicity or ethnic community.

As said, this was what Du Bois meant by his use of the word nation, which he used off and on in the twentieth century. A number of Black and white intellectuals did the same. An ethnic group that was trapped inside a country, an ethnic group that had aspirations to form a separate country, an ethnic group that lost a country and that resided in another country, or an ethnic group that was associated with a country as the predominant ethnic group of that country before it became another country's colony was called a "nation," and sometimes a "nation within a nation." This was done in the nineteenth and twentieth centuries by Europeans and Americans. Black Americans engaged in this kind of writing as well, particularly from the twentieth century on. Paul Robeson engaged in this kind of writing. He did not even believe that Black people were a full ethnic group or a full ethnic community, which his phrase "kind of nation" indicated. But what Robeson did not seem to realize was that Black people were not interested in taking on an African identity or an "African nationality."

And he was wrong to say that they had no nationality. They saw themselves as Americans, which was their nationality and which they had accepted as their national identity since the nineteenth century, when Whites in America began accepting such an identity. And something else that Robeson did not see and that Stuckey did not see over the length of writing his book (and that other Black and white historians have not seen) is that an African identity is not a *national* identity, but rather a *continental* identity. Black people do not live on the African continent, where an African identity would be logical thinking. Black people are thoroughly Americans, which many Black people have been saying since the nineteenth century, including saying that they were more American than most white people, who functioned so much of the time in violation of what America stood for.

Vincent P. Franklin is the other Second-Wave Black historian whose work I wish to critique in this chapter. His study was *Black Self-Determination*.[24] This book was also marred by the author's strong Black nationalist thinking and assumptions, and particularly by his confusion between ethnic group and country, or ethnic community and country, and also by his use of the concept of self-determination, the title of the book and the concept around which the book was written.

Franklin knew what nationalism meant (i.e., its reference to nation-state or country). He also knew that self-determination was a phrase that was associated with nationalism and also a country, which meant that a country sought independence and the right to determine its internal development and its external or foreign relations. Franklin took the concepts of nationalism and self-determination and applied them to Black people and their history in America, and this, along with his Black nationalist thinking, produced the difficulties and flaws of his study.

Franklin used these two words and some comparative comments about ethnic groups and countries to project an image—a false one—that Black people constituted an ethnic group that aspired to form a country within or without America. At the outset of his book he remarked, "In Western Europe from the 1780s to the 1880s, the French, German, and Italian nations were engaged in campaigns for 'national self determination.'" On the same page, he said,

However, once these former colonial territories became "sovereign states," distinct ethnic groups, possessing separate languages, cultural institutions, and heritages within these societies, oftentimes began to demand "ethnic self-determination." These cultural groups conceived of themselves "as oppressed, discriminated against, or dominated by the central government." Thus, the French in Canada, the Biafrans in Nigeria, the Huttu in Burundi, the Basques in Spain, the Muslims in Lebanon, and other Asian, African, and American ethnic groups are engaged in a "quest for self-determination because as individual human beings they feel oppressed, discriminated against, or dominated in the political system of which they are a part."[25]

Franklin's move into comparative history to try to explain something about Black history was bold and imaginative. But it was not a very extensive effort, and it was skewed to produce an image and understanding that Black people, as an ethnic group in America, sought independent nationhood. Franklin's comparative effort involved no contrasting of Black history with other histories that might contradict the evidence he was drawing on or the image and understanding he was seeking to project. In his comparative efforts, Franklin asserted that countries pursuing independence or ethnic groups pursuing autonomy or nation-state status exhibited the values of resistance and self-determination. He argued that Blacks in America had always exhibited the same values, since the days of slavery. These were core values of Black life, Franklin argued, and for him they were Black nationalist values and not just simply values of Black ethnicity or of Black community life. Franklin saw no other values that Black people might have that would also be core values since the days of slavery. He wrote in his study,

When we examine the cultural beliefs and practices that developed among enslaved Afro-Americans we find that this value of "resistance against oppression" was pervasive. This cultural value was found in the secular "songs of resistance" that most of the slaves knew and sang among themselves. Through these songs and folktales the enslaved Afro-Americans taught their children and themselves that through wit, quickness, guile, and courage they could outmaneuver even the strongest overseer, outsmart the meanest master, and elude the most relentless patrollers.[26]

The number of Black slaves who were whipped or in other ways brutalized by masters and overseers and others over the course of their slave history should have cautioned Franklin about talking in such absolutist, singular terms about the slaves, about how *all* of them had wit and quickness, and how *all* of them outmaneuvered and outsmarted their white oppressors. This is romantic thinking and not historical scholarship, and it distorts the reality of Black slave life, particularly during the nineteenth century, when the institution was the most oppressive, suppressive, and exploitative. These workings of the system did produce resentment and resistance on the part of Black slaves, and even demands for more autonomy or self-determination for Black slave life.

But the oppressive slavery of the South in the nineteenth century also produced other kinds of personality traits and social responses on the part of Black slaves, and thus other kinds of values as well, such as submission, obedience, humility, deference, and cooperation. These values might well be expressed or exhibited expediently or manipulatively by Black slaves, but they were their values as slaves nonetheless, and part of their intellectual and psychological realities. It is appropriate here to recall what Booker T. Washington said about the ravages that slavery inflicted upon Black people: "The greatest injury that slavery did my people was to deprive them of that sense of self-independence, habit of economy, and executive power, which are the glory and destruction of the Anglo Saxon Race."[27]

Franklin's view of Black slave life had no sense of the tragedies of that life. That was because Franklin did not give credence to either an African Holocaust or an African–Black Holocaust that greatly affected the ability of Black slaves to resist or to assault the institution of slavery, to say nothing about the White over Black structure and system, especially the more rigid way it functioned on slave plantations and farms. Gladys-Marie Fry presented a discussion of the relationship between Black slaves and the white patrollers that appeared before Franklin's study and contradicted the essentially untragic and idyllic image that he presented of Black slaves and Black slave life in the South of the nineteenth century. In *Night Riders in Black Folk History*, she described how white patrollers were able to exercise effective power over slaves and to compel obedience. "Thus, as his oral tradition records, much of the constraint and coercion employed against the Black to force him into disciplined obedience was produced by playing on this fear of and belief in the supernatural."[28] These were times when Black slaves did not outwit, outmaneuver, or outsmart their white oppressors.

But what was a glaring weakness of Franklin's study in his effort to show that Black slaves were nationalistically oriented and that the origins of Black nationalism could be found in Black slave life, especially of the nineteenth century, was that he did not point out how Black slaves used other psychological traits, responses, and values to extract some benefit from slavery. Through submitting, showing obedience or deference, or cooperating and promoting harmony between themselves and their white oppressors on plantations and farms, Black slaves helped to maintain the institution of slavery and its oppressive and exploitative character. They were also able, through the same means, to extract some benefits from the institution of slavery, such as more for their diet, some days of rest, more recreational activities, some festive days, special bonuses, or some acreage to farm for personal or family consumption or to sell agricultural produce for money. The white masters and overseers used the "whip and the carrot" to make Blacks slaves and to maintain them as slaves, and to maintain the institution of slavery itself.

Black slaves learned to use contradictory psychological traits, contradictory personal and social traits, and contradictory values to gain some benefits and advantages as slaves. This helped to produce the diunital method of cognition that, in turn, helped Black slaves to be flexible in their thinking and social behavior on plantations and farms. Black slaves were not one-dimensional people, as much scholarship has indicated, whether it was the old racist scholarship that projected Black slaves in racist, stereotyped ways or the new Black and White scholarship that projects romantic, idyllic images of slaves. Black slaves were a complicated people, and Black slave life was complicated. Unable to overthrow slavery no matter how resentful, hostile, or resistant they were, they learned how to mitigate the slave institution in effective ways and to use a wide variety of means to gain some autonomy and self-determination for their separate existence on plantations and farms. Autonomy and self-determination were not associated with nationalism, not even Black nationalism for Black slaves, but rather with their ethnic existence, which they sought to augment as slaves.

At one point in his book Franklin made a statement that showed the great influence that his Black nationalist thinking had on his research and writing, and the way it led him into romanticizing Black history: "The possibility of integration into American society as equal citizens appeared remote at best. Emigration, on the other hand, was a viable alternative, given the enforcement of the Fugitive Slave Law, and had great potential for bringing about freedom from oppression and self-determination.[29]

The very last thing that could be said about Black people in antebellum America was that "emigration . . . was a viable alternative" for them. Most Black people were slaves and were not going anywhere. Most nonslave Blacks rejected emigration from America, and most of those who did go, which was in the 1850s, went to Canada. This was Black nationalism in Black history, but it was a fringe activity, done on an impromptu or spontaneous basis and not out of a sense of tradition or out of a Black nationalist ideological commitment. In the late nineteenth century, Pap Singleton and Henry Adams led some Blacks out of the South to try to establish some all-Black towns in the West. The effort was not that successful. Franklin was wrong to call this a manifestation of Black nationalism. It was the implementation of a Black separate life in America in a different manner, to gain a greater autonomy and self-determination, but there was never at any time thoughts of constructing a separate Black country in America. Franklin was correct to see that Bishop McNeal Turner, Chief Sam, and Marcus Garvey were Black nationalists, as all three black leaders favored Black emigration from America to Africa, though none had much success in their efforts.

One of the primary reasons for Turner, Chief Sam, and other Black nationalists in the late nineteenth and early twentieth centuries not having success with Black nationalist advocacy was Booker T. Washington. The latter was a special problem for Franklin in his study on Black nationalism. The problem stemmed from two sources: the traditional one that portrays Booker T. Washington as an "Uncle Tom" and an "accommodationist" who sold out the interest of Black people in the late nineteenth and early twentieth centuries, and Franklin's confused thinking about nationalism, which was confused because he did not distinguish it from Black ethnicity or the Black ethnic community and its indigenous, nonnationalistic activities. Like so many other Black scholars (and white ones as well), Franklin did not do much research on Washington to write about him in his book.

For instance, he said that Washington did not consider Black religion to be a religion of self-determination among Blacks. This view is far from being correct. In 1890 Washington created quite a stir, particularly among the Black clergy, with an article he wrote on them and the Black Church, which was critical of both of them, and which received the praise of Ida Wells (Barnett).[30] He criticized the Black clergy and the Black church for being too otherworldly and for being characterized by ignorance and immorality, because neither was doing much to help Black people modernize and develop in America. Christianity of a this-worldly "Protestant Ethic" kind formed an important part of Washington's Black modernization and development ideology. He established a seminary at Tuskegee Institute that provided Tuskegee students and the young leaders that the institute produced and sent into the rural areas to lead and help rural Blacks with the kind of religion that Washington wanted them to have and the kind he wanted them to impart to rural Blacks. In 1893, in another article, he said "that kind of religion which will help him fill not only his heart, but his stomach, clothe and shelter his body and surround him with some of the conveniences and comforts of life, is the kind that is best for the Negro."[31]

In the final chapter of his study, entitled "The Challenge of Black Self-Determination," Franklin said of Washington that he appealed to Black self-determinationist values in his "call for the support of black controlled businesses, schools, and other social and economic institutions." Then, in the same breath, he contradicted himself, saying, "Fortunately (or unfortunately), Washington did not represent the values and interests of the black masses and therefore should not be considered their leader."[32]

It was strange enough that Franklin contradicted his own views about Washington, but it was incredible that he would say that Washington was not the leader of the "black masses," which he was. None other than Du Bois thought that. In *The Souls of Black Folk*, he wrote, "Today he stands as the one recognized spokesman of his ten million followers. [He] arose as essentially the leader not of one race but of two—a compromiser between the South, the North, and the Negro."[33]

What Du Bois was saying of Washington was that he was a gargantuan leader because he was not only a leader of 10 million Black people, but was a leader of many white people, providing pivotal leadership between northern and southern Whites and between these two regions of the country. Du Bois was actually describing how important Washington was not only to Black people, but also to white people and America. Yet the scholarship on Washington, including Louis Harlan's two volumes on the Tuskegeean, presents Washington as some kind of "political boss" or "provincial" Black leader with narrow and self-defeating interests for Black people.[34]

In the late 1960s Harold Cruse wrote two books explaining the enormity of Booker T. Washington's leadership in America, which was a modernization leadership to him.[35] In 1970 Robert Factor wrote extensively on Booker T. Washington's leadership in *The Black Response to America* (which Harlan ignored, as he did Cruse's books, in writing his volumes on the Tuskegean), in which he provided a rather full discussion of Washington as a modernization leader.[36] In 1978 William Toll not only regarded Washington as a modernization leader, but as a revolutionary modernization leader, talking of him and Paul Friere and Frantz Fanon in the same breath, a thesis and discussion that Lois Harlan also ignored (although he apparently read Toll's book, because it was cited in the bibliography in the second volume of his biography of Washington).[37] I myself had written of Washington as a modernization leader in 1978 as part of an article written on another Black leader, Kelly Miller.[38] There were some white contemporaries of Washington who understood that Washington was not only a modernization leader but a revolutionary one. One such person was Thomas Dixon, who wrote racist works on Blacks but who still said the following of Washington:

Mr. Washington is not training Negroes to take their place in any industrial system in the South in which the white man can direct or control him. He is not training his students to be servants and come at the beck and call of any man. He is training them *all* to be masters of men, to be independent, to own and operate their own industries, plant their own fields, buy and sell their own goods, and in every shape and form destroy the last vestige of dependence on the white man for anything.[39]

This was revolutionary thinking if there ever was such thinking, and Washington also tried to implement this kind of thinking in practical ways when he was the leader of Blacks in America between 1895 and 1915. Washington sometimes used the word revolution to describe his program to help Blacks. In the early 1890s he wrote, "let . . . them see . . . as they have seen year after year these educated young men and women revolutionize and regenerate whole communities."[40] In 1900, in *The Future of the American Negro*, Washington remarked, "In a word, a complete revolution has been wrought in industrial, educational, and religious life of this whole community by reason of the fact that they had this leader."[41] When Washington did not use the word revolution to describe his leadership or his program for Black people, he used images in his writings or speeches to do so. In describing the program for Black people in his Atlanta Address of 1895 (in his autobiography, *My Larger Education*, published in 1912, three years before his death) Washington said, "I felt that we needed a policy, not of destruction, but of construction; not of defense, but of aggression . . . a policy . . . of . . . advance."[42]

The image and reality of Washington as a modernization leader, and a revolutionary modernization leader at that, did not appear on any page in Harlan's two-volume study of the Tuskegean. This was also true of Franklin's writing on Washington in his book *Black Self-Determination*, which was more of the kind of *flight scholarship* on Washington that continues to be typical of First- and Second-Wave Black historians. Franklin went to such an extreme in this matter. He denied Washington was a Black nationalist (which he was not), even though he met all of the criteria of that label the way Franklin wrote about it in his study. And he even said to historians that they should not regard Washington as the leader of Black people, when historical evidence clearly confirms this. Franklin was trying to undo and even make history, instead of just writing it and encouraging other historians to do the same.

Third-Wave Black historiography will reclaim Washington from the scholarship, by Black and white scholars, that has denigrated and suppressed knowledge of him as a human being and as the primary and, indeed, beloved leader of Black people during twenty critical years of their trek "up from slavery." Washington was often referred to as the "Wizard" by Black and white people, reflecting the brilliance and awe of his leadership. W.E.B. Du Bois wrote history, sociology, and historical sociology about this period, which included writing about Black modernization, development, and progress under Washington's leadership. Black people are still in this general phase of their history—"up from slavery" to contemporary development—which Third-Wave Black historiography would refer to as the Fifth Phase of Black history. It would also indicate that this phase had its origins in the 1860s. In the next and final chapter, there is a discussion of Third-Wave Black historiography's conception of the phases and processes of Black history.

Chapter 8

Third-Wave
Black Historiography II

Third-Wave Black historiography conceives of Black history, like the other three forms of Black historiography, as having its initial origins in West and Central Africa, from whence came most of the black slaves to North America. However, its practitioners would not feel bound to put Black history into any conventional or accepted periodization scheme for discussion or analytical purposes, to which First- and Second-Wave Black historians have adhered. Third-Wave Black historians also would be under no compulsion, political, philosophical, or ideological, to write only on Black people and Black history. White people relate directly and indirectly to Black people and their history in America, and thus having critical knowledge and understanding of them and how they have made history in this country, and how they relate to American history, which Third-Wave Black historiography could provide, would be a way of augmenting the critical knowledge and understanding of Black history. White people and their racist behavior are directly and indirectly related to the phases and processes of Black history that Third-Wave Black historiography focuses on as part of its subject matter, and that really cannot be understood properly or critically without dealing with White racism; namely, the white supremacist/ebonicistic expression of it and concrete White racist behavior. We'll be look-ing at these phases and processes in some detail in this chapter.

Third-Wave Black historiography will be committed to the his-torical canonical requirement of research in primary and second-ary materials and evidence, but its practitioners would not feel the inhibition that canonical historians feel in utilizing social science theories and knowledge (or even philosophy, for that matter) as means to interpret historical evidence. These kinds of knowledge are critical to understanding the phenomenon of racism and white people functioning in America as racists, and Third-Wave Black historiography will make extensive use of them. It would even be in a position to contribute knowledge about racists and racism in American history that can augment the philosophical and social science understanding of these phenomena.

While Black historians since precursors start Black history in Africa, the other major historical practice to date has been to dis-cuss Black history within the periodization of general American history. As determined by the history profession over the years, the periods of American history are the colonial, early national, antebellum, civil war and reconstruction, Populist and Progressive period, twentieth century before World War II, post–World War II period, and sometimes what is called contemporary history from the 1960s on. First- and Second-Wave Black historians invariably seek to place Black history within those time and ideological frame-works, usually to talk about Black participation within these frame-works, although in different ways: First-Wave Black historians write on Black history, having an interest to show how Black people partici-pated in and affected white people and larger American history, while Second-Wave Black historians are primarily interested in talking about Black people in a given period, and not showing much of their relationship to white people or larger American history.

Third-Wave Black historians would not feel compelled to accept the history profession's periodization scheme of American history, and might wish to alter conceptualization and periodization. They might wish to call the colonial period the New England period. The history profession looks upon New England as a limited region of America, but the English, through colonies and with the aid of other Europeans, created an entire area in North America that was really New England (i.e., an area where English civilization was transplanted to North America and altered there). The history of America grew out of this earlier history. So the next period in American history might not be the early national period, but New England to America, to be able to focus sharply on this transition to see what was left behind and what continued on and how it continued on. The next period would be the dissolution of America, followed by the restoration of America. The latter period would be followed by the period of accelerated national development, and so on. Third-Wave Black historiography would write on each of these differently conceived periods of history by integrating the history of Black and white people and showing how these two peoples and these two histories interacted with each other to help produce the realities of each period.

For instance, it was during the history of New England, as differently conceived, that the White over Black structure and system was constructed in America, which was done by white and Black people and functioned to reproduce this New England history or period in American history. After all, this New England history, from Maine to Georgia, centered strongly in white people using Black people to their advantage. It also involved Black people trying to utilize culture and institutions they helped to construct to their advantage. Traditional historical writing has greater difficulty in dealing with historical reality in this manner. A historical sociology would have less difficulty, and would be able to assess this kind of history in a critical manner, focusing on the direct and indirect ways that white people and Black people contributed to each other's history, and the direct and indirect ways that both peoples contributed to the New England period of American history. Third-Wave Black historiography would take this approach, based on its use of a critical historical sociological methodology, to all the newly conceived periods of American history.

Third-Wave Black historiography would not be interested in a superficial or less than full assessment of the way Black people have helped to contribute to American history and to construct American culture, society, and civilization. This is something that the history profession, dominated by white male historians, has always resisted. I remember the time when white historians thought nothing of saying to young Black historians seeking to make professional history careers that they should study the history "of their own people," meaning the history of Black people, which was then usually referred to as "Negro history." But those same historians offering that guidance, as a rule, did not even believe that there was such a subject as Black history, although they did know about "race relations," and this was what they thought "Negro history" was about. But what young Black historians were really being told, myself among them, was that they should not think of writing on the larger American history, as this was the exclusive right of white male historians.

First-Wave Black historians as a rule did not, and to this day do not, write on larger American history; that is to say, write textbooks on American history or write monographs on some general period of American history, save one exception: the period the profession calls the Civil War and Reconstruction period. This was a period, eventually, that white historians could accept Black historians writing about. This was, after all, a period of American history in which professional Black historians would be interested, and there would always be pressure put on the history profession to open up that area of research and writing to Black historians. There were also white historians who rejected the blatant racist writing on the Civil War and Reconstruction period in American history. They were interested in change in that historiography, and they welcomed "outside" input—up to a point.

John Hope Franklin, in a recent publication of some of his articles written between 1938 and 1988, said that he regarded himself as a historian who happened to be Black.[1] Franklin was not denying that he was Black or in any way diminishing this personal reality. He was simply saying that as a Black historian he could write and was entitled to write, because of his qualifications as a professional historian, on any aspect of American history and on any aspect of White history and the larger American history. Articles in his book and his other publications testify to his ability and interest, such as *The Militant South 1800–1861*, which was about white people in the antebellum South.[2] Du Bois began his professional historical writing with a book that was about white people and the way they created and dealt with the social problems of suppressing the African slave trade to America, and the institution of slavery itself. In 1972 Earl Thorpe wrote about southern white slaveholders and the South in *The Old South: A Psychohistory*.[3] Nell Irvin Painter published a history of the United States between the late nineteenth and early twentieth centuries entitled *Standing at Armageddon: The United States, 1877–1919.*[4] Although not about American history but about European penetration into Africa, David Levering Lewis's *The Race to Fashoda* falls into this category of historical writing.[5]

Third-Wave Black historiography would assert the principle that Black historians can write on any aspect of American history, including White history and the larger American history. Indeed, Third-Wave Black historiography would make a distinction between White history and American history, the same as it would make a distinction between Black history and American history, while it saw both particular histories, in interaction, functioning in an overwhelming manner to make American history and American society. After all, at the center of that society from the seventeenth century on was the White over Black structure and system, the general reproductive agency of American history and society.

Third-Wave Black historiography would also make it clear that White history is paradoxical and ironic. It is American history, but it is also *anti-American history*. This is not something with which white historians seriously deal. Thinking themselves critical in their historiography, they say that white people have not always lived up to America's ideals, beliefs, and values, or the lofty morality embedded in them. This skirts the real critical discussion, and also ignores or avoids the clear reality that white people in America have for centuries perverted and subverted American ideals, beliefs, values, morality, precious documents, institutions, and social relationships. This was not aberrational behavior, but continuous behavior, conscious and unconscious; manifestations of White history that de-ethicalized and abnormalized American history, making it function contrary to its own ideals and sublime purposes. Blacks were victims (as well as others in the country) of White history and de-ethnicalized and abnormalized American history, making their existence in America very oppressive and considerably tragic. But white people, in their characteristically racist and irrational, pathological, and immoral fashion, blamed Black people for their considerably blighted condition in America as slaves and nonslaves. Whites viewed themselves as guiltless, innocent, and nonresponsible, and talked about the "innocence of America." Showing his understanding of this kind of behavior, Nathan Huggins wrote in *Black Odyssey*,

Racism and racial caste . . . have been, in their turn, studied as the "tangle of pathology" of blacks. . . . Very little thought has been given to the general health of the society that created and sustains them. Society and its historians have treated all these phenomena as aberrations, marginal to the main story.[6]

Huggins also talked about the way white people, including white historians in America, marginalized the reality and the significance of slavery in American history and society. "Like the framers of the Constitution, they have treated racial slavery and oppression as curious abnormalities—aberrations—historical accidents to be corrected in the progressive upward reach of the nation's history."[7]

The abnormalities were in the personalities, thinking, and social behavior of white people, which were embedded in the White over Black structure and system (i.e., the culture and social institutions), and thus the social life and history of America. This guaranteed that most Whites would be socialized as racists, a socialization that would be continuous over their lifetimes, compelling them to act as racists wherever they went in America and in their participation in American culture and institutions over their lifetime. Abnormally (i.e., irrationally, pathologically, and immorally) was the normal way that white people have interacted with Black people in this country. Interacting with them any other way has been marginal and aberrational.

Third-Wave Black historiography would deal fully with White racism in America (namely, white supremacy/ebonicism), and would no longer let this reality escape historical scholarship, especially the way white supremacy/ebonicism affected white people intellectually, psychologically, morally, and spiritually, and the impact these racist- as well as slavery-produced afflictions had on white people and affected American culture and social institutions. When the history of white people or the larger American history are not treated as critically as Third-Wave Black historiography would do, it prevents Black people from making their full case about the tyrannical, oppressive, and exploitative ways that white people and the larger history of the country have related to them. It makes it appear as if Black people have been the debilitated ones, showing the crippling afflictions and deficiencies, or "inner disturbances," that they turned against a psychologically healthy and guiltless, innocent, and nonresponsible white population that has been generous and helpful to a fault toward Black people. Blacks are unable to talk with seeming rationality or truth about the tyrannical, perverted, and exploitative way that American institutions have functioned against them over the length of their historical existence in the country.

In short, Black people are robbed of the full legitimacy of their complaint against Whites and America, and the legitimacy of and justification for the responses they make in America against a people and a country that does them great harm. This is the continuing African–Black Holocaust in America. Third-Wave Black historiography will consciously write history, observing the rules of scholarship but also motivated by the thought that a greater truth tells a more accurate story, and the greater truth about the way white people and the larger American history have related to Blacks would provide Blacks with reliable knowledge and truth that would stand as sources of legitimacy and justification for social and historical action in America.

Third-Wave Black historiography would be forceful in arguing that American Black slavery was a dictatorial, oppressive, and exploitative institution, and in this form it related to American history, culture, and social life. There was a time when historians had this view of American slavery, without the greater knowledge that present-day historians have of the institution. In the early twentieth century, white historians such as Ulrich Phillips and others endeavored to take the dictatorship, oppression, and exploitation out of American slavery; in short, to get white men especially, but other white people and America, off the hook. Slavery was a contradiction to all notions that America was a free society, had free institutions, and that America was a land of opportunity for all, the rhetoric that white male Americans fed themselves and those who would listen to them. Slavery and its twin, White racism, which reinforced and helped to perpetuate it, indicated that many white people had serious personality afflictions and that American culture and social institutions had been infested with these afflictions that perverted and subverted them.

Slavery, as the Ulrich Phillips kind of scholarship had it, was not to be portrayed as a blight on American history or American society, or on white people, which this kind of scholarship equated with American history and society (i.e., "white society," "white America," and "white civilization"). Even as slaveholders and supporters of slavery, white people were to be guiltless, innocent, and nonresponsible, and by the same delusory thinking and slight-of-hand scholarship, white people, and especially white men who were primarily the slaveholders, were not to be judged tyrannical, oppressive, and exploitative of Blacks. Nathan Huggins wrote in *Black Odyssey*, "American historians, nevertheless, have conspired with the Founding Fathers to create a national history, teleologically bound to the Founders' ideals rather than reality."[8]

But the situation is more complicated than Huggins indicated. The historians he had reference to were white historians. But in a curious way, a number of Black historians also participate in this "conspiracy," or at least reinforce and perpetuate it. There are Black historians who project idyllic images of Black life under slavery and who essentially ignore the tyrannical, oppressive, and exploitative character of American slavery, projecting an image of slavery, intended or not, as being paternalistic, benevolent, and concerned for the fullness of Black humanity. This projects the image, even if not intended, of guiltless, innocent, and nonresponsible white slaveholders. White historians who project idyllic images of Black slave life or who do not stress the dictatorial, oppressive, and exploitative character of American slavery also participate in or reinforce the conspiratorial effort to take slavery out of American slavery. All of this kind of historical writing encourages historians to present the following kind of typical image of American slavery in textbooks read by college and university students:

The treatment of slaves ranged all the way from hideous sadism to gentle paternalism. On some plantations, slaves found themselves continuously beaten; on others, never. Some slaves were always hungry; others ate nearly as well as white folks. Some slaves were poorly clad and housed that they drew sympathy from neighboring whites and blacks. Others lived so well that they were envied by poor whites and exhibited as model specimens to visiting foreigners. The major cause of this variation in treatment was not so much the region or plantation size, as the personalities involved.[9]

The authors of the textbook wanted to get away from the generalities of slavery, which they said kept "breaking down." So they focused on the variations to be found within the institution and described these variations in such a way that the lives of most Black slaves were ignored and the way the institution functioned toward most Black slaves was also ignored. The authors focused on extremes of treatment, and thus gave the impression and projected the image that slavery was half this and half that: half cruel and half benevolent, half enlightened and half blighted, that half the slaves were equal to white people even though they were slaves; in short, that half the slaves were not even slaves, but were more like agricultural workers whose humanity and personal interests were taken into full account and accommodated, not by their masters, but by people who were more like benevolent agricultural employers. Gone from this image of slavery was the fact and the reality that slaveholders owned people, and owned them for generations, including the slaves who were treated badly and those who were treated better.

White masters had the right to work slaves during most of the hours of the day and to take the fruits of their labor for their own profit. They had the right, and carried out the right, of denying Black slaves, including badly treated slaves and better treated slaves, political and civil rights. They had the right to deny Black slaves an education, even a rudimentary education of learning how to read and write. They had the right to confine Black people to physical and geographical locations. They required Black slaves, even those they treated better, to show them deference, and to show deference to all white people. They required Black slaves, including the slaves they treated better, not to show anger, hostility, or defiance in their presence, not to look them straight in the eyes when talking to them, not to grimace or make a fist when talking to them, and immediately to leave their presence when they were dismissed and not to come into their presence unless beckoned.

White masters had the right to beat any of their slaves. They had the right to buy and sell them. They had the right to regard them as property, as they did cows, fences, trees, or rivers. They had the right to be abusive toward Black slaves, they had a right to humiliate them, they had a right to denigrate them and to treat them all as if they were children or some kind of "pets." They had a right to extend privileges to their slaves and a right to take privileges back. They had a right to decide which slaves could court and mate and have families. They had a right to break up families. White male slaveholders and other white males had a right to abuse Black female slaves sexually and to ignore their feelings or interests. They had a right to uproot slaves from an area, from family, from friends, and from familiar surroundings, and a right to punish slaves severely if they did not want to make the move.

All these descriptions are *generalities* about American slavery, and they are generalities that reflect the reality of the dictatorial, oppressive, and exploitative character of the institution. The ethnic identity and the cultural and social life that Black people developed as slaves in America were developed within this context. Whatever mitigation or variation that occurred in the institution occurred within this context. And it might be added that this whole dictatorial, oppressive, and exploitative context was promoted, enforced, and protected by constitutions, political institutions, and the legal system and law. There was the *rule of slave law* in America that did not promote rights, justice, or fairness, but rather the denial of rights, the denial of justice, the denial of fairness, and the legal right of people to be lawless and abusive toward other people. This was also true of racist laws and the *rule of racist law* that reinforced slave laws and slavery. Dictatorial, oppressive, and exploitative slavery, and the rule of racist and slave law, had an impact on the thinking of white people and on the culture and institutions of America, and Third-Wave Black historiography will investigate and delineate these impacts.

It all relates to getting at the "deeper" understanding of American history and life that is required to help get at the "deeper" understanding of Black history and life in America and the historical ways that Black people have responded to historical domination, exploitation, and continued, varied abuse. In other words, this is getting at the deeper understanding of how Black people have responded historically to the oppressive, exploitative, and abusive

White over Black structure and system and the African–Black Holocaust that it helped to create and perpetuate in American history and Black history to assault, exploit, and abuse Black people.

This also means, then, that Black history itself has to be probed and discerned in a deeper manner. This would be the object of a Third-Wave Black historiography, which would assert that this deeper assessment, among other things, would require knowing and understanding the *phases and processes* of Black history, which a critical historical sociological approach would make it possible to do in the most effective manner. The phases and processes, obviously, would have their origins in Africa. There would be five broad phases of Black history that a Third-Wave Black historiography would delineate and discuss, and four historical–social processes: the *Disruption, Destruction, Retention*, and *Transformation* historical–social processes. White people appeared in all the phases and processes of Black history, as well as Black people, and this joint, interactive participation would be critical to evaluating the phases and processes in Black history. What follows is an extended discussion of the phases and processes of Black history, presented as a general outline of these matters.

The First Phase would be the West and Central African background of Black people, the history and life of the people who were transported to the Western Hemisphere as slaves, who were the original ancestors of Black people and who produced the immediate and second ancestors of Black people. The First Phase of Black history would include the history of the three West and Central African kingdoms of Ghana, Mali, and Songhay, and the cultural and social life of those kingdoms. This means that Third-Wave Black historians would not only be dealing with history, but also realities that would fall under the academic disciplines of cultural anthropology and sociology.

As said in the previous chapter, Third-Wave Black historiography would make use of extrinsic theories and make them part of its historical sociological methodology. There would be cultural anthropological and sociological theories and knowledge that Third-Wave Black historians would have to know thoroughly and use to understand the culture and social life of the black people who became slaves in North America. Historians, including Black historians, usually deal rather superficially with the West and Central African cultural and social background of Black slaves. It means that they are not knowledgeable enough about the original cultural and social traits, and thus would not recognize easily what cultural and social traits survived in slavery and among the Black population in America.

Much of the survival would have to be in the form of transformed traits; that is, traits joined together with the new European American cultural and social fare, or that would be adapted to the slave experience itself, which would also be transformed traits, such as the diunital method of cognition, which was the transformed West and Central African holistic method of cognition that the slave experience wrought. Transformed original African cultural and social attributes were, by definition, *Black* cultural and social attributes. Thus, finding more African survivals among Black slaves and the ongoing Black population would not prove that Black people were Africans, but that they were black and Black people of black African descent; that Black ethnicity and Black culture and social life were of black African descent. But as can also be seen, Black people, and to an important extent Black ethnicity, Black culture, and Black social life, were also of European American descent, which Third-Wave Black historiography would also always maintain.

The Second Phase of Black history would be the African–Black Holocaust phase as it occurred through the seventeenth and nineteenth centuries. This phase emerged during the continuing White/European assault against Western and Central Africa and the black people there, which had been going on since the late fifteenth century. This assault was the African Holocaust, carried out by European countries, trading companies, and individual shippers (including pirates). The African Holocaust involved an assault against kingdoms, villages, tribes, clans, and families for the purpose of getting control of human bodies that Whites/Europeans wanted to use for their own purposes. These people were aided by some Western and Central Africans. Some Black historians seek to deny this collaboration, or seek to find a justification for it by emphasizing the ways black Africans were compelled to collaborate. There was compulsion, but there was also motivations of power, greed, and opportunities for wealth on the part of many collaborators.

Thus, the African Holocaust has to draw in and analyze the African collaboration as part of its total assessment. The Holocaust disrupted West and Central African history, culture, and social life, and then through a continuous process of capturing, enslaving, and transporting slaves, planting slavery in the Western Hemisphere, and grossly exploiting black slave labor, Western and Central African cultural traits and Western and Central Africans were destroyed. The African Holocaust was extended to North America in the seventeenth century, where in time it became the African–Black Holocaust, which involved the same disruption of histories and disruption and destruction of cultural and social traits and human beings, and the horrendous process of their reduction to slavery and their enslavement in North America. This holocaustic experience continued intensely over the eighteenth century and much of the nineteenth century, a period of 230 years.

The phase of the African–Black Holocaust also witnessed, as part of its reality, the establishment of the White over Black hierarchical social structure and social system that, in turn, helped to produce and perpetuate the reality of the African–Black Holocaust. White racism (i.e., white supremacy/ebonicism) inundated the White over Black structure and system, and enslaved and nonenslaved Black people and their lives constituted the lower portion of the structure and system. Thus, the African–Black Holocaust was rooted in North America as an integral part of the general reproductive agency of American history, culture, and social life. The African–Black Holocaust was a daily experience for Black people in North America for 230 years. It was so not only because of a daily slave existence for most Black people, but also because of the perversion and subversion of American ideals, beliefs, and values.

White maintenance of Black chattel slavery helped to pervert and subvert these idealities. White racism also played a strong role by de-ethicalizing and abnormalizing these idealities, making them function in a racist manner toward Black people, which helped to perpetuate slavery in America. In short, Whites perverted and subverted America to maintain Blacks in a daily holocaustic experience. Thus, an integral part of the African–Black Holocaust, the White over Black structure and system that helped to establish and perpetuate it, and the general and daily functioning of America—not as an aberration or departure from the main functioning of the country, but as integral to its functioning, and of which Black people were victims during the Second Phase of their history in America—was White irrationality, pathology, and immorality, and an essential lack of conscience on the part of white people when interacting with Black people.

The Third Phase of Black history grew out of the Second Phase, the African–Black Holocaust phase, commencing during the late seventeenth and early eighteenth centuries and continuing until past the mid-nineteenth century. This means that the Third and Second Phases of Black history overlapped. The Third Phase was the phase when black African slaves produced Black slaves, when original black African ancestors produced a Black ancestral group that in turn produced and reproduced Black people in America. This was the phase of Black history when Black ethnicity was planted and when the Black ethnic culture and social life were initially constructed. This ethnicity and construction was done mainly by Black slaves, who transformed an African (accepted in retrospect) continental identity and African ethnic identities into a single Black identity, even if this identity could not be publicly projected in a positive, forceful manner; and when Black slaves joined African survivals with new cultural and social fare and adapted survivals to their slave experience that helped to produce their Black ethnicity and the Black culture and social life.

The Third Phase of Black History also saw the establishment (even creation) of nonslave Blacks in America. They existed in the northern and southern part of the country. These Black people were, and more or less remained, an anomaly in American history and social life. They were not slaves, but they were not free people either, because they were not white. They were not subjected directly to slave laws, but were treated very much like slaves by the application of racist laws and other racist practices. This meant that the Black life that nonslave Blacks constructed in the North and South was directly affected by racist laws and other racist practices, and strongly indirectly affected by slave laws and slavery. The various racist and slave manifestations were part of the White over Black structure and system, which put nonslave Blacks and their lives alongside Black slaves and essentially regarded both groups of Blacks and their social lives as one people and one life, the bottom portion of the White over Black structure and system.

While nonslave Blacks and Black slaves were lumped together in America and dominated, controlled, and exploited by Whites, these two groups of Black people grew up differently in America, and functioned in a considerably different manner in the country, as the Third Phase of Black history indicates. First and foremost, most nonslave Blacks in this phase of Black history were geographically separated from most Black slaves, living in the North while most Black slaves lived in the South. The nonslave Blacks, most of whom previously had been slaves, constructed the Black community that northern Black slaves eventually joined and to which southern Black slaves fled during the eighteenth century and the first half of the nineteenth century. The nonslave Blacks and their community in the North (as well as the nonslave Blacks and their community in the South), were not dominated, controlled, or exploited as much by the White over Black structure and system, or victimized as much by the African–Black Holocaust, as Black slaves and their community, North and South. The Third Phase of Black history eventually established a Cotton Curtain that separated northern nonslave Blacks and southern Black slaves and nonslave Blacks, resulting in a serious division among Black people and a variegated kind of development among them.

The Fourth Phase of Black history began in the late seventeenth and early eighteenth centuries, overlapping the Second and Third Phases, and extended into the first half of the twentieth century. This is the Phase where Black people consciously or unconsciously began identifying with the developing and finally constructed American identity and with European American culture, and claiming them all as their own. These activities were done differently by Blacks in the South (that is, Black slaves) and by nonslave Blacks, especially those in the North. The Black slaves in the South, from the late seventeenth century through the first half of the nineteenth century, laid claim to European American culture more than they did to the developing or finally constructed American identity. From the late seventeenth century on Black slaves began grabbing European American cultural and social traits that resembled the African (in retrospect) cultural and social traits that they brought to North America with them, and that would enable them to hold onto these traits, even in a modified manner; or they latched onto new environmental situations, such as the corn-shucking activity that permitted them to employ certain African (in retrospect) cultural and social traits, even if in a transformed manner and without the same full meaning.

Assimilating and utilizing European American culture to hold onto cultural and social traits or to construct a new, synthetic culture, Black slaves erected a historical–cultural–social wall between themselves and Western and Central Africans that incoming West and Central African slaves had to confront and relate to and that separated especially Black slaves from their original African (in retrospect) history and homeland. This compelled and facilitated Black slaves turning to European American cultural and social attributes, identifying with them, and assimilating and using them. But this identifying, assimilating, and using was not done to have an American identity, but primarily for reasons of survival and for cultural and social construction. The European American cultural and social traits were assimilated by Black slaves especially and became part of their being, and thus their partial and unconscious identity with the American identity and their unconscious claim on it.

In the North, during the Fourth Phase of Black history, nonslave Blacks identified directly with the American identity and publicly claimed it as their identity and the identity of all Black people in America, as their birthright. They sought to participate directly in what were now called, especially in the nineteenth century, American culture and social life, not only to claim, but to implement their American identity. They did this throughout the nineteenth century. They were joined by southern Blacks (that is, former Black slaves) in the late nineteenth century, when they, in the 1860s and 1870s, began claiming their American identity and American citizenship. This continued under the leadership of Booker T. Washington and the local leaders he provided for Black people in the South. It was in the late nineteenth and early twentieth centuries that the two separate Black communities in America began to come together as a single community in the country. This single community claimed themselves to be Americans, and struggled against or cooperated with white Americans to get them to accept the American identity of Black people, their American citizenship, and their rights as American citizens. In the 1940s, 1950s, and 1960s, this historical thrust of well over two centuries achieved significant gains.

The Fifth Phase of Black history (which will likely give way to a Sixth Phase) began in the 1860s when 4 million Black people and a dominated, controlled, and grossly exploited community was *released* from slavery. These Blacks and their community were not set free in America, and strong and numerous obstacles were erected against both becoming free. Indeed, in the late nineteenth century, millions of Black people, many former slaves, were reduced to another form of servitude in the South, by racism, indebtedness sharecropping, peonage labor, disfranchisement, segregation, and violence that carried on into the next century. But despite their suppression, which was also caused by northern White indifference as well as collaboration with southern Whites, the former Black slaves and their descendants made efforts to modernize and develop, as individuals, as a group of people, and as a community, launching a modernization and development phase of Black history that continues to the present day.

In the 1880s Booker T. Washington inaugurated his leadership of southern Blacks, which was a modernization and development leadership. Between 1895 and 1915 he accelerated that leadership, concentrating it and his modernization and development programs among rural Blacks in the South. Most Black people in the country lived in the South, and most of that aggregate lived in rural areas. Washington saw the urbanization of the South as a threat to the modernization and development of Blacks, which he thought would occur best on the land rather than in cities. But the Tuskegean witnessed the continued urbanization of America and the increasing movement of Blacks to cities, and thus the trend toward urbanization among Blacks, and he realized he had to deal with it. He met this situation by creating an urban-based leadership, South and North, which he did through the National Negro Business League and other Black organizations. His goal was to build an urban Black middle class that would be a leadership class for Black people and function not only to modernize and develop Blacks living in cities, but also to unite the two segments of the Black community in America and to construct it as a single national community.

The effort to build a national Black community (with variations, of course) and to carry this community through modernization and development has been going on since the death of Booker T. Washington, and in many ways building on the foundations he laid. That modernization and development process also involved Black middle-class urban people leading Blacks to claim their American identity and to attain full citizenship and full citizenship rights in the country. That effort was accelerated in the 1950s and 1960s, led by southern Black middle-class people who were descendants of the Black middle class that Washington had helped to build in the South between the 1880s and his death in 1915. The Black middle class continues to function as the leadership class of Black people, and continues to try to lead millions of Black people and the national Black community in contemporary development.

While Third-Wave Black historiography would divide Black history into five broad phases, it would also insist that the phases are not sharply separated from each other, and that they overlap with each other and affect each other. Only one of the phases ever dissipated, and that was the First Phase. The Second, Third, and Fourth Phases continue to exist and function in the Fifth Phase, affecting its development. Black people have never had the requisite power to end any of their phases of history or fully to complete a phase of their history. The African–Black Holocaust phase continues on in Black history, sometimes functioning in an awesome manner, as it is presently in the national Black community destroying so many young Black people and seriously weakening that community and its efforts to continue modernizing and developing.

Blacks still have not completed the Third Phase of their history, as they still have not understood themselves to be, on a widely accepted basis, an ethnic group in America. Their focus is primarily still on race and themselves being a racial group and a racial community. There is still no concepts of a national Black ethnic group and a national Black ethnic community among Black people. While Black people consider themselves to be Americans and strongly assert that identity, they still have not secured their citizenship or citizenship rights in the country. Black people were victims of White racism in the 1970s and 1980s that saw diminishment of their national citizenship and their national citizenship rights, and this racist assault continues. Only a solid construction of a national Black ethnic community and its full modernization and development can enable Blacks to jettison all the previous phases of their history and have only one phase to function in and to complete, although this would not end phases in Black history, as others would emerge in time.

But ending or completing phases of Black history prior to the Fifth Phase and being able to carry out the Fifth Phase successfully requires that Black people know in a full manner the historical–social processes of Black history that appear in the phases of that history and that seriously affects how they function. Third-Wave Black historiography would consciously seek to help Black people understand the broad processes of their history. As said previously, there are four such historical–social processes: the Disruption, Destruction, Retention, and Transformation processes. These processes had their genesis in the Second Phase of Black history, where the Disruption and Destruction processes first appeared. They continued during the Third Phase of Black history, where the Retention and Transformation processes were added. The Third, Fourth, and Fifth Phases of Black history evidenced all four processes, which interacted with and impacted each other in each phase, helping to shape the contours of each phase. All four of the historical–social processes of Black history became part of and were reproduced by the White over Black structure and system.

Each phase of Black history from the Second Phase on evidenced the White over Black structure and system, which generally determined how the four historical–social processes functioned in each phase. It should be recalled that the White over Black structure and system involved three broad features, meaning that the general reproductive agency of American history and social life involved three such features: people (namely white and Black people), cultural features, and social features. People participated in the cultural and social features, making them what they were and reproducing them as they interacted with each other in a dominant–subordinate pattern to reproduce the general structure and system.

Since the historical–social processes were part of the White over Black structure and system and reproduced by it, white people and Black people participated in these processes, helping to determine each of their realities as they occurred and continued to occur in American history and Black history. This is another way of saying that white and Black people have interacted with each other to help shape each of the phases of Black history, and Black history generally in America. Precursor and First-Wave Black historians always accepted White involvement in the making of Black history. Second-Wave Black historians talk less about this involvement, and some want to get white people out of Black historical writing and thus out of Black history altogether. But that simply cannot be done except by distorting or suppressing the full reality of Black history. Third-Wave Black historiography would have as one of its major objectives showing how white people have interacted with Black people to help make Black history, how Black people have interacted with white people to help make White history, and how the two of them have interacted together to help make American history.

As said before, the Disruption and Destruction processes first appeared during the Second Phase of Black history. The Whites/Europeans initiated these two processes, and thus the historical–social processes in Black history. The Disruption process was initiated by such people seeking slaves in Africa, which was expanded and continued by the trading of weapons and other goods for slaves, encouraging African kingdoms, African villages, and groups of Africans to war and intrude upon each other, and by Africans capturing each other to sell to white traders or to trade each other for weapons or other goods. Disruption of kingdoms, life in villages, and clan and family life occurred when Africans were removed from such places and institutions. Cultural and social practices were disrupted by these removals. Disruption of African psychologies and thinking occurred in the captures, while being stored in slave facilities, during ship doctors's inspections, and during the Middle Passage to the Western Hemisphere.

Black Africans played roles in the Disruption process. They also played roles in the Destruction process, which was initiated in Western and Central Africa by Whites/Europeans and black Africans when both groups killed black Africans in the process of capturing others to make them slaves. Black Africans died in the forced marches to slave facilities and in slave facilities and on slave ships. Villages were destroyed during captures. Families were destroyed during captures and in slave facilities and on slave ships. The sanity of many Africans was destroyed during these activities, as were ethnic identities and loyalties and authority figures, authority symbols, and authority lines. Many cultural and social traits were destroyed.

The Disruption and Destruction processes continued when African slaves arrived in North America, continuing the Second Phase of Black history. Disruption of African psychologies and African thinking in particular continued, as black Africans were put on a physically different land and were forced to relate to people who were physically and culturally and socially different from them, who treated them with such hostility and cruelty, and who were bent on making them slaves. The auction-block inspections, the buying and selling of slaves, and the separation of family members disrupted the lives of Africans. The breaking-in process that converted Africans into slaves did the same. The slave institution of which Black Africans became the central elements continued the Destruction process initiated in Africa. Lingering ethnic identities, loyalties, and languages were destroyed, as well as traditional authority figures and symbols and many original cultural and social traits. African slaves died during the break-in process or in trying to escape from their slave reality.

The Third Phase of Black history introduced the Retention and Transformation processes of Black history and was the first phase where all four historical–social processes occurred, which would continue on through all other phases of Black history. The Disruption process continued, in a general way, when the institution of slavery disrupted, on a permanent basis and in a considerable way, the relationship of African (in retrospect) slaves with Africa and black Africans. The Black slaves who emerged in America as offspring of African and Black slaves had their relationship disrupted with Africa and black Africans, and even African slaves that kept coming into the country on a smuggled basis until the mid-nineteenth century. Such Africans met considerable hostility and rejection from indigenous Black slaves until they became part of the new ethnicity and indigenous slave community. The Disruption process divided northern nonslave Blacks from southern Black slaves, and also from the nonslave Blacks in the South, including the slaveholders among them. Nonslaveholding nonslave Blacks had a disrupted relationship with Black slaves, who were segregated on slave plantations and farms. The thinking of nonslave Blacks in the North and South was frequently disrupted and confused by their anomalous status in America.

The Destruction process also continued in the Third Phase of Black history. Generally speaking, Africans becoming Black people, destroyed the existence of Africans in America. Black slave women were a primary element in this destruction process, giving birth to Black people rather than Africans. The development of a Black identity among Black slaves, even if it was not projected forcefully or openly on slave plantations and farms, destroyed the possibility of an African identity being accepted by Black slaves, which negative views about Africa, Africans, and an African identity that white people and Black slaves had also functioned to destroy. That means that the future of Black people as Africans in America was destroyed, as well as an African history in America.

The Third Phase of Black history also saw the introduction of the Retention and Transformation processes. African slaves and Black slaves generally retained their original biological or racial characteristics. The retention could not be total, because these group attributes fell under the Disruption process when white men and African and Black slave women produced children who were lighter in complexion. They also fell somewhat under the Destruction process when the children of white men and African and Black slave women were so light that they could "pass" for white.

The slave institution did much to promote the Retention process in Black history during its initial appearance in the Third Phase of that history. Slavery confined Africans and Black slaves to plantations and farms and prevented extensive interaction between white people and slaves, thus preventing extensive amalgamation and permitting Black slaves generally to hold onto their original biological or racial characteristics. Slavery confined the retention of African cultural and social survivals primarily among Black slaves, with the assumption that they were inferior, which aided slaves in holding onto them. The belief that the African (in retrospect) retentions were considered inferior by itself aided Retention. The existence of Black ethnicity and a Black culture and social life, which were continuously held at the bottom of the White over Black structure and system in the South during the Third Phase of Black history, were, through this means, retained in that history.

The Transformation process emerged during this time frame. This process functioned generally to transform Africans (accepted in retrospect) into Black people, a new ethnic group of the black race that had been transplanted from Africa to the Western Hemisphere, and specifically into the Americas. Slavery played a role in the Transformation process by forcing former Africans to look away from their original homeland and to look strongly, if not in a stronger manner, at the new land to which they had come and would now live, and to which they would have to adapt. The Transformation process involved an alteration in the perception of Africans as to who they were and would now have to be, even if a full focus on the latter was not as yet possible. The Transformation process involved both acculturation and assimilation.

Acculturation is a combination cultural and social process that involves people who come to a cultural and social situation, evidencing their own cultural and social attributes, and who have to learn and adjust to the new cultural and social fare. This also involves, as a requirement and as a means to facilitate learning and adjustment, losing some or a lot of their original cultural and social attributes. African slaves had to acculturate in America and it helped to transform them. They also transformed themselves by fusing new cultural and social attributes with original ones to create new, synthetic cultural and social traits. They were transformed when they had to adapt original traits to new physical surroundings.

While the original African slaves acculturated, the Black slaves born in America assimilated. Assimilation applies to people born in a cultural and social context to indigenous people. They assimilate or learn and internalize the culture and social life around them. In the case of Black slaves that meant assimilating and internalizing the Black culture and social life into which they were born, but also, as much as it was possible or permitted, the culture and social life of white people and of America. Assimilation functioned to help transform black people born in America into Black people. The latter, acting as *Black* people, helped to perpetuate Black people and Blackness, and thus aided the Retention process of Black history by helping to retain Black ethnicity and Black culture and social life. But assimilation also helped Black slaves born in America to become Americans, however slow or difficult that was, and thereby functioned to promote the Transformation process that was turning the mass of Black people into Americans. Nonslave Blacks assimilated more quickly and more of the European American heritage and the American identity.

The Retention and Transformation processes also played strong roles in the Fourth Phase of Black history. This was the phase where Black people sought to establish their American identity and to achieve citizenship and citizen rights. This was initially done by northern nonslave Blacks, who were eventually joined by former slaves who pursued the same objectives. Both groups of Blacks used the Retention process for these purposes. They held onto their blackness and Blackness. Nonslave Blacks also organized Black organizations, such as antislavery societies and state conventions and other kinds of political groups to pursue their goals. Black churches played a role in these activities. In the late nineteenth century other Black organizations, like the Afro-American Council and the Negro American Academy, plunged into this activity. In the twentieth century Blacks organizations, such as the National Association of Colored Women, the Pullman Porter and Maids Union, and much later the Southern Christian Leadership Conference, pursued and sought to lead Blacks in pursuit of an American identity and citizenship and citizenship rights.

In the late nineteenth century Booker T. Washington led Black people in the South, most Black people in America, in using the Retention process to attain their American objectives. He created his own Black leaders and his own Black organizations, such as the Farmers and Workers Conferences and the National Negro Business League, and utilized other Black organizations, such as national Black churches, Black fraternal societies, and Black newspapers, to help southern and northern Blacks to achieve their American goals. But with southern Blacks, Washington's approach was on a long-term rather than a short-term basis. In his view, White racism, which was extremely vicious, was against Blacks at this time pursuing their Americanity. It was necessary for Blacks to build themselves up as a people and to build up group power, which would take some years, but would be used to help Blacks pursue their American identity and citizenship goals. Blacks did this in the South in the 1950s and 1960s, redeeming Washington's long-term leadership and his long-term use of the Black Retention process.

Throughout the length of the Fourth Phase of Black history, Black people used the Transformation process of their history to achieve a publicly accepted American identity and American rights. The Transformation process not only involved assimilation, as said before, but also involved integration. The latter was a combination cultural and social process of participation, meaning an individual or a group participating in the culture and social life of their community or country. Black slaves engaged in integration throughout the 230 years of slavery in America. They participated in the American economy, in America's religious institutions (when they attended white churches in the South), and in white families as servants or cooks. Through this participation they learned aspects of the American culture and assimilated it and made it a part of themselves, meaning they made Americanness part of themselves, which would be the springboard for their conscious, public quests for American objectives during and following the war between the United States and the Southern Confederacy and in the postwar period.

Northern nonslave Blacks made use of assimilation and integration to utilize the Transformation process by assimilating American political culture and participating with Whites in antislavery and abolition societies, and in political parties. They participated in the army and navy of the United States during the mid-century war with the conscious purpose of trying to end slavery in America and to help Blacks attain American objectives. They, along with southern Blacks, integrated into or participated in the Spanish–American War, World War I and World War II, and the Korean War, to quest for and legitimize American claims. In the twentieth century Blacks helped to create and participated in biracial organizations, such as the National Association for the Advancement of Colored People and the National League on the Urban Conditions of Negroes (the Urban League), and later the Congress of Racial Equality, as part of the Transformation process of their history, to push that process toward achieving American goals. From the 1930s to the 1960s Blacks participated in the Democratic Party to help implement the Transformation part of their history and to achieve transformation objectives.

The Disruption and Destruction processes also functioned during the Fourth Phase of Black history, with white people and Black people implementing them. Whites initiated the Disruption process when they disrupted the new relationship that a number of Blacks thought they would have with American life, and were even promised after the War of Independence. Blacks fought in that war, helping to defeat the English. Some Blacks were released from slavery for their participation, but then they had to face strong racism and rigid segregation that suppressed and/or retarded their ability to participate fully in American life.

In the late eighteenth century and throughout the first half of the nineteenth century Whites disrupted Black life by their colonization schemes to induce Blacks to leave America, or to deport them. There were Blacks who favored and implemented colonization. Black thinking was disrupted and confused about colonization and leaving America, at least to some extent, throughout the first half of the nineteenth century. Blacks reflected disrupted and confused thinking when they labeled their institutions and organizations African but then referred to themselves most of the time as Negroes or Colored people. During the 1830s, 1840s, and 1850s Black participation in American politics was disrupted by their disenfranchisement. This disruption continued in the North well beyond the mid-century war because of continuing disenfranchisement and Black political apathy.

Blacks in the South who participated in the region's politics in the postwar period had this participation disrupted by disenfranchisement during the late nineteenth and early twentieth centuries. In the 1850s Black life was disrupted in the North by thousands of Blacks fleeing to Canada. In the late nineteenth and early twentieth centuries Black thinking was disrupted and confused and Black life was disrupted by Black migratory or emigration schemes. Disrupted and confused thinking about emigration occurred in the post–World War I period with the Garvey propaganda and program. In the 1950s and 1960s the Black struggle for liberation in America was disrupted and confused by the numerous approaches by which Blacks conducted the struggle, in which they found themselves opposed to each other and Whites.

The Destruction process began in the late eighteenth century when Black men died in the War for Independence. This kind of manifestation of Destruction occurred a number of times during the Fourth Phase of Black history, as Blacks died in a number of

American wars, and considerably in vain, because these expressions of patriotism and commitment to America did not pay off in big political and civil rewards. Indeed, it sometimes led to repression and more destruction, as occurred after the Civil War, when many Blacks were killed in the South, and following World War I. In the 1830s a number of Northern Blacks were killed by white mobs, and intermittently during this phase of Black history Blacks were killed by white mobs. The national citizenship and national citizenship rights that Black people gained in the 1860s and 1870s were destroyed before the close of the nineteenth century, and continued to be destroyed until the 1950s and 1960s.

Blacks were killed during the 1930s when southern Whites renewed their lynching of Black people. A large number of Blacks died during the liberation struggle of the 1950s and 1960s. Between the late nineteenth century and the first half of the twentieth century, a number of Blacks killed each other over arguments, family or lover quarrels, in the pursuit of criminal objectives, or as an indirect way of retaliating against or killing white people. In the nineteenth and twentieth centuries the minds of numbers of Blacks were destroyed by the racist-inundated world in which they had to live.

The Fifth Phase of Black history has seen the active functioning of the Retention process. During the mid-nineteenth-century war Black slaves engaged in activities that put pressure on Congress and President Lincoln to end slavery. After the war, they pooled meager resources to buy land and establish schools. In the latter half of the nineteenth century Blacks in the South and North, aided by Whites who participated in the Retention process, established a number of Black colleges, which were really, in most cases, only more or less high schools, but which would become genuine higher education institutions. Booker T. Washington encouraged former Black slaves to buy land and become individual farmers, and to build schools, homes, and churches in rural areas.

In the late nineteenth and early twentieth centuries, Blacks in the North and South established businesses and some industries. In this same period they established newspapers and magazines to educate and entertain themselves and to encourage themselves in modernization and development. Black intellectuals formed a "think tank," the Negro American Academy, at the close of the nineteenth century that functioned in the twentieth century. From the late nineteenth century to the 1920s, Blacks developed their aesthetic culture: their music, dance, theatre, humor, and art, which produced a "Renaissance" in the 1920s. Throughout the first half of the twentieth century Blacks increased the numbers in their middle class, their numbers of professional people, and their numbers of professional organizations. In the 1960s Blacks developed Black Power and Black politics, and also produced a large number of professional Black scholars and organizations for these scholars, such as the National Council of Black Studies. Throughout the twentieth century Black women's clubs, societies, and professional organizations constituted manifestations of the Retention process and helped to promote it.

The Transformation process was implemented in the 1860s and 1870s, when former Black slaves and nonslave Blacks functioned as elected officials in southern state governments, until their ouster. Blacks also participated in the U.S. Congress until their ouster in the opening years of the twentieth century. Black farmers joined with white farmers in the Populist movement to augment their power and income, but their efforts were not very successful. Northern Blacks joined the Progressive movement at the turn of the twentieth century to try to increase the political power of Blacks, to augment their opportunities in the American economy, and to move their standard of living toward that of Whites in America. Blacks sought to take advantage of the New Deal of the 1930s with its various governmental programs with respect to housing, farm ownership, employment, and artistic activities.

From the 1930s on Blacks, functioning through biracial organizations such as the NAACP and the Urban League and through the Democratic Party, sought to gain access to national, state, and county government social programs to augment their group existence. They employed these same institutions, as well as a plethora of human relations councils, to try to get civil rights bills and fair-employment-practice laws passed by American governments. In the 1940s and 1950s Blacks pressured the U.S. government to integrate the armed forces, and to open up advancement channels for Blacks in the armed services. In the 1950s Blacks, along with white allies, pressured the Supreme Court into declaring segregated education illegal, as well as the general practice of segregation in American life, which would open up educational and economic opportunities for Blacks in America. In the 1960s Blacks demanded that the U.S. government provide them with economic assistance and social programs as it did white Americans, to augment their standard of living and their modernization and development in the country.

The Retention and Transformation processes had to work against the Disruption and Destruction processes of the Fifth Phase of Black history, as they were hindered in their functioning by these processes. The Disruption process was implemented when Blacks from the North and Blacks from the South, former slaves and nonslave Blacks, could not agree on the objectives that former slaves should pursue after the mid-century war, with northern Blacks wanting them to pursue political and civil rights while southern Blacks were more interested in education and economic objectives. In the late nineteenth century Black thinking was disrupted by the virulent White racist public assault against their psychology and their public image. This kind of disruption actually continued throughout the twentieth century, with the movies, radio, and television promoting it by assaulting the Black psychology and publicly disparaging the Black public image. Black politics and Black efforts to modernize and develop in the late nineteenth and early twentieth centuries were disrupted when Booker T. Washington and other Black leaders disagreed over political objectives and strategies of modernization and development. This kind of disruption also occurred in the 1920s, when Marcus Garvey and indigenous Black middle-class leaders clashed about these matters.

The same kind of clash occurred in the 1960s and 1970s, when a number of established Black leaders criticized the Black Power ideology and the Black Power movement, which focused broadly on Black modernization and development, and particularly the modernization and development of the Black community, rather than just the civil rights aspects of that thrust. Blacks in the twentieth century standing against assimilation and integration disrupted Black politics and Black efforts to modernize and develop. Black conservatives who in the 1980s and into the 1990s attacked the Black use of the national government to help augment and develop Black life promoted the Disruption process. Those middle-class Black people who insisted that Black people were Africans, African Americans, or Afro-Americans when most Black people regarded themselves as Black people did the same thing.

The Destruction process began in the Fifth Phase of Black history when southern Whites killed Black people who tried to vote, buy land, become independent farmers, and establish schools. In the late nineteenth and early twentieth centuries, southern Whites killed some Black people who became successful in business. They destroyed the homes and businesses of some successful people. Southern Whites killed Blacks who sought to migrate from the South to live and work in the North to augment their incomes and their standard of living. During economic depressions or recessions over the nineteenth and twentieth centuries, the livelihood of many Blacks was destroyed when they lost their jobs and incomes. In the late nineteenth and early twentieth centuries Blacks lost lucrative occupations, such as caterers or racehorse jockeys. From the late nineteenth century to the present moment, white policemen, of various kinds, have killed a large number of Black people. Over the same time period a large number of Black people have died from diseases and poor health care. Since the 1960s many Blacks have died from using drugs, supplied by white and Black people.

In the 1940s, the 1950s, and the 1960s, and even afterward, when Blacks have rioted in cities, they have destroyed property and businesses owned by Blacks, jobs and incomes that Blacks once had, and the decent or augmented lifestyle that Blacks once had. Black families have continuously been destroyed over the past several decades by the payment practices of the American welfare system. The Black community itself has been undergoing slow destruction by Blacks killing Blacks, by the continuing larger number of Black youth not finishing public school and not finding work, and by Black middle-class people no longer wishing to be a part of the Black community or wanting to help other Black people modernize and develop.

The discussion of the phases of Black history shows that the phases overlapped. The processes of Black history, as just seen, overlapped the phases themselves, simply because the processes functioned in all the phases, except the very first one. The history of Black people in America shows that the historical–social processes that they have to know well, and that they have to try to control and use, are the Retention and Transformation processes. These are the twin *motor powers* of Black history (which correspond roughly to the separate and integrated tracks and movements of that history). The Retention process is the one that seeks to retain Black people as a physical and human reality in America. It also seeks to continuously augment the power of Black people in America, and also their cultural (aesthetic as well as social; i.e., ideals, values, norms) and social life in America, including relations between Black men and women, Black adults and children, and the Black social classes. The Retention process, in short, seeks to build up and retain Black Power, Black ethnicity, and the national and local Black communities.

Black Power and a powerful Black existence in America makes it possible for Blacks to use the Transformation process of their history more effectively. With greater power Blacks have the means to assimilate and integrate better in America, and greater wherewithal to demand and secure their American identity and their rights and freedom in the country. Using the Retention and Transformation processes diunitally and effectively, Blacks have the means to exert considerable control over and considerably diminish the Disruption and Destruction processes that plague them and their history in America. In short, they have a greater means to move against the White over Black structure and system, to diminish it, and even try to destroy it, which Blacks ultimately have to do to be fully free in the country.

The other important thing that greater control over and use of the Retention and Transformation processes in diunital interaction does for Black people is that it makes it possible for them to live in America and to make history in the country with a greater balance and harmony, and with a greater sense of realism. The Retention process emphasizes and clarifies that Black people are an ethnic group in America of the black race and of black African descent. This process connects Black people to Africa and Africans, and the history, culture, and social life of both, as well as to other black people in the Western African Extensia. It keeps a path continuously open to develop relationships with other black peoples from Africa in the Western African Extensia.

The Transformation process emphasizes and clarifies that Black people are to some extent of white biological descent, and that they are also of European descent, as historical assimilators of, participators in, and contributors to the European heritage of America and the specific American cultural and social heritage. The Retention process emphasizes, protects, and promotes the Black ethnic identity of Blacks, while the Transformation process emphasizes, protects, and promotes the American identity of Blacks. Functioning diunitally, they emphasize, protect, and continuously promote the Black American identity, and thus the continuous balanced, harmonious, and realistic character of the Black identity in America. The two processes also make it possible, in a balanced, harmonious, and realistic manner, for Blacks to maintain their historical relationship with both of their historical, cultural, and social heritages, and to be able to make creative uses of them. Third-Wave Black historiography would endeavor to promote all of these dimensions of Black people and their history in America and as part of the historical black African Presence in the world, in their case, as people of black African descent.

W.E.B. Du Bois once said that Black people in America had a "double-consciousness." He meant two things by that, one negative and the other positive. The negative consideration was that Black people historically had had to view themselves from the perspective that White racists had of them and the oppressive, exploitative, and hostile world (the Disruption and Destruction processes) in which they forced Black people to live: "A world which yields him no true self-consciousness, but only lets him see himself through the revelation of the other world."[10] The positive side of the "double-consciousness" identity and psychology was the view that Black people had of themselves; who they were, who they could be, and what they were capable of achieving that contradicted the White racist depictions and conclusions. This "double-consciousness" reality of Blacks, Du Bois said, was full of tension and anxiety: "two warring ideals in one dark body, whose dogged strength alone keeps it from being torn asunder."[11]

The two "warring ideals" were thus the two different identities that Black people had in their "double-consciousness": the racist identity that white people had for them and the identity that they had of and for themselves that they wanted white people and America to accept—their Black and American identities, or their singular, combined Black American identity (Retention and Transformation processes). Du Bois wanted Black people to move from a previous oppressive and debilitating "double-consciousness" to a different one that a Black American identity would create and augment and that Black people had historically been struggling to project and hold onto in America. It is necessary to return partially to a quotation presented earlier in the work:

The history of the American Negro is the history [of] this longing to merge his double self into a better and truer self. In this merging he ... would not Africanize America, for America has too much to teach the world and Africa. He would not bleach his Negro soul in a flood of white Americanism, for he knows Negro blood has a message for the world. He simply wishes to make it possible for a man to be both a Negro and an American, without being cursed and spit upon by his fellows.[12]

Du Bois's description of the situation reflected his use of what I would call the Africancentric and Blackcentric perspectives in diunital interaction. He rejected the idea that Black people were Africans, but regarded them to be of black African descent. He therefore condemned efforts to try to Africanize Black people and America, although he knew full well the African Presence was in Black people and America in the form of inheritance and descent and that it affected both. Du Bois's comments show that he regarded Black people as a distinctive kind of black people, born and raised in America and greatly formed by America, who were Americans and not Africans. They also were not white people; that is, white people with "dark skins." They were Black people, unique and different in many ways from other black people, and even from white people who were their fellow citizens.

Du Bois believed that Black people in America had a "message" for white people, America, and black people elsewhere, because of their European American heritage and the way they had transformed and retained that heritage by their original African and subsequent Black heritage. This double heritage, this other mani-festation of the positive dimension of the "double-consciousness" psychology and reality, would be the basis from which Blacks in America would provide their "message"—their interpretation of history, the world, and what was real or good and bad in it—and that would be a perspective for others to peruse. Third-Wave Black historiography would not have the objective of trying to present the Black "message" to the world, but it would seek to provide the best understanding of Black history possible. If Blacks seek to use this understanding as one of the means to try to construct a world message, so be it.

Notes

1. INTRODUCTION

1. Joseph E. Holloway, ed., *Africanisms in American Culture* (Bloomington: Indiana University Press, 1990), xx.

2. Lee Sigelman and Susan Welch, *Black Americans' Views of Racial Inequality: The Dream Deferred* (New York: Cambridge University Press, 1991), xi; "Polls Say Blacks Prefer to Be Called 'Black,'" *Jet*, February 11, 1991, 8; *Jet*, May 30, 1994, 37; *Jet*, August, 1994, 46.

3. Sigelman and Welch, *Black Americans' Views of Racial Inequality*, xi.

4. Henry Louis Gates, Jr., *Loose Canons: Notes on the Culture Wars* (New York: Oxford University Press, 1992), Ch. 8.

5. Sterling Stuckey, *Slave Culture: Nationalist Theory & the Foundations of Black America* (New York: Oxford University Press, 1987). V. P. Franklin, *Black Self-Determination: A Cultural History of the Faith of the Fathers* (Westport, Conn.: Lawrence Hill, 1984).

6. Julius Lester, ed., *The Seventh Son: The Thought and Writings of W.E.B. Du Bois*. Vol. 1 (New York: Vintage Books, 1991), 154–169.

7. W.E.B. Du Bois, "An Open Letter to the Southern People (1887)," in *Against Racism: Unpublished Essays, Papers, Addresses, 1887–1961*, ed. Herbert Aptheker (Amherst: University of Massachusetts Press, 1985), 1–2.

8. W.E.B. Du Bois, *The Suppression of the African Slave Trade to the United States of America 1638–1870* (Baton Rouge: Louisiana State University Press, 1969).

9. W.E.B. Du Bois, *The Philadelphia Negro: A Social Study* (New York: Schocken Books, 1967).

10. W. D. Wright, *Racism Matters* (Westport, Conn.: Praeger, 1997), Ch. 2.

11. Ivan Van Sertima, *They Came Before Columbus* (New York: Random House, 1976).

12. Larry Rohter, "An Ancient Skull Challenges Long-Held Theories," *New York Times*, October 26, 1999, F4–5.

13. Molefi Kete Asante, *Kemet, Afrocentricity and Knowledge* (Trenton, N.J.: African World Press, 1990), 12.

14. Ibid., 15.

2. FIRST- AND SECOND-WAVE BLACK HISTORIANS I

1. Quoted in Clarence E. Walker, *Deromanticizing Black History: Critical Essays and Reappraisals* (Knoxville: University of Tennessee Press, 1991), 5.

2. William Cooper Nell, *The Colored Patriots of the American Revolution* (New York: Arno Press and the *New York Times*, 1969).

3. William Wells Brown, *The Negro in the American Rebellion: His Heroism and His Fidelity* (New York: Johnson Reprint Corporation, 1968).

4. George Washington Williams, *History of the Negro Race in America from 1619 to 1880*. 2 vols. (New York: Bergman, 1968).

5. Dickson D. Bruce, Jr., "The Ironic Conception of American History: The Early Black Historians, 1883–1915," *The Journal of Negro History* 69, no. 2 (1984): 53.

6. Reinhold Niebuhr, *The Irony of American History* (New York: Charles Scribner's Sons, 1952).

7. Harry L. Watson, *Liberty and Power: The Politics of Jacksonian America* (New York: Noonday Press, 1990), 12–13.

8. Abraham Lincoln, "Address on Colonization to a Deputation of Negroes," in *Lincoln on Black and White: A Documentary History*, ed. Arthur Zilversmit (Belmont, Calif.: Wadsworth, 1971), 96.

9. Earl E. Thorpe, *Negro Historians in the United States* (Baton Rouge, La.: Fraternal Press, 1958), 15–17.

10. Williams, *History of the Negro Race*, vol. 1, p. 25.

11. Benjamin Brawley, *A Social History of the American Negro* (New York: Macmillan, 1970).

12. Nell, *The Colored Patriots of the American Revolution*, 120.

13. Theodore S. Hamerow, *Reflections on History and Historians* (Madison: University of Wisconsin Press, 1987), Ch. 11.

14. John Hope Franklin, "On the Evolution of Scholarship in Afro-American History," in *The State of Afro-American History: Past, Present, and Future*, ed. Darlene Clark Hine (Baton Rouge: Louisiana State University Press, 1986), 13–22.

15. Ibid., 15.

16. Carter G. Woodson, *Education of the Negro to 1861* (New York: Arno Press, 1968); Carter G. Woodson and Charles H. Wesley, *The Negro in Our History*, 11th ed. (Washington, D.C.: Associated, 1966); Carter G. Woodson,

ed., *The Mind of the Negro as Reflected in Letters Written during the Crisis, 1800–1860* (New York: Russell & Russell, 1969); Carter G. Woodson, *The African Background Outlined: Or Handbook for the Study of the Negro* (New York: New American Library, 1969); Carter G. Woodson, *African Heroes and Heroines,* 2d ed. (Washington, D.C.: Associated, 1944).

17. Franklin, "On the Evolution of Scholarship in Afro-American History," 14–15.

18. W.E.B. Du Bois, *Black Reconstruction in America: An Essay toward a History of the Part Which Black Folk Played in the Attempt to Reconstruct Democracy in America, 1860–1880* (New York: Atheneum, 1970).

19. Franklin, "On the Evolution of Scholarship in Afro-American History," 16.

20. Ibid., 18.

21. Earl Thorpe, *Negro Historians in the United States* (Baton Rouge: Fraternal Press, 1958), Ch. 2.

22. Benjamin Brawley, *The Negro Genius: A New Appraisal of the Achievement of the American Negro in Literature and the Fine Arts* (New York: Dodd, Mead, 1937).

23. Alain Locke, *The Negro and His Music* (New York: Arno Press and the *New York Times*, 1969); Alain Locke, *Negro Art: Past and Present* (New York: Arno Press and the *New York Times*, 1969).

24. John Tierney with Lynda Wright, "The Search for Adam and Eve," *Newsweek*, January 11, 1988, 47.

25. J. A. Rogers, *Sex and Race: Negro–Caucasian Mixing in All Ages and All Lands.* 3 vols. (St. Petersburg, Fla.: Helga M. Rogers, 1967, 1972); J. A. Rogers, *World's Great Men of Color.* 3 vols. (New York: Macmillan, 1972).

26. Quoted in J. A. Rogers, *Africa's Gift to America: The Afro-American in the Making and Saving of the United States* (St. Petersburg, Fla.: Helga M. Rogers, 1961).

3. FIRST- AND SECOND-WAVE BLACK HISTORIANS II

1. John Hope Franklin, "On the Evolution of Scholarship in Afro-American History," in *The State of Afro-American History: Past, Present, and Future,* ed. Darlene Clark Hine (Baton Rouge: Louisiana State University Press, 1986), 14.

2. W.E.B. Du Bois, *The Souls of Black Folk: Essays and Sketches* (Greenwich, Conn.: Fawcett, 1961); W.E.B. Du Bois, *The Negro* (New York: Oxford University Press, 1970); W.E.B. Du Bois, *The Gift of Black Folk: The Negroes in the Making of America* (New York: Washington Square Press, 1970); W.E.B. Du Bois, *Black Folk Then and Now: An Essay in the History and Sociology of the Negro Race* (New York: Octagon Books, 1973).

3. W.E.B. Du Bois, *John Brown* (New York: International, 1962).

4. Herbert Aptheker, *Afro-American History: The Modern Era* (New York: Citadel Press, 1991), 57.

5. Manning Marable, *W.E.B. Du Bois: Black Radical Democrat* (Boston: Twayne, 1986).

6. W. D. Wright, "The Socialist Analysis of W.E.B. Du Bois" (Ph.D. diss., University of Michigan, 1986).

7. W.E.B. Du Bois, "Sociology Hesitant," 1904, manuscript, the Du Bois Papers, reel 82, pp. 5–6, University of Massachusetts Archives.

8. W.E.B. Du Bois, "The Study of the Negro Problems," in *W.E.B. Du Bois on Sociology and the Black Community*, ed. Dan S. Green and Edwin D. Driver (Chicago: University of Chicago Press, 1978), 82.

9. W.E.B. Du Bois, "The Laboratory in Sociology at Atlanta University," in ibid., 61.

10. W.E.B. Du Bois and Rushton Coulborn, "Mr. Sorokin's Systems," in *Book Reviews by W.E.B. Du Bois*, comp. and ed. Herbert Aptheker (Millwood, N.Y.: KTO Press, 1977), 190.

11. W.E.B. Du Bois, "Stealing a Continent," in ibid., 174–175.

12. John Hope Franklin, "The New Negro History," *The Journal of Negro History* 43, no. 2 (1957): 95–97; Franklin, "On the Evolution of Scholarship in Afro-American History," 22.

13. Benjamin Quarles, "Black History Unbound," *Daedalus* 103, no. 2 (1974): 165–166.

14. Thomas C. Holt, "Wither Now and Why?" in *The State of Afro-American History: Past, Present, and Future*, ed. Darlene Clark Hine (Baton Rouge: Louisiana State University Press, 1986), 5.

15. Vincent Harding, "Beyond Chaos: Black History and the Search for the New Land," in *Amistad I*, ed. John A. Williams and Charles F. Harris (New York: Vintage Books, 1970), 267–292.

16. Quoted in John W. Blassingame, "The Afro-Americans: From Mythology to Reality," in *The Reinterpretation of American History and Culture*, ed. William H. Cartwright and Richard L. Watson (Washington, D.C.: National Council for Social Studies, 1973), 53.

17. Ibid., 54–55.

18. Sheila S. Walker, "Expanding Our Worldview Beyond the U.S.," *CAAS Newsletter* 2, no. 1 (1991): 1.

19. Robert L. Harris, Jr., "Coming of Age: The Transformation of Afro-American Historiography," *The Journal of Negro History* 67, no. 2 (1982): 118.

20. Ibid., 116.

21. Vernon J. Dixon and Badi G. Foster, eds., *Beyond Black or White: An Alternate America* (Boston: Little, Brown, 1971).

22. Mary White Ovington, *Half a Man: The Status of the Negro in New York* (New York: Hill and Wang, 1969), 100.

23. Lerone Bennett, Jr., *The Negro Mood and Other Essays* (Chicago: Johnson, 1964), 51.

24. Joseph White, Jr., "Guidelines for Black Psychologists," *The Black Scholar* 1, no. 5 (1970): 57.

25. Du Bois, *The Souls of Black Folk*, 17.

26. Harris, "Coming of Age: The Transformation of Afro-American History," 116.

27. Nathan I. Huggins, "Integrating Afro-American History into American History," in *The State of Afro-American History: Past, Present, and*

Future, ed. Darlene Clark Hine (Baton Rouge: Louisiana State University Press, 1986), 166.

28. L. D. Reddick, "A New Interpretation for Negro History," *The Journal of Negro History* 22, no. 1 (1937): 20.

29. Herbert Aptheker, *American Negro Slave Revolts* (New York: Columbia University Press, 1943).

30. Kenneth M. Stampp, *The Peculiar Institution: Slavery in the Antebellum South* (New York: Random House, 1956).

31. Stanley Elkins, *Slavery: A Problem in American Institutional and Intellectual Life* (New York: Grosset & Dunlap, 1963).

32. John W. Blassingame, *The Slave Community: Plantation Life in the Antebellum South* (New York: Oxford University Press, 1972); George P. Rawick, *From Sundown to Sunup: The Making of the Black Community* (Westport, Conn.: Greenwood Press, 1972); Eugene D. Genovese, *Roll, Jordan, Roll: The World the Slaves Made* (New York: Pantheon Books, 1974).

33. Leslie Howard Owens, *This Species of Property: Slave Life and Culture* (New York: Oxford University Press, 1976); Albert J. Raboteau, *Slave Religion: The Invisible Institution in the Antebellum South* (New York: Oxford University Press, 1978); Thomas L. Webber, *Deep Like the Rivers: Education in the Slave Quarter Community, 1831–1865* (New York: W. W. Norton, 1978); Herbert Gutman, *The Black Family in Slavery and Freedom, 1750–1925* (New York: Pantheon Books, 1976); Nathan I. Huggins, *Black Odyssey: The Afro-American Ordeal in Slavery* (New York: Vintage Books, 1977); Lawrence W. Levine, *Black Culture and Black Consciousness: Afro-American Folk Thought from Slavery to Freedom* (New York: Oxford University Press, 1977).

34. George P. Rawick, ed., *The American Slave: A Composite Autobiography*, 41 vols. (Westport, Conn.: Greenwood Press, 1972–1979); Norman P. Yetman, ed., *Life Under the "Peculiar Institution": Selections from the Slave Narrative Collection* (New York: Holt, Rinehart and Winston, 1970).

35. Laurence Shore, "The Poverty of Tragedy in Historical Writing on Southern Slavery," *South Atlantic Quarterly* 85, no. 2 (1986): 147–148.

36. Ibid., 147.

37. I. A. Newby, "Historians and Negroes," *The Journal of Negro History* 56, no. 1 (1969): 33.

38. Lerone Bennett, Jr., "The White Problem in America," in *The White Problem in America*, by the editors of *Ebony* (Chicago: Johnson Publishing, 1966), 1–10.

39. Samuel Du Bois Cook, "A Tragic Conception of Negro History," *The Journal of Negro History* 45, no. 4 (1960): 222.

4. ORTHOGRAPHY, HISTORY, AND BLACK ETHNICITY

1. Winthrop D. Jordan, *White over Black: American Attitudes toward the Negro 1550–1812* (Baltimore, Md.: Penguin Books, 1968), 7.

2. George M. Frederickson, *The Arrogance of Race: Historical Perspectives on Slavery, Racism, and Social Equality* (Middletown, Conn.: Wesleyan University Press, 1988), 3.

3. Ibid., 160.

4. Quoted in Edmund S. Morgan, "The Education of a Saint," in *American Life, American People*, vol. 1, ed. Neil Larry Shumsky and Timothy J. Crimmins (New York: Harcourt Brace Jovanovich, 1988), 19.

5. Ibid.

6. Robert D. Marcus and David Burner, eds., *America First Hand*, vol. 1: *From Settlement to Reconstruction*, 2d ed. (New York: St. Martin's Press, 1992), 49.

7. Quoted in Jordan, *White over Black*, 159.

8. Quoted in Gary B. Nash, *Red, White & Blacks: The Peoples of Early North America* (Englewood Cliffs, N.J.: Prentice Hall, 1992), 139.

9. Quoted in Leonard Dinnerstein and Kenneth T. Jackson, eds., *American Vistas 1607–1877*, 3d ed. (New York: Oxford University Press, 1979), 39–40.

10. Quoted in Silvio A. Bedini, *The Life of Benjamin Banneker* (New York: Charles Scribner's Sons, 1972), 82.

11. Judith Cocks to James Hillhouse, Marietta, March 8, 1795, in *Slave Testimony: Two Centuries of Letters, Speeches, Interviews, and Autobiographies*, ed. John Blassingame (Baton Rouge: Louisiana State University Press, 1977), 7.

12. James Hope to Dr. Master (Beverley Tucker), Jones Borough, November 16, 1834, in ibid., 12.

13. Usa Payton to Dear Master (Beverley Tucker), St. Louis, February 23, 1851, in ibid., 14.

14. Quoted in Robert S. Starobin, ed., *Blacks in Bondage: Letters of American Slaves* (New York: View Points, 1974), 26.

15. Thomas Rightso to John Walker, Canadday, December 5, 1850, in Blassingame, *Slave Testimony*, 154.

16. W.E.B. Du Bois, *The Souls of Black Folk: Essays and Sketches* (Greenwich, Conn.: Fawcett, 1961), 72.

17. W.E.B. Du Bois, "The Revelation of Saint Orgne the Damned," in *W.E.B. Du Bois Speaks: Speeches and Addresses 1920–1963*, ed. Philip S. Foner (New York: Pathfinder Press, 1970), 112–113.

18. W.E.B. Du Bois, "The Future of Africa: Address to the All-African People's Conference, Accra," in *The Seventh Son: The Thought and Writings of W.E.B. Du Bois*, vol. 2, ed. Julius Lester (New York: Vintage Books, 1971), 661.

19. W.E.B. Du Bois, "A Program of Reason, Right and Justice for Today," in ibid., 676.

20. Kenneth Thompson, *Beliefs and Ideology* (New York: Tavistock, 1986).

21. Nicolas Abercrombie, Stephen Hill, and Bryan Turner, *The Dominant Ideology* (London: George Allen & Unwin, 1980).

22. W.E.B. Du Bois, "The Souls of White Folk," in *W.E.B. Du Bois: A Reader*, ed. Meyer Weinberg (New York: Harper & Row, 1970), 304.

23. W.E.B. Du Bois, *The Negro* (New York: Oxford University Press, 1970), 8.

24. Ibid., 9.

25. Bernard Lewis, *Race and Slavery in the Middle East: An Historical Enquiry* (New York: Oxford University Press, 1990), 16.

26. Ibid., 17.

27. W.E.B. Du Bois, "The Conservations of Races," in Foner, *W.E.B. Du Bois Speaks: Speeches and Addresses 1890–1919*, 73–85.

28. Barbara J. Fields, "Ideology and Race in American History," in *Region, Race, and Reconstruction: Essays in Honor of C. Vann Woodward*, ed. J. Morgan Kousser and James M. McPherson (New York: Oxford University Press, 1982), 144.

29. K. Anthony Appiah and Amy Gutmann, *Color Consciousness: The Political Morality of Race* (Princeton, N.J.: Princeton University Press, 1996), 38; Tommy L. Lott, *The Invention of Race: Black Culture and the Politics of Representation* (Malden, Mass.: Blackwell, 1999), 50.

30. Adolph Reed, Jr., *Class Notes Posing as Politics and Other Thoughts on the American Scene* (New York: New Press, 2000), 84.

31. Mary C. Waters, *Ethnic Options: Choosing Identities in America* (Berkeley and Los Angeles: University of California Press, 1990), 7.

32. Milton M. Gordon, *Human Nature, Class, and Ethnicity* (New York: Oxford University Press, 1978), 106–113.

33. Benjamin B. Ringer and Elinor R. Rawless, *Race-Ethnicity and Society* (New York: Routledge, 1989), 4–5.

34. Stephen Steinberg, *The Ethnic Myth: Race, Ethnicity, and Class in America* (Boston: Beacon Press, 1989).

5. WHITES/EUROPEANS AND THE ORIGINS
OF THE AFRICAN IDENTITY

1. Sir E. A. Wallis Budge, *A History of Ethiopia: Nubia & Abyssinia*, vol. 1 (Oosterhout N.B., The Netherlands: Anthropological, 1970), vii.

2. George Washington Williams, *History of the Negro Race in America from 1619 to 1880* (New York: Bergman, 1968), vol. 1, p. 13.

3. W.E.B. Du Bois, *Darkwater: Voices from Within the Veil* (New York: Schocken Books, 1969), 74.

4. John G. Jackson, *Introduction to African Civilizations* (Secaucus, N.J.: Citadel Press, 1970), 65.

5. Williams, *History of the Negro Race in America*, 13.

6. Frank M. Snowden, Jr., *Before Color Prejudice: The Ancient View of Blacks* (Cambridge: Harvard University Press, 1983), 8.

7. Budge, *A History of Ethiopia*, vii.

8. James E. Brunson and Runoko Rashidi, "The Moors of Antiquity," in *Golden Age of the Moor*, ed. Ivan Van Sertima (New Brunswick, N.J.: Transaction, 1992), 36.

9. Ibid., 28, 36.

10. J. A. Rogers, *Sex and Race: Negro–Caucasian Mixing in All Ages and All Lands* (St. Petersburg, Fla.: Helga M. Rogers, 1967), vol. 1, p. 86.

11. Lloyd A. Thompson, *Romans and Blacks* (Norman: University of Oklahoma Press, 1989).

12. Jack D. Forbes, *Black Africans & Native Americans: Color, Race and Caste in the Evolution of Red–Black Peoples* (New York: Basil Blackwell, 1988), 67.

13. Ibid., 79.

14. Ibid., 16.

15. Ibid., 11.

16. Ivan Van Sertima, ed., *Nile Valley Civilizations* (Journal of African Civilizations, 1985), 17.

17. Ibid.

18. Yosef ben-Jochanan, "Questions and Answers," in *New Dimensions in African History: The London Lectures of Dr. Yosef ben-Jochanan and Dr. John Henrik Clarke*, ed. John Henrik Clarke (Trenton, N.J.: Africa World Press, 1991), 77.

19. Gerald Massey, *A Book of the Beginnings: Egyptian Origines in the British Isles*, vol. 1 (London: Williams and Northgate, 1881), 28.

20. ben-Jochanan, "Questions and Answers," 77.

21. Herodotus, *The Histories*, rev. ed., with an intro. and notes by A. R. Burn (New York: Penguin Books, 1972), 283.

22. Henrico Stephano, *Thesaurus Graecae Linguae*, vols. 1–2 (Paris: Excudebut Ambrosius Firmin Didot, 1831–1856), 2703.

23. Charlton T. Lewis and Charles Short, eds., *A Latin Dictionary* (Oxford: Clarendon Press, 1966), 69.

24. Robert H. Hood, *Begrimed and Black: Christian Traditions of Blacks and Blackness* (Minneapolis, Minn.: Fortress Press, 1994), 25.

25. Michael Avi Yonah and Israel Shatzman, *Illustrated Encyclopaedia* (New York: Harper & Row, 1975), 23.

26. Bernard Lewis, *Race and Slavery in the Middle East: An Historical Inquiry* (New York: Oxford University Press, 1990), 51.

27. Ibid., 50.

28. Banna to L. Tappan, Westville, March 12, 1841, in *Slave Testimony: Two Centuries of Letters, Speeches, Interviews, and Autobiographies*, ed. John Blassingame (Baton Rouge: Louisiana State University Press, 1977), 38.

29. Abram Blackford to Mary B. Blackford, Monrovia, February 14, 1846, in ibid., 64.

30. William C. Burke to Mrs. Mary C. Lee, Mount Rest Clay-Ashland, February 20, 1859, in ibid., 103.

31. Williams, *History of the Negro Race*, vol. 1, p. 14.

32. Hollis R. Lynch, *Edward Wilmot Blyden: Pan-Negro Patriot 1832–1912* (New York: Oxford University Press, 1970), 67.

33. Abiola Irele, *The African Experience in Literature and Ideology* (London: Heinemann Educational Books, 1981), 96.

34. Lynch, *Edward Wilmot Blyden*, 61–62.

35. Knife Abraham, *Politics of Black Nationalism: From Harlem to Soweto* (Trenton, N.J.: Africa World Press, 1991), Chs. 2–5.

36. Quoted in Irele, *The African Experience in Literature and Ideology*, 68.

37. Ibid., 69–78.

38. Ibid., 70.

39. Kwame Nkrumah, *Consciencism* (London: Heinemann Educational Books, 1964).

40. Ali A. Mazrui, "On the Concept of 'We Are All Africans,'" *American Political Science Review* 57, no. 1 (1963): 90.

41. M. Itua, "Africans Do Not Want to Be Africans," in *The Black Think Tank*, ed. Naiwu Osahon (Lagos, Nigeria: International Coordinating Committee of the 7th Pan African Congress, 1992), 4.

42. Quoted in Kwame Anthony Appiah, *In My Father's House: Africa in the Philosophy of Culture* (New York: Oxford University Press, 1992), 73.

43. Ibid., 76.

44. Ibid., 80.

45. Molefi Kete Asante, *The Afrocentric Idea* (Philadelphia: Temple University Press, 1987), 6.

46. Ibid., 10.

6. BLACKS AND THE RETROSPECTIVE AFRICAN IDENTITY

1. Winthrop D. Jordan and Leon F. Litwack, *The United States: Conquering a Continent*, vol. 1, 7th ed. (Englewood Cliffs, N.J.: Prentice Hall, 1991), 51.

2. Melville J. Herskovits, *The Myth of the Negro Past* (Boston: Beacon Press, 1990).

3. John Edward Philips, "The African Heritage of White America," in *Africanisms in American Culture*, ed. Joseph E. Holloway (Bloomington: Indiana University Press, 1990), 225–239.

4. John Henrik Clarke, "African-American Historians and the Reclaiming of African History," in *African Culture: The Rhythms of Unity*, ed. Molefi Kete Asante and Kariamu Welsh Asante (Trenton, N.J.: African World Press, 1990), 157–158.

5. John Henrik Clarke, *Christopher Columbus and the Afrikan Holocaust: Slavery and the Rise of European Capitalism* (New York: A & B, 1992), 90.

6. Benjamin Quarles, *The Negro in the Making of America*, rev. ed. (New York: Collier Macmillan, 1969), 95.

7. Chris Dixon, *African American and Haiti Emigration and Black Nationalism in the Nineteenth Century* (Westport, Conn.: Greenwood Press, 2000), 178.

8. Sylvia M. Jacobs, *The African Nexus: Black American Perspectives on the European Partitioning of Africa, 1880–1920* (Westport, Conn.: Greenwood Press, 1981), 26.

9. W.E.B. Du Bois, *Book Reviews by W.E.B. Du Bois*, comp. and ed. Herbert Aptheker (Millwood, N.Y.: KTO Press, 1977), 8.

10. W.E.B. Du Bois, *Darkwater: Voices from within the Veil* (New York: Schocken Books, 1969), 71.

11. Quoted in John Hope Franklin, "George Washington Williams and Africa," in *Historical Judgments Reconsidered: Selected Howard University Lectures in Honor of Rayford W. Logan*, ed. Genna Rae McNeil and Michael R. Winston (Washington, D.C.: Howard University Press, 1988), 3.

12. Quoted in Martin Staniland, *American Intellectuals and African Nationalists, 1955–1970* (New Haven, Conn.: Yale University Press, 1991), 178.

13. Quoted in ibid., 179.

14. Quoted in ibid., 184.

15. David Walker, *David Walker's Appeal, in Four Articles; Together with a Preamble, to the Coloured Citizens of the World, but in Particular, and Very Expressly, to Those of the United States of America* (New York: Hill and Wang, 1965).

16. Marilyn Richardson, ed., *Mary W. Stewart: America's First Black Political Writer, Essays and Speeches* (Bloomington: Indiana University Press, 1987).

17. Frederick Douglass, *My Bondage and My Freedom* (Chicago: Johnson, 1970), 184.

18. Ibid., 338.

19. Frederick Douglass, *The Life and Times of Frederick Douglass* (New York: Crowell–Collier, 1962), 468.

20. Robert G. Weisbord, *Ebony Kinship: Africa, Africans, and the Afro-American* (Westport, Conn.: Greenwood Press, 1973), 22.

21. Martin Robison Delaney, *The Condition, Elevation, Emigration, and Destiny of the Colored People of the United States Politically Considered* (New York: Arno Press and the *New York Times*, 1968).

22. Philip S. Foner and George E. Walker, eds., *Proceedings of the Black State Conventions, 1840–1865*, vols. 1–2 (Philadelphia: Temple University Press, 1970).

23. Quoted in ibid., vol. 1, p. 68.

24. Leonard P. Curry, *The Free Black in Urban America 1800–1850: The Shadow of the Dream* (Chicago: University of Chicago Press, 1981), 236–237.

25. B. A. Botkin, ed., *Lay My Burden Down: A Folk History of Slavery* (Chicago: University of Chicago Press, 1945); Julius Lester, *To Be a Slave* (New York: Dell, 1968); Norman P. Yetman, *Life Under the Peculiar Institution: Selections from the Slave Narrative Collection* (New York: Holt, Rinehart, and Winston, 1970).

26. Robert S. Starobin, ed., *Bondage: Letters of American Slaves* (New York: View Points, 1974).

27. Charles L. Blockson, *The Underground Railroad: First-Person Narratives of Escapes to Freedom in the North* (New York: Prentice Hall, 1987).

28. Molefi Kete Asante, *The Afrocentric Idea* (Philadelphia: Temple University Press, 1987), 9.

29. Houston A. Baker, Jr., *The Journey Back: Issues in Black Literature and Criticism* (Chicago: University of Chicago Press, 1980), 21.

30. Booker T. Washington, "A Speech at the Memorial Service for Samuel Chapman Armstrong," in *The Booker T. Washington Papers*, vol. 3, *1889–95*, ed. Louis R. Harlan, Stuart B. Kaufman, and Raymond Smock (Urbana: University of Illinois Press, 1974), 320.

31. Booker T. Washington, *The Future of the American Negro* (New York: New American Library, 1969), 99.

32. Ibid.

33. Richardson, *Mary W. Stewart*, 50; Weisbord, *Ebony Kinship*, 20.

34. Richardson, *Mary W. Stewart*, 75.

7. THIRD-WAVE BLACK HISTORIOGRAPHY I

1. Hine, "Lifting the Veil, Shattering the Silence: Black Women's History in Slavery and Freedom," in *The State of Afro-American History: Past, Present, and Future*, ed. Darlene Clark Hine (Baton Rouge: Louisiana State University Press, 1986), 223.

2. Darlene Clark Hine, *Hine Sight: Black Women and the Reconstruction of American History* (New York: Carlson, 1994); Evelyn Brooks Higginbotham, *Righteous Discontent: The Women's Movement in the Black Baptist Church, 1880–1920* (Cambridge: Harvard University Press, 1993); Deborah Gray White, *Too Heavy a Load: Black Women in Defense of Themselves, 1894–1994* (New York: W. W. Norton, 1999).

3. Paul Veyne, *Bread and Circuses: Historical Sociology and Political Pluralism*, abridged ed. (London: Allen Lane, Penguin Press, 1990), 2.

4. Dennis Smith, *The Rise of Historical Sociology* (Philadelphia: Temple University Press, 1991), 3.

5. Ibid., 1.

6. W.E.B. Du Bois, *The Negro* (New York: Oxford University Press, 1970), 90.

7. Ross Poole, *Morality and Modernity* (New York: Routeledge, 1991), ix.

8. W.E.B. Du Bois, *The World and Africa: An Inquiry into the Part Which Africa Has Played in World History* (New York: International, 1965), 23.

9. John Hope Franklin, "Foreword: W. E. Burghardt Du Bois, Pioneer Historian of the Slave Trade," in W.E.B. Du Bois, *The Suppression of the African Slave Trade to the United States of America 1638–1870* (Baton Rouge: Louisiana State University Press, 1969), 10.

10. Quoted in August Meier and Elliott Rudwick, *Black History and the Historical Profession, 1915–1980* (Urbana: University of Illinois Press, 1986), 297.

11. Sterling Stuckey, *Slave Culture: Nationalist theory and the Foundations of Black America* (New York: Oxford University Press, 1987); V. P. Franklin, *Black Self-Determination: A Cultural History of the Faith of the Fathers* (Westport, Conn.: Lawrence Hill, 1987).

12. Stuckey, *Slave Culture*, 14.

13. Ibid., 3.

14. Francis Bebey, *African Music: A People's Art* (New York: Lawrence Hill, 1969), 92–113.

15. Ibid.

16. Gilbert Osofsky, ed., *Puttin' On Ole Massa: The Slave Narratives of Henry Bibb, William Wells Brown, Solomon Northrop* (New York: Harper & Row, 1969).

17. Quoted in John W. Blassingame, ed., *Slave Testimony: Two Centuries of Letters, Speeches, Interviews, and Autobiographies* (Baton Rouge: Louisiana State University Press, 1977), 182.

18. Quoted in Charles L. Blockson, *The Underground Railroad: First-Person Narratives of Escapes to Freedom in the North* (New York: Prentice Hall, 1987), 175.

19. Quoted in Julius Lester, *To Be a Slave* (New York: Dell, 1968), 86.

20. Stuckey, *Slave Culture*, 126.

21. W.E.B. Du Bois, "A Negro Nation Within the Nation," in *W.E.B. Du Bois Speaks: Speeches and Addresses 1920–1963*, ed. Philip S. Foner (New York: Pathfinder Press, 1970), 77–86.

22. Stuckey, *Slave Culture*, 291–292.

23. Ibid., 328.

24. V. P. Franklin, *Black Self-Determination: A Cultural History of the Faith of the Fathers* (Westport, Conn.: Lawrence Hill, 1987), 7.

25. Ibid.

26. Ibid., 78.

27. Booker T. Washington, "A Speech at the Memorial Service for Samuel Chapman Armstrong," in *The Booker T. Washington Papers*, vol. 3, *1889–95*, ed. Louis R. Harlan, Stuart B. Kaufman, and Raymond Smock (Urbana: University of Illinois Press, 1974), 320.

28. Gladys-Marie Fry, *Night Riders in Black Folk History* (Knoxville: University of Tennessee Press, 1975), 46.

29. Franklin, *Black Self-Determination*, 101–102.

30. Booker T. Washington, "The Colored Ministry: Its effects and Needs," in *The Booker T. Washington Papers*, vol. 3, *1889–95*, ed. Louis R. Harlan, Stuart B. Kaufman, and Raymond Smock (Urbana: University of Illinois Press, 1974), 71–75; Ida B. Welles to Booker T. Washington, Memphis, Tennessee, November 30, 1890, in ibid., 108.

31. Booker T. Washington, "A Speech before the New York Congregational Club," in ibid., 283–284.

32. Franklin, *Black Self-Determination*, 195.

33. W.E.B. Du Bois, *The Souls of Black Folk: Essays and Sketches* (Greenwich, Conn.: Fawcett, 1961), 43–44, 47.

34. Louis R. Harlan, *Booker T. Washington: The Making of a Black Leader 1856–1901* (New York: Oxford University Press, 1972); Louis R. Harlan, *Booker T. Washington: The Wizard of Tuskegee, 1901–1915* (New York: Oxford University Press, 1983).

35. Harold Cruse, *The Crisis of the Negro Intellectual* (New York: William Morrow, 1967); Harold Cruse, *Rebellion and Revolution* (New York: William Morrow, 1968).

36. Robert L. Factor, *The Black Response to America: Men, Ideals, and Organizations from Frederick Douglass to the NAACP* (Reading, Mass.: Addison-Wesley, 1970).

37. William Toll, *The Resurgence of Race: Black Social Theory from Reconstruction to the Pan African Conferences* (Philadelphia: Temple University Press, 1979).

38. W. D. Wright, "The Thought and Leadership of Kelly Miller," *Phylon* 39, no. 2 (1978): 180.

39. Thomas Dixon, Jr., "Booker T. Washington and the Negro," in *The Poisoned Tongue: A Documentary History of American Racism and Prejudice*, ed. Stanley Feldstein (New York: William Morrow, 1972), 203.

40. Booker T. Washington, "A Speech at Old South Meeting House, Boston," in Harlan, Kaufman, and Smock, *The Booker T. Washington Papers*, vol. 3, p. 201.

41. Booker T. Washington, *The Future of the American Negro* (New York: New American Library, 1969), 119.

42. Booker T. Washington, *My Larger Education: Being Chapters from My Experience* (Miami, Fla.: Mnemosyne, 1969), 107.

8. THIRD-WAVE BLACK HISTORIOGRAPHY II

1. John Hope Franklin, *Race and History: Selected Essays, 1938–1988* (Baton Rouge: Louisiana State University Press, 1989).

2. John Hope Franklin, *The Militant South 1800–1861* (Cambridge: Harvard University Press, 1956).

3. Earl E. Thorpe, *The Old South: A Psychohistory* (Durham, N.C.: Seeman Printery, 1972).

4. Nell Irvin Painter, *Standing at Armageddon: The United States, 1877–1919* (New York: W. W. Norton, 1987).

5. David Levering Lewis, *The Race to Fashoda: European Colonialism and African Resistance to the Scramble for Africa* (New York: Weidenfeld & Nicolson, 1987).

6. Nelson I. Huggins, *Black Odyssey: The Afro-American Ordeal in Slavery* (New York: Vintage Books, 1977), xvi.

7. Ibid., xii.

8. Ibid.

9. Winthrop D. Jordan and Leon F. Litwack, *The United States: Conquering a Continent*, vol. 1, 7th ed. (Englewood Cliffs, N.J.: Prentice Hall, 1991), 294.

10. W.E.B. Du Bois, *The Souls of Black Folk: Essays and Sketches* (Greenwich, Conn.: Fawcett, 1961), 16.

11. Ibid., 17.

12. Ibid.

Selected Bibliography

Abercrombie, Nicolas, Stephen Hill, and Bryan Turner. *The Dominant Ideology*. London: George Allen & Unwin, 1980.

Appiah, Kwame Anthony. *In My Father's House: Africa in the Philosophy of Culture*. New York: Oxford University Press, 1992.

Appiah, Kwame Anthony, and Amy Gutmann. *Color Consciousness: The Political Morality of Race*. Princeton, N.J.: Princeton University Press, 1996.

Aptheker, Herbert. *American Negro Slave Revolts*. New York: Columbia University Press, 1943.

———. *Afro-American History: The Modern Era*. New York: Citadel Press, 1991.

Asante, Molefi Kete. *The Afrocentric Idea*. Philadelphia: Temple University Press, 1987.

———. *Kemet, Afrocentricity and Knowledge*. Trenton, N.J.: African World Press, 1990.

Baker, Houston A., Jr. *The Journey Back: Issues in Black Literature and Criticism*. Chicago: University of Chicago Press, 1980.

Bebey, Francis. *African Music: A People's Art*. New York: Lawrence Hill, 1969.

Bennett, Lerone, Jr. *The Negro Mood and Other Essays*. Chicago: Johnson, 1964.

Blassingame, John W. "The Afro-Americans: From Mythology to Reality." In *The Reinterpretation of American History and Culture*, edited by William H. Cartwright and Richard L. Watson. Washington, D.C.: National Council for Social Studies, 1973.

———, ed. *Slave Testimony: Two Centuries of Letters, Speeches, Interviews, and Autobiographies*. Baton Rouge: Louisiana State University Press, 1977.

Brawley, Benjamin. *The Negro Genius: A New Appraisal of the Achievement of the American Negro in Literature and the Fine Arts*. New York: Dodd, Mead, 1937.

———. *A Social History of the American Negro*. New York: Macmillan, 1970.

Brown, William Wells. *The Negro in the American Rebellion: His Heroism and His Fidelity*. New York: Johnson Reprint Corporation, 1968.

Bruce, Dickson D., Jr. "The Ironic Conception of American History: The Early Black Historians, 1883–1915." *The Journal of Negro History* 69, no. 2 (1984): 53–62.

Brunson, James E., and Runoko Rashidi. "The Moors of Antiquity." In *Golden Age of the Moor*, edited by Ivan Van Sertima. New Brunswick, N.J.: Transaction, 1992.

Budge, Sir E. A. Wallis. *A History of Ethiopia: Nubia & Abyssinia*. Vol. 1. Oosterhout, N.B., The Netherlands: Anthropological, 1970.

Clarke, John Henrik. "African American Historians and the Reclaiming of African History." In *African Culture: The Rhythms of Unity*, edited by Molefi Kete Asante and Kariamu Welsh Asante. Trenton, N.J.: African World Press, 1990.

———, ed. *New Dimensions in African History: The London Lectures of Dr. Yosef ben-Jochanan and Dr. John Henrik Clarke*. Trenton, N.J.: African World Press, 1991.

Cook, Samuel Du Bois. "A Tragic Conception of Negro History." *The Journal of Negro History* 45, no. 4 (1960): 219–240.

Cruse, Harold. *The Crisis of the Negro Intellectual*. New York: William Morrow, 1967.

———. *Rebellion and Revolution*. New York: William Morrow, 1968.

Curry, Leonard P. *The Free Black in Urban America 1800–1850: The Shadow of the Dream*. Chicago: University of Chicago Press, 1981.

Delaney, Martin Robison. *The Condition, Elevation, Emigration, and Destiny of the Colored People of the United States*. New York: Arno Press and the *New York Times*, 1968.

Dixon, Chris. *African American and Haitian Emigration and Black Nationalism in the Nineteenth Century*. Westport, Conn.: Greenwood Press, 2000.

Dixon, Vernon J., and Badi G. Foster, eds. *Beyond Black or White: An Alternate America*. Boston: Little, Brown, 1971.

Douglass, Frederick. *The Life and Times of Frederick Douglass*. New York: Crowell–Collier, 1962.

———. *My Bondage and My Freedom*. Chicago: Johnson, 1970.

Du Bois, W.E.B. *The Souls of Black Folk: Essays and Sketches*. Greenwich, Conn.: Fawcett, 1961.

——. *The World and Africa: An Inquiry into the Part Which Africa Has Played in World History.* New York: International, 1965.

——. *The Philadelphia Negro: A Social Study.* New York: Schocken Books, 1967.

——. *Darkwater: Voices from within the Veil.* New York: Schocken Books, 1969.

——. *The Suppression of the African Slave Trade to the United States of America 1638–1870.* Baton Rouge: Louisiana State University Press, 1969.

——. "The Conservation of the Races." In *W.E.B. Du Bois Speaks: Speeches and Address 1890–1919,* edited by Philip S. Foner. New York: Pathfinder Press, 1970.

——. *The Gift of Black Folk: The Negroes in the Making of America.* New York: Washington Square Press, 1970.

——. *The Negro.* New York: Oxford University Press, 1970.

——. "The Revelation of St. Orgne the Damned." In *W.E.B. Du Bois Speaks: Speeches and Address 1890–1919,* edited by Philip S. Foner. New York: Pathfinder Press, 1970.

——. "The Souls of White Folk." In *W.E.B. Du Bois: A Reader,* edited by Meyer Weinberg. New York: Harper & Row, 1970.

——. *Black Folk Then and Now: An Essay in the History and Sociology of the Negro Race.* New York: Octagon Books, 1973.

Elkins, Stanley. *Slavery: A Problem in American Institutional and Intellectual Life.* New York: Grosset & Dunlap, 1963.

Factor, Robert L. *The Black Response to America: Men, Ideals, and Organizations from Frederick Douglass to the NAACP.* Reading, Mass.: Addison-Wesley, 1970.

Fields, Barbara J. "Ideology and Race in American History." In *Region, Race, and Reconstruction: Essays in Honor of C. Vann Woodward,* edited by J. Morgan Kousser and James M. McPherson. New York: Oxford University Press, 1982.

Foner, Philip S., and George E. Walker, eds. *Proceedings of the Black State Conventions, 1840–1865.* Vols. 1–2. Philadelphia: Temple University Press, 1970.

Forbes, Jack D. *Black Africans & Native Americans: Color, Race and Caste in the Evolution of Red–Black Peoples.* New York: Basil Blackwell, 1988.

Franklin, John Hope. *The Militant South 1800–1861.* Cambridge: Harvard University Press, 1956.

——. "The New Negro History." *The Journal of Negro History* 43, no. 2 (1957): 89–97.

——. "On the Evolution of Scholarship in Afro-American History." In *The State of Afro-American History: Past, Present and Future,* edited by Darlene Clark Hine. Baton Rouge: Louisiana State University Press, 1986.

——. *Race and History: Selected Essays, 1938–1988.* Baton Rouge: Louisiana State University Press, 1989.

Franklin, V. P. *Black Self-Determination: A Cultural History of the Faith of the Fathers.* Westport, Conn.: Lawrence Hill, 1984.

Frederickson, George M. *The Arrogance of Race: Historical Perspectives on Slavery, Racism, and Social Equality.* Middletown, Conn.: Wesleyan University Press, 1988.

Fry, Gladys-Marie. *Night Riders in Black Folk History.* Knoxville: University of Tennessee Press, 1975.

Gates, Henry Louis, Jr. *Loose Canons: Notes on the Culture Wars.* New York: Oxford University Press, 1992.

Genovese, Eugene D. *Roll, Jordan, Roll: The World the Slaves Made.* New York: Pantheon Books, 1974.

Hamerow, Theodore S. *Reflections on History and Historians.* Madison: University of Wisconsin Press, 1987.

Harding, Vincent. "Beyond Chaos: Black History and the Search for the New Land." In *Amistad I*, edited by John A. Williams and Charles F. Harris. New York: Vintage Books, 1970.

Harlan, Louis R. *Booker T. Washington: The Making of a Black Leader 1856–1901.* New York: Oxford University Press, 1972.

———. *Booker T. Washington: The Wizard of Tuskegee, 1901–1915.* New York: Oxford University Press, 1983.

Harlan, Louis R., Stuart B. Kaufman, and Raymond Smock, eds. *The Booker T. Washington Papers.* Vol. 3, *1889–95.* Urbana: University of Illinois Press, 1974.

Harris, Robert L., Jr. "Coming of Age: The Transformation of Afro-American Historiography." *The Journal of Negro History* 67, no. 2 (1982): 107–121.

Herskovits, Melville J. *The Myth of the Negro Past.* Boston: Beacon Press, 1990.

Higginbotham, Evelyn Brooks. *Righteous Discontent: The Women's Movement in the Black Baptist Church, 1880–1920.* Cambridge: Harvard University Press, 1993.

Hine, Darlene Clark. *Hine Sight: Black Women and the Reconstruction of American History.* New York: Carlson, 1994.

Holloway, Joseph E., ed. *Africanisms in American Culture.* Bloomington: Indiana University Press, 1990.

Hood, Robert H. *Begrimed and Black: Christian Traditions of Black and Blackness.* Minneapolis, Minn.: Fortress Press, 1994.

Huggins, Nathan I. *Black Odyssey: The Afro-American Ordeal in Slavery.* New York: Vintage Books, 1977.

Irele, Abiola. *The African Experience in Literature and Ideology.* London: Heinemann Educational Books, 1981.

Itua, M. "Africans Do Not Want to Be Africans." In *The Black Think Tank*, edited by Naiwu Osahon. Lagos, Nigeria: International Coordinating Committee of the 7th Pan African Congress, 1992.

Jackson, John G. *Introduction to African Civilizations.* Secaucus, N.J.: Citadel Press, 1970.

Jacobs, Sylvia M. *The African Nexus: Black American Perspectives on the European Partitioning of Africa, 1880–1920.* Westport, Conn.: Greenwood Press, 1981.

Jordan, Winthrop D. *White over Black: American Attitudes toward the Negro 1550–1812*. Baltimore, Md.: Penguin Books, 1968.

Lester, Julius. *To Be a Slave*. New York: Dell, 1968.

———, ed. *The Seventh Son: The Thoughts and Writings of W.E.B. Du Bois*. Vol. 1. New York: Vintage Books, 1971.

Levine, Lawrence W. *Black Culture and Black Consciousness: Afro-American Folk Thought from Slavery to Freedom*. New York: Oxford University Press, 1977.

Lewis, Bernard. *Race and Slavery in the Middle East: An Historical Enquiry*. New York: Oxford University Press, 1990.

Lewis, Charton T., and Charles Short, eds. *A Latin Dictionary*. Oxford: Clarendon Press, 1966.

Locke, Alain. *The Negro and His Music*. New York: Arno Press and the *New York Times*, 1969.

———. *Negro Art: Past and Present*. New York: Arno Press and the *New York Times*, 1969.

Lott, Tommy L. *The Invention of Race: Black Culture and the Politics of Representation*. Malden, Mass.: Blackwell, 1999.

Marable, Manning. *W.E.B. Du Bois: Black Radical Democrat*. Boston: Twayne, 1986.

Marcus, Robert D., and David Burner, eds. *America First Hand*. Vol. 1. 2d ed. New York: St. Martin's Press, 1992.

Mazrui, Ali A. "On the Concept of 'We Are All Africans.'" *American Political Science Review* 57, no. 1 (1963): 88–97.

Meier, August, and Elliott Rudwick. *Black History and the Historical Profession, 1915–1980*. Urbana: University of Illinois Press, 1986.

Morgan, Edmund S. "The Education of a Saint." In *American Life, American People*. Vol. 1, edited by Neil Larry Shumsky and Timothy J. Crimmins. New York: Harcourt Brace Jovanovich, 1988.

Nash, Gary B. *Red, White & Blacks: The Peoples of Early North America*. Englewood Cliffs, N.J.: Prentice Hall, 1992.

Nell, William Cooper. *The Colored Patriots of the American Revolution*. New York: Arno Press and the *New York Times*, 1969.

Niebuhr, Reinhold. *The Irony of American History*. New York: Charles Scribner's Sons, 1952.

Nkrumah, Kwame. *Consciencism*. London: Heinemann Educational Books, 1964.

Owens, Leslie Howard. *This Species of Property: Slave Life and Culture*. New York: Oxford University Press, 1976.

Painter, Nell Irvin. *Standing at Armegeddon: The United States, 1877–1919*. New York: W. W. Norton, 1987.

Quarles, Benjamin. *The Negro in the Making of America*. Rev. ed. New York: Collier Macmillan, 1969.

———. "Black History Unbound." *Daedalus* 103, no. 2 (1974): 163–178.

Raboteau, Albert J. *Slave Religion: The Invisible Institution in the Antebellum South*. New York: Oxford University Press, 1978.

Rawick, George P. *From Sundown to Sunup: The Making of the Black Community*. Westport, Conn.: Greenwood Press, 1972.

Reed, Adolph, Jr. *Class Notes Posing as Politics and Other Thoughts on the American Scene*. New York: New Press, 2000.

Richardson, Marilyn, ed. *Mary W. Stewart: America's First Black Political Writer, Essays and Speeches*. Bloomington: Indiana University Press, 1987.

Ringer, Benjamin B., and Elinor R. Rawless. *Race, Ethnicity and Society*. New York: Routledge, 1989.

Rogers, J. A. *Sex and Race: Negro–Caucasian Mixing in All Ages and All Lands*. 3 vols. St. Petersburg, Fla.: Helga M. Rogers, 1967, 1972.

———. *World's Great Men of Color*. 3 vols. New York: Macmillan, 1972.

Sertima, Ivan Van. *They Came before Columbus*. New York: Random House, 1976.

———, ed. *Nile Valley Civilizations*. Journal of African Civilizations, 1985.

Sigelman, Lee, and Susan Welch. *Black Americans' Views of Racial Inequality: The Dream Deferred*. New York: Cambridge University Press, 1991.

Shore, Laurence. "The Poverty of Tragedy in Historical Writing on Southern Slavery." *South Atlantic Quarterly* 85, no. 2 (1986): 147–164.

Smith, Dennis. *The Rise of Historical Sociology*. Philadelphia: Temple University Press, 1991.

Snowden, Frank M., Jr. *Before Color Prejudice: The Ancient View of Blacks*. Cambridge: Harvard University Press, 1983.

Staniland, Martin. *American Intellectuals and African Nationalists, 1955–1970*. New Haven, Conn.: Yale University Press, 1991.

Starobin, Robert S., ed. *Bondage: Letters of American Slaves*. New York: View Points, 1974.

Stephano, Henrico. *Thesaurus Graecae Linguae*. Vols. 1–2. Paris: Excudebut Ambrosius Firmin Didot, 1831–1856.

Thompson, Kenneth. *Beliefs and Ideology*. New York: Tavistock, 1986.

Thompson, Lloyd A. *Romans and Blacks*. Norman: University of Oklahoma Press, 1989.

Thorpe, Earl E. *Negro Historians in the United States*. Baton Rouge, La.: Fraternal Press, 1958.

———. *The Old South: A Psychohistory*. Durham, N.C.: Seeman Printery, 1972.

Toll, William. *The Resurgence of Race: Black Social Theory from Reconstruction to the Pan African Conferences*. Philadelphia: Temple University Press, 1979.

Veyne, Paul. *Bread and Circuses: Historical Sociology and Political Pluralism*. Abridged ed. London: Allen Lane, Penguin Press, 1990.

Walker, Clarence E. *Deromanticizing Black History: Critical Essays and Reappraisals*. Knoxville: University of Tennessee Press, 1991.

Walker, David. *David Walker's Appeal, in Four Articles: Together with a Preamble, to the Coloured Citizens of the World, but in Particular, and Very Expressly, to Those of the United States of America*. New York: Hill and Wang, 1965.

Washington, Booker T. *The Future of the American Negro*. New York: New American Library, 1969.

Waters, Mary C. *Ethnic Options: Choosing Identities in America.* Berkeley and Los Angeles: University of California Press, 1990.

Watson, Harry L. *Liberty and Power: The Politics of Jacksonian America.* New York: Noonday Press, 1990.

Webber, Thomas L. *Deep Like the Rivers: Education in the Slave Quarter Community, 1831–1865.* New York: W. W. Norton, 1978.

Weisbord, Robert G. *Ebony Kinship: Africa, Africans, and the Afro-American.* Westport, Conn.: Greenwood Press, 1973.

White, Deborah Gray. *Too Heavy a Load: Black Women in Defense of Themselves, 1894–1994.* New York: W. W. Norton, 1999.

White, Joseph, Jr. "Guidelines for Black Psychologists." *The Black Scholar* 1, no. 5 (1970): 52–57.

Woodson, Carter G. *The African Background Outlined: Or Handbook for the Study of the Negro.* New York: New American Library, 1969.

———, ed. *The Mind of the Negro as Reflected in Letters Written during the Crisis, 1800–1860.* New York: Russell & Russell, 1969.

Woodson, Carter G., and Charles H. Wesley. *The Negro in Our History.* 11th ed. Washington, D.C.: Associated, 1966.

———. *Education of the Negro to 1861.* New York: Arno Press, 1968.

Wright, W. D. "The Thoughts and Leadership of Kelly Miller." *Phylon* 39, no. 2 (1978): 180–192.

———. *Racism Matters.* Westport, Conn.: Praeger, 1997.

Yetman, Norman P., ed. *Life under the "Peculiar Institution": Selections from the Slave Narrative Collection.* New York: Holt, Rinehart, and Winston, 1970.

Index

Achebe, Chinua, 114, 115
Afer, 106
Africa: African diaspora, 17–18; "African ethnicity" a misnomer, 168; African Extensia, 18, 51, 140, 164; African Extensia and sub-divisions predicated on distinction between black Africans and people of black African descent, 19, 133; African Extensia predicated on black people being original human beings, 19; African identity a continental, not national identity, 178; African identity a retrospective identity, 107, 119, 124, 126, 130, 163, 168, 169, 171, 200; "African nationalism" a misnomer, 6; African Presence, 119, 123, 164, 214; ancient Greek word, not indigenous to Africa, 16; a continent, not a country, 108–109; lack of African consciousness among Black slaves, 109, 121–122, 164, 168–169; subdivisions of the African Extensia: Southern African Extensia, Eastern African Extensia, Northern African–Black Holocaust, 118, 125–126, 146, 153, 163–164, 171–172, 180, 192, 198–199, 202

Africancentric Perspective: accepts the concept and reality of African Holocaust, 118; Afrocentric Perspective, 17; cannot relate to the African Extensia, and Western African Extensia, 19, 22, 51; does not relate to tragedies in black Africa history, 117; illogical concept, 188; improper method for analyzing Black history and life, 20; interacts with Black-centric Perspective, 126, 215; method to analyze black African history and life, 20; not same as Africancentric Perspective, 19–20

ABOUT THE AUTHOR

W. D. Wright is Professor of History Emeritus at Southern Connecticut State University.